1,000,000 Books

are available to read at

—◆—

www.ForgottenBooks.com

—◆—

Read online
Download PDF
Purchase in print

ISBN 978-1-331-64571-9
PIBN 10217310

This book is a reproduction of an important historical work. Forgotten Books uses
state-of-the-art technology to digitally reconstruct the work, preserving the original format
whilst repairing imperfections present in the aged copy. In rare cases, an imperfection in
the original, such as a blemish or missing page, may be replicated in our edition. We do,
however, repair the vast majority of imperfections successfully; any imperfections that
remain are intentionally left to preserve the state of such historical works.

1 MONTH OF
FREE
READING

at

www.ForgottenBooks.com

By purchasing this book you are eligible for one month membership to ForgottenBooks.com, giving you unlimited access to our entire collection of over 1,000,000 titles via our web site and mobile apps.

To claim your free month visit:

www.forgottenbooks.com/free217310

English
Français
Deutsche
Italiano
Español
Português

www.forgottenbooks.com

Mythology Photography **Fiction**
Fishing Christianity **Art** Cooking
Essays Buddhism Freemasonry
Medicine **Biology** Music **Ancient
Egypt** Evolution Carpentry Physics
Dance Geology **Mathematics** Fitness
Shakespeare **Folklore** Yoga Marketing
Confidence Immortality Biographies
Poetry **Psychology** Witchcraft
Electronics Chemistry History **Law**
Accounting **Philosophy** Anthropology
Alchemy Drama Quantum Mechanics
Atheism Sexual Health **Ancient History**
Entrepreneurship Languages Sport
Paleontology Needlework Islam
Metaphysics Investment Archaeology
Parenting Statistics Criminology
Motivational

NATIONAL DUTIES

AND OTHER

SERMONS AND ADDRESSES

BY

JAMES MARTINEAU

Hon. LL.D. Harv.: S.T.D. Lugd. Bat.
D.D. Edin.: D.C.L. Oxon.

LONGMANS, GREEN, AND CO.

39 PATERNOSTER ROW, LONDON
NEW YORK AND BOMBAY
1903

A.174316

PRINTED BY
WOODFALL AND KINDER, LONG ACRE
LONDON

PREFATORY NOTE.

———◆———

THE Sermons contained in this Volume are a small selection from the manuscripts left to us by our Father, and were written for the most part during the earlier period of his ministry in Liverpool; but were afterwards delivered (in their present revised form) during the term of his London ministry at Little Portland Street Chapel. To make this clear, we have given the dates at the end of each.

Although not included by him when producing his two Series,—the "Endeavours" (in 1843 and 1847) and the "Hours of Thought" (in 1876 and 1880)—we have felt that they would be welcomed and found helpful by many; and we owe to Dr. James Drummond's kindness the judicious choice, from among a much larger number, of what seem to be the most valuable and characteristic.

GERTRUDE MARTINEAU.
EDITH MARTINEAU.

5, ELDON ROAD,
    HAMPSTEAD,
        February, 1903.

CONTENTS.

NATIONAL DUTIES.

XX.

ADDRESSES ON VARIOUS OCCASIONS.

NATIONAL DUTIES.

I.

𝕿𝖍𝖊 𝕲𝖗𝖔𝖚𝖓𝖉 𝖔𝖋 𝕹𝖆𝖙𝖎𝖔𝖓𝖆𝖑 𝖀𝖓𝖎𝖙𝖞.

I.

ISAIAH lx. 12.

" The nation and kingdom that will not serve thee shall perish."

IN every crisis of public strife, when irreconcilable
principles have tried their strength in the open field,
the Old Testament has risen into higher favour with
religious men; has seemed to become richer, deeper,
grander than before; and to speak with a directness
and reality that almost take its antiquity away. The
peasants of Germany called their leader the Sword of
Gideon, and took Westphalia for their Promised Land.
The Huguenots besieged in La Rochelle pondered the
story of Sennacherib's host, and prayed the prayer of
Hezekiah. If you peep over the shoulder of Cromwell's
trooper, reading his Bible in the hay-loft ere he flings

B

himself upon the straw to sleep, the page on which
the lantern shines tells of Barak at the brook or
Jephtha on the road. The cry of public humiliation
or thanksgiving sets itself to the harp of David, or
takes up the strains of Isaiah. At such times prophets
speak more to the heart than apostles, and the Christian
gospel is harder to apply than the Hebrew annals.
Something of this is no doubt due to the greater purity
and spirituality of the religion of Christ; to the
intensity of passion awakened in an age of conflict, and
seeking fuel from divine support; and the readiness
with which the older scriptures respond to this lower
mood of mind. But this is not all; men who have no
savage taste, no sympathy with the jealousy and wrath,
the vindictiveness and partiality, attributed by the
triumphant or the despairing to their Jehovah, feel
the same fact; and are conscious in days of political
excitement of an interval difficult to fill between the
lessons of evangelists and the duties and interests of
the time. The true reason is this; that Judaism is
national, Christianity universal; religion in the one is
concentrated into the kingdom of Israel, in the other
widened into the kingdom of heaven; works in the one
upon a map of this world, amid an historic people, on
the margin of great empires, and along the lines of
spreading colonization; stands in the other neutral to
the distinctions of race and the vicissitudes of destiny,
and speaks only to the spirit that is alike in all. Hence

in an age which stirs questions of public polity, in which the heart of the world is seething with new and nobler aims, and the tribes of men are drawn off by the inspiration of special genius, it is the Hebrew scriptures alone that give response to their uppermost affections ; uttering the prayer and recording the heroism of men who testified for the monarchy of God ; breathing the strains of exile from their native land ; hurling **defiance** at oppressors, or breaking into songs of deliverance, or predicting the reign of justice on earth ; in every way alive with the feelings of men astir in the fields, and blown upon by the open air of history. The Old Testament is the expression of an intense *nationality,*—a nationality consecrated by faith, and guarded by a sense of loyalty to the living God. The expression may be often fierce and wild, for it comes out of the soul of men neither better nor wiser than might be found elsewhere ; but it is *real,* and meets the case of those who are tossed upon like contests and exposed to like temptations.

To look for the same function from the Christian records is totally to mistake their nature, and to reverse the character of the religion which they exhibit at its origin. Christianity is Judaism bursting all its bounds, flinging away its exclusions and negations, substituting the human race in the place of Israel, and bringing all into divine relations. In contradicting the narrowness of the Law, and proclaiming the universality of the gospel, it necessarily restricts itself to those elements of duty and faith which are alike for every mind, those few and simple spiritual truths which are independent of clime and era, of youth and age, of class and section, of tribe and even world.   It is the religious doctrine *of human nature,* whensoever living, wheresoever placed ; and takes no notice therefore of the differences of feelings and obligation between the man and the woman, the servile or the free, the Tartar or the Saxon, the states-man or the artisan, the mediæval baron or the modern merchant.   It deals with the world as if it had no map and no history, but were, like the heaven to which it points, an assemblage of spiritual units, each with the same trust and the same concerns.   It was a matter of the utmost moment to draw forth, and set for awhile as in a burning focus before the eye, this funda-mental ground of divine truth and duty ; to claim an infinite sanctity for every soul ; to offer the communion and presence of God to all ; and to lay this privilege bare by tearing off the web of particular relations that hide it from the view.   To the Greek boasting of his wisdom, to the Roman of his sway, to the German of his freedom, to the Jew of his election, it was needful and wholesome to reveal the consecrated root of humanity that bore every blossom of them all, and make them conscious of the heavenly dew and nourishing wind that fed them into life.   Of so great consequence was this, that this truth was made to stand out in isolated intensity, and its evangelical teachers were screened from every apprehension that might distract them from it. They were permitted to believe that history was at an end, that the earth was brought to its last time; that all local colouring was on the point of being wiped out, and that a kingdom was to come with one uniform admission, faith in an eternal representative of God. The picture that lay before the imagination of the first Christians was in this respect like the conception which modern believers have of the eternal life; where are neither rich nor poor, sick nor healthy, infant born nor hoary head laid low; which has no charts of its oceans, no atlas of its lands; where moon no longer changes, and no twilight harbingers the sun. In their writings therefore there is no provision for the continuance of this world; no account is taken of any inheritance it may have given us, or any bequest we have to leave to it; no importance is attached to its external conditions, whose remedy will soon be found in their extinction; and no duty in regard to them is enjoined, but to bear with patience, to obey with quietness, and stand aloof. It is therefore no wonder that the Christian scriptures are not, in any direct way, a manual for the merchant or the statesman; and, saying little of the duties arising from social and historical *differences,* insist rather on what springs from spiritual community and our natural equality in the sight of God. That which is sent to reveal the universal cannot be called in question for looking to that alone, and even forgetting that the special has to be.

Consider too the *historical theatre* on which Christianity appeared and spread; and ask yourself whether, if the religion itself had been ever so inclined to expound the patriot's duty, there was really anything suitable to be said. We doubtless owe to the Roman Empire a grand field for the diffusion of Christian truth; a world-wide realm was the proper scene for the mission of a universal faith. But we owe to it also this countervailing grudge; that it has prevented, or at least disturbed, to this very hour, the growth of any genuine nation upon the earth. Taking its rise from an Italian city, and widening its circle during eight centuries, it wiped out the independent life and pushed back the landmarks of historic tribes, wherever its eagles advanced; its genius for organization enabled it to hold what it acquired, and purchase content by material order and military fear; till from the Tigris to the Atlantic, from Dacia to the Southern Nile, one vast area, with the Mediterranean between, was embraced by the cordon of legions; and within it not a dialect but two could speak without shame at its own barbarism; not an ancestry be honoured a hundred leagues from the Tiber without confession of provincialism, not an hereditary worship be paid without turning to the catalogue and seeing whether the god stood in the niches of the Pantheon. Over this wide territory you might travel by land or water; you might trade; you might rest and settle; you might plant and build, enjoy or study; but you could make no law, call no meeting, denounce no tax, deserve no civic office, take no practical interest in anything that binds the private citizen to the public memoirs of the world. Power was encamped over the nations; and they died down into mere crowds of individuals. No life-blood circulated through their territorial frame; no pulses of simultaneous sympathy could beat; no common pride could animate them, and therefore even common shame soon ceased to agitate; and in the absence of scope for any nobler passion, they yielded themselves to private ends, and multiplied their pleasures and their gains.

A religion sent forth over such a world can say nothing of the commonwealth; on the side of the political virtues it must present a blank; and so terrible did the omission seem to the Christian teachers, so mutilated did human nature look under this incapacity, that it was evidence to them against the longer existence of the disjointed world that entailed it; and the allegiance and self-sacrifice that were not wanted here they transferred to the invisible realm, and bespoke for "a better country, even a heavenly." What would have been patriotism under better terrestrial conditions became joyous, affectionate, devoted "fellow-citizenship with the Saints"; what would have been loyalty took the upward and ideal direction, and became a simple willingness to spend and be spent in the service of the "King of Saints." And these were real and living affections, bursting with pure fire into the vacant spaces of the human soul, and kindling it all with a fresh enthusiasm. They silently organized the inner life of the Church, and by spontaneously creating and harmonizing the whole work of the moral faculties, enabled the Christians to remain amid the sphere of the Roman State, and yet sit free of it; to determine their own duties, settle their own disputes, balance their own relations, administer their own institutions, and take no notice of the courts, the schools, the prisons, the temples around them. The system which thus grew up, being self-luminous, came out more brightly as the shades gathered upon the empire; it soon appeared to the discerning the rising energy of the world; and notwithstanding its heavenly seclusion from affairs, in order to keep together a spiritual society, it had to come to the rescue when the civil ties gave way, and save mankind from anarchy. Thus the Church, by decay of other agencies, was re-introduced into the secular business of human nature, took it up as its secondary function, and absorbed it into its prior maxims and ideas. Thus it was, that first favoured by Roman power and tranquillity, the universal *religion*

shaped a universal *Church;* and then, compelled by
Roman weakness and confusion, the universal Church
succeeded to universal *empire.* In the Roman Catholic
theory this earth is under a theocracy; the temporal
circle of interests and duties is of divine appointment,
like the spiritual; but though belonging to the same
system, is natural instead of supernatural; ordinary,
not special; referred therefore to lower functionaries,
but supervised and brought to account by the higher.
States are the local administrators of the One all-
comprehensive hierarchy; to which there is an appeal
on every human thing; from which there is appeal
on none.   It is quite clear that this doctrine leaves no
scope for the free development of any nationality; it
contemplates the human race as *one,* and undertakes
the charge of its unity; it does not so oppose the
spiritual to the temporal as in adopting the one to
refrain from the other; but including the lower in the
higher, prescribes conditions that penetrate them both.
Thus, no people can escape the ecclesiastic leading-
strings, or unconditionally assert the right of their
own moral life; a programme of fundamental laws is
handed in to them by the priests, to which their first
loyalty is due; and only with the reservation of these
provisos may they unfold their own being, throw
a heroism into their history, and take the vow to
their own law, and fling their affections into their
native air.

Not less discouraging, though in a different way, to any national feeling, has been the doctrine of the Reformation. While Catholicism adopted this world into its system, only bade it sit at the foot of the sacred steps, Protestantism ignored and repelled it,— hurled it into the devil's lap,—and said, "There, take it from our sight, it is none of ours."   The temporal was regarded not as the divine at a lower stage and less unmixed, but as the utterly *un*divine; and was set in sharp contradiction to the spiritual; so that the two spheres of the early Christians were restored in all their original antithesis, and the disciple, though present in the body on the scene of human things, was to live in a higher converse and walk by faith instead of sight.   His relation to God,—everything belonging to his religion,—was a thing which he had all to himself, a supernatural transaction between heaven and his own personality, which might take place as well if he were alone in space; which might indeed be repeated, if Divine grace so willed, upon his right hand neighbour and his left, but was still not made a social affair by happening individually over and over again; and had the effect of taking a man out of natural society instead of twining him more closely into it; of making him indifferent to the affairs of this life and look down upon the world as a profane assemblage of carnal things.   The grand effect of the Protestant *Regeneration* was to snatch the convert clear away from the tastes of this state, and set him prematurely into those of another; to hold his affections loose from property, reputation, beauty, knowledge, art, country, family and friends, and induce him to accept Christ as the equivalent and substitute for all. Whoever places Christian perfection in this absolute escape of the soul from the conditions of place and time, and self-extinction in the eternal at once, looks upon the world as an evanescent accident, and history as a devil's drama, and politics as the gambling table of unregenerate men. Religious persons will touch none of these things; or if they do, it will be only through the painful necessity which still clogs them with the dead weight of a fallen nature; they will do it, not with hearty zeal, but with disdainful shame, and apologies for venturing so near to the core of evil and temptation. For the most part they ask nothing of the State except to *be let alone* to live their own higher life, and work apart in their prayerful and missionary way, for the freer course of the kingdom of God. This is the origin of the low modern doctrine of Politics; which delivers to the *Individual* whatever is sacred and binding and holy; and then hands over all the leavings to the State; which would have a *Body* politic without a *Soul;* which denies to Law any *moral* character as the expression of an organized public *conscience*, and treats it as a mere preventive guard, holding clear the space for the

development of personal faculty.   Hence it is that in
all Protestant lands the historical functions and
evolutions of the world have struggled on without a
consecration ; nationalities have formed themselves by
force of circumstances, not by enthusiasm of affection
and co-operation of resolute will ; and governments,
instead of being the natural outcome and embodiment
of a people's best life, and so surrounded by their
trust and reverence, have become the standing objects
of vigilant suspicion.   Great as the benefits are which
we owe to the champions of the Reformation in the
sixteenth and seventeenth centuries, and accustomed
as we are to look to the Puritans as the founders of
our modern liberties, we have reason to thank God
that their success was not greater, and to bless the
true national instinct which barred their further way.
They cared little for their country except as a theatre
for their faith ; that they belonged to it was one of
the accidents of nature which they despised, and was
indifferent to the ordinances of grace which they
revered.   Cromwell, the Huntingdon brewer, was an
Englishman ; but Cromwell, the Saint, was one of the
Lord's people.   Coligny, the Admiral, was citizen of
France ; but Coligny, the Huguenot, fought for a
State within the State, for separate fortresses and
troops and guarantees and consistories, which would
have established and intermixed two federated nations
upon the same soil.   The sympathies of the Protes-

tants were with each other all over the world, and not
with the land of their birth and the institutions of
their inheritance. Their strife was at home, their
friendships abroad. Their correspondence, their
preachers, their literature, were European; they
prayed passionately for their brethren, tamely for
their country, whose history they cared not to study;
whose ornamental arts they despised; whose poetry
was too warm with the blood of generous life for
them; whose cathedrals they stripped and white-
washed; whose lordly timbers they cut; and whose
whole Past they would have cleansed away as a Baby-
lonish mess of horrors. Their aim was not patriotic,
but cosmopolitan; not so much to guard the honour
and unity of England as to gather the whole world
into an Evangelical Alliance. Had they fully triumphed
in their aim, and shorn the flowing locks which history
had grown so richly and so long, this earth would
have presented a dismal and an ugly spectacle. As it
is, they balanced their many services by bequeathing
to us the degrading doctrine of politics, which empties
out from them every noble colouring of Moral desire
and reduces them to an organization of police; which
makes the State exist for the claims of individuals,
instead of the individual for the ennoblement of the
commonwealth; which totally detaches all religious
sentiment, all historical knowledge and enthusiasm
from the criticism and estimate of public affairs, and

is not ashamed to try them by the standard of the meanest selfishness or a vapid philanthropy. In short, they left us with nothing sacred and inspiring to us between individual piety and universal love; no intermediate resting-place for zeal, affection and effort; no means of consecrating and glorifying this actual world of seas and lands, of hills and streams, of oppressions and liberties, of tradition, life, and poetry, in which our lot is cast. Between religious people who try to love everybody, and worldly who look only to themselves, no scope was allowed for middle admirations to kindle and carry away the generous natural heart.

Sacerdotal and evangelical *régime* are alike inadequate to the real exigencies of mankind. This earth is made for something else than to be managed by priests and converted by saints, and reduced by both to a mere threshold of eternity. It has a value on its own account, and so long as the sunshine warms its heart will remain dear to men in a thousand ways that monks and missionaries never notice. These have been too long left without recognition and consecration. In the applied gospel of modern times we must have *room for the world*,—a welcome for its noblest forces, a benediction for its struggles of Honour and Right, a divine interpretation of its history and its various humanity. Between the individuality that insulates each, and the kingdom of heaven that embraces all, there is the home, the neighbourhood, the country, spreading round us widening circles of sacred claim. Besides the moment at which we live and the eternity to which we go, we belong to historic ages whose pulses beat in us to-day, and should quicken us with some glow of reverent thought and higher duty. How, from the pale light of a universal religion, to win some rich and holy colours for these closer human relations; how to harmonize the mystic breathings of the One Spirit with divergent affections of the manifold nature and various lot; how, with Christian mind to rise above nature, at the loss of no natural love for the familiar friend, the native land, the inherited trust; this is the problem which, from the failure of past times and the needs of the present, it yet remains for our Christianity to solve.

LIVERPOOL, 1854.
LONDON, 1866.

II.

The Ground of National Unity.

ISAIAH lx. 12.

"The nation and kingdom that will not serve thee shall perish."

I**T** is a curious fact that in the professed and organized doctrines of our times there is no provision whatever for justifying and enforcing the special duties and affections of the citizen. They are absolutely un-recognized in every creed and every church. They work their way into such acknowledgment as they have by irresistible force of nature, from the human and lay end of society, as accidents foreign to the codes of faith and morals. Religious persons do not know what to make of them, and remain in a state of uneasy relation toward them ; and are usually withdrawn into quite another sphere in proportion to the growth of a deep personal piety. There is a large fund indeed of public spirit and self-sacrifice ready for moments of exigency. But it is either of spontaneous

and unregulated origin ; or it is a treasure derived from
Pagan sources, and flows in through the avenues of
ancient literature still happily open in our schools
and universities. Devout Christians, as well as mere
utilitarians, often lament the heathen training of our
educated youth, and wonder what our children can
have to do with Troy and Athens, Rome and Carthage.
But it was a blessed inconsistency, a truly Providential
infatuation, that led Melancthon to follow up the vernacular Bible with the Greek and Latin Grammar ; to
proclaim war against monarch barbarism, ally himself with the new learning of Reuchlin and Erasmus,
and encourage the enthusiasm of ecclesiastical studies.
He thus provided unconsciously for an order of sentiments and admirations which the catechism and
the confession omitted and practically disallowed ; and
gave to the heart of many generations a perception of
the beauty of this life and world, the nobleness of
Gentile nature, and the divine grandeur of public
Law, which no evangelistic discipline of itself would
have secured. The infusion into the character of
Christian nations of certain elements of Pagan faith
and feeling brings together no doubt some unreconciled
tendencies, but, like many other practical contradictions, prevents the tyranny of half truths, and keeps
alive the everlasting kernel of good which God stored
in his ancient heathendom, till we can prepare the
Christian soil to grow it.

The opposition which the Reformers set up between *Law and Gospel* is the origin of the modern theory of State and Church. The former belonged to the natural man, the latter to the spiritual; and as these two were contrary in every attribute, no terms were too strong for the abasement of the one or the exaltation of the other. The contrast of earth and heaven, night and day, darkness and light, are insufficient, says Luther, to represent the chasm that separates the sphere of Works from that of Faith, the moralities of the natural Will from the assurance and affection of the regenerate heart. The Christian's soul sits free of all sense of obligation; no burthen weighs upon his conscience; the traces of remorseful tears in a face uplifted before God are the sure signs of unconversion,—the proof that he knows not what is appointed him to offer, and worries himself with a vain sacrifice. The rules of right are quite indifferent to religion and have no wings to help us in the least up into the mountain of our God; but, like the plodding ass upon the dusty plain and common road below, will only carry our store of gainful merchandise, and serve the uses of secular and selfish life. They are for the body and its habits; but are quite foreign to the soul and its aspirations. When the empires of morals and religion have thus been cut off from contact, and all holy authority drawn up into heaven, it seems difficult to say why the duties should be observed at all;

stripped of sanctity and awfulness, what remains to them that they should still speak with the voice of command? It is expedient to observe them, says the Reformer, for sake of convenience and order; they are conditions of a treaty of social peace, by adhering to which we can keep down the war of passion and greediness, and render the earth a habitable place. In themselves, the Moral Laws are arbitrary impositions (says Zwingli), like the rules by which a household is regimented and organized; prescribing when the bell shall be rung or the walk be taken, and where the children shall change their shoes. Other arrangements might have served as well, and by being established would have become right; but the great thing is to have *some* working customs; and as these are here, and are well understood, it is proper for new-comers to fall in with them.

The Gospel and the Law being thus sharply distinguished,—the soul alone being subjected to faith, the body alone to Morals,—if there were a group of souls with the right faith it made a *Church;* if an assemblage of bodies with the same Morals, it made a *State.* Man being both corporeal and spiritual, the same community of persons may constitute both; meeting together *in Church,* they deal with all that concerns them in their divine relation, and find free scope for their love, and trust, and conscience; meeting together in *State* membership, they absent

themselves from whatever is holy and noble, and
treat of their comforts and their gains, and consider
how to give the largest range to the desires and
faculties that are alien to God. The Church taking
only the soul, and the State only the body, each goes
apart with its own, and as a counterpart to a dis-
embodied religion produces materialism in politics;
which does not profess to meddle with anything beyond
the self-interest of men and the passions that disturb
its unembarrassed pursuit; which performs its function
as if they were only acquisitive animals, with limbs
that may be hurt and capital that may be stolen;
which undertakes to mount guard over both; but
having secured these conditions of physical well-being,
knows nothing of any higher life, and passes rigid as
a policeman through the dense and struggling
humanities where guilt hides its revelry, and temptation snatches its victim, and sorrow stifles its
prayer.

Now it is false that man is entirely made up of
body and goods on one hand, and the *soul* on the
other, in the narrow theological sense; and it is therefore false that he can be rightly ruled by the partnership of doctrinal reliance and personal selfishness.
There is a vast middle range which you can neither
Calvinize nor corrupt; which is neither evangelistic
nor sordid; which lies between the highest peaks of
contemplative faith, and the rag-market of human

nature where the air is tainted and the very light no longer clean. There are a host of natural affections and generous enthusiasms which do not want conversion like a culprit, and will not be beaten like Luther's lazy ass—manly nobleness, womanly tenderness, childlike trust; the patience of knowledge, the inspiration of beauty, the indignation at wrong; all the impulses which enrich our world with truth, art, and public justice;—these are left at large by the protestant classification, and float uneasily between heaven and earth. Flung off by professional religion, as not spiritual, they go about without a blessing; having no call to play sentinel over body and goods, they shrink from the adoption of Law. They belong not to the soul alone, for they love this earth and taught Pagans how to glorify it. They belong not to the body alone, for they conquer its appetites and make it the organ of heroic life. Their very function and joy are found midway,—to put a soul into the substance of the world, that its matter may cease to be material, and its spirit cease to be invisible; to work out divine suggestion into *form*, that something of God may abide with us from morn to night, and we may not be for ever tossed between the frost and fire; to *realize* conscience in visible life and public expression, that all the holiness in the universe may not be hid in the upper heaven and the secret heart, but may vindicate an empire in the open business of to-day. These parts

of our nature, which are neither selfish nor evange-
listical, the moralities and reverences of this life, the
admiration we have for *embodied* justice and heroism
are the proper ground of social and political union.
Their office is to spread an influence both ways ;
upwards into religion, to colour and humanize it ;
downwards into Law, to give it the dignity of an idea.
The restriction of the State to mere police regulation
has nothing to recommend it beyond the pedantic
formula to which Luther's false partition of human
life gave the only sense it ever had. A State is the
corporate expression of a people's mind ; there is no
reason whatever for permitting its material self-interest
to speak in legislation, and leaving its moral convictions and higher sentiments to remain the accidents
of individuals, private and unorganized. And whenever they attain sufficient unanimity and intensity they
will pay small respect to doctrinaire prohibition, will
lay their rightful hand on statute-book and institution,
and inscribe there the record of their conscience, their
will, and their religion.

How little the protestant theory, which charges the
Church with the souls, and the State with the bodies
of mankind, agrees with the facts, appears from a
very simple consideration. Since all men have souls,
there can be no limit to the range of the Church ; and
since all men have bodies, there can be no limit to
the range of the State, till the whole race be brought

under one Catholic Polity. At least, no other bar to perpetual extension of sway would exist, except the mechanical difficulty of propagating the same administrative force over a wide area of human space. No *inner* limit would arise from any changing quality of function ; the work to be done would be homogeneous, and the instruments for its accomplishment the same. Yet, if there be any one lesson which history unambiguously teaches, it is the impossibility of a universal Church, and much more of a universal empire. Not even that divine religion which disowned all lineage and equalized all orders, which brought together Jew and Greek at the same table, which swept by its missionaries over a world of fused and levelled nationalities, and clasped by its hierarchy a society that crumbled in the hand of Proconsuls and the grasp of legions, was able to harmonize the genius of East and West, and shape a worship in which both would kneel. And if protection of body and goods by the same arm of power constitutes a State and fulfils its essential conditions, then the ideal of a Polity was almost realized under Trajan and the Antonines ; and British India must be preferred to the turbulent glories of the Hellenic States. Yet neither of these could be called the true *native country* to any one of the millions whose *birth-place* lay within their limits ; and notwithstanding the perpetual improvement of their law, and effective organization of their protective force, they are

examples not of natural cohesion, but of artificial
arrest of dissolution. The reason is obvious; it is not
that there is any *want of a common interest*, but that
there is *nothing else ;* that the material bond is shame-
fully visible, and because it does not hurt the body,
chafes and reproaches the spirit; that the facts of
to-day are intolerable beside the traditions of the past,
and before the face of strangers the physiognomy of
superseded history grows sad. It is because the rulers
and the ruled have nothing in common but body and
goods, that the relation, said to affect these alone, is
unstable and melancholy. The intelligence of common
speech, the fervour of common admirations, the inheritance of a common ancestry, the glow of a
common music and poetry and faith are wanting;
and the attempt is ever vain to replace these, the ideal
cement of nations, by reliance on the real interest of
individuals.

The fact is, the conception of society, as made up of
so many individuals, each with his personality complete
and rounded off, and bringing into the common stock
his antecedent outfit of capacities and rights, is an
empty fiction. Individuality is not brought into Society,
but is first made there ; and whatever constitutes man
a person rather than *a thing*, his consciousness of right
and wrong, his perception of a divine beauty and meaning in the world, his power of reflective and independent
will, he first finds when he looks into other eyes, and

catches from the Promethean fires of a kindred sympathy. The growth of a common self-sacrifice is the
prior condition of any self-assertion of private natures;
and moral unity is found in groups before it culminates
in isolation. You that suppose it the perfection of
society that it shall let the individual alone and simply
make a clear space for the play of his faculties,—say,
what do you mean by "*the individual*"? When and
where did he ever appear? Do you mean some wild man
of the woods, anthropomorphous, but not yet human?
Or the half solitary savage, mastered by passion, or
lying in wait for predatory intelligence? These are
the only creatures provided beforehand by mere plastic
nature, independent of the informing God, to serve as
raw material of the historic world; and all that converts
these species into men, self-knowledge, self-sacrifice,
reverencing Law set on fire with Love and serving
God, is kindled by the looks of other faces, flushed
and lighted by the pulsations of a common heart. It
is an ungrateful mistake to turn round upon the power
that has set us on our feet, and say: Now that it has
done this good thing it shall do no more, and it is time
that our emancipator should be chained. It may be
indeed that the very best thing achieved by civilised
Society is the development of special force of individual
character, and an intense energy of personal conviction
and conscience. But these are neither entitled nor
enabled to set up for themselves, and divorce their

connection with the world.   They are the advanced posts
of adventurous conscience, which, held by solitary
prowess in one age, are but won for the public empire in
the next; and those who seize them are not to hold them
as their own, but to occupy them in trust for mankind,
till the advancing host comes up.   Indeed, without this
hope that what is a lonely position now will be a settled
and social truth hereafter, individuality itself would lose
its chief and fostering encouragement, lose its nobler
form, and wither into egotism and self-will.   It is not
true, therefore, that the community exists for the sake
of the individual, and that the highest end attained
by government is the security for personal development; unless you add the supplemental truth, that the
individual soul is itself the blossom and the fruit of
social union, and has its ripest blessing not when it
hangs in air ripe and beautiful of itself, but when it
drops for others upon the soil already rich with fallen
foliage of the past.   With all our Protestant and
Christian respect for personal rights, we cannot afford
entirely to part with the old Greek idea, that the
commonwealth is lord of the citizen, and entitled to
use him and his transient existence as the organ
and nutriment of its permanent and comprehensive
life.

What is it then in his nature that renders Man
political?   He might have common *fears* inducing
him to submit to stronger power; but that would

make only a *Camp.* He might have common *interests*, leading him to subordinate his personal to the public Will ; but that would make only a *Company.* Not till we say, He has a common *sense of justice*, do we touch the spring from which the State arises. That which gives efficacy to an external authority over him is the existence and consciousness of a righteous authority within him ; and the whole force and significance of Law to him depends on this, that it embodies and interprets the voice of Right within his heart. Where this condition fails,—where selfish ambition leaps into the throne of power, and usurps the language and insignia of public Right, men may indeed hold their peace under the bribe of security or the fruitlessness of protest ; but they obey with secret shame ; a meanness clings to the very safety of their body and the increase of their goods ; they feel as if their country were turned into a camp of freebooters, where the rule may be vigorous and orderly, but has nothing of the intrinsic majesty of Law. But for the inner Conscience, the secret reverence for a higher in contrast with a lower, man might be *broken in* like a brute, but could not be *ruled* as a citizen. The function of the State is simply to give external form and expression to that portion of the Moral Law of God which the Society generally owns and has the means of enforcing ; nor is there any other limit to its legislative rights, than that it speaks truly the common conscience and attempts

nothing beyond the public power. To this paramount
righteousness of Law, this function of interpreting the
eternal rectitude of God in the heart of man, all lower
ends, all the expediences of temporal good, must be
subservient. Within the same Society there is a long
train of moral positions in the collective march ; from
the noble pioneers who explore and prepare the front
to the lagging rear that halts and must be forced along.
Of the great assemblage of people there is not one
without special opportunities for particular notice of
some element and part of what is right and good.
Its physical position, its special industry, its traditional antecedents, its natural temperament, its
language, examples, and literature, combine to form a
character and consciousness distinct from those of
other tribes ; and awaken a perception of some side
of nobleness or justice, some blessing of truth and
faith, disallowed or undiscovered elsewhere. This it
is that constitutes at once that nation's duty and its
right. Not only has it a title to assert and vindicate
itself as an authorized constituent of this human world ;
but it is essentially *a trust* deposited with us from the
great hand of Providence, to be preserved and improved
for the family of peoples. To record and embody in
the public law of each land its permanent and united
convictions, to cling to them so long as they shine with
the clear light of conscience, and uphold them in the
face of dissentient and even raging nations, is the

contribution due to the general Moral code of history and the world. It is the right of national unity, it is the form of national duty, it is the expression of national reverence, by which alone the warning is escaped, "the Nation and Kingdom that will not serve me shall perish."

LIVERPOOL, 1854.
LONDON, 1866.

III.

The Grounds and Inner Duties of National Unity.

———◆———

ISAIAH lxvi. 8.

"Shall the earth be made to bring forth in one day? or shall a nation be born at once?"

WERE there no such thing in human nature as a sense of right and wrong, organized Society would be impossible. There might be co-operative clubs, mutual assurance companies, industrial partnerships, for the achievement of gainful ends ; but of such associations the principle is self-interest, the purpose is single and select, the rules are an arbitrary mechanism without pretension to natural obligation, and the whole system dissoluble by the human will which created it. These conditions could never, by any mere extension of scale, constitute *a State;* which is not a fabricated economy of man, but a spontaneous growth determined into existence by God ; which is not a contrivance for some preconceived object, but an organism co-extensive with the whole of life ; which speaks with force not of mere collective self-will free to change its voice from day to day, but of an eternal equity above the reach of mood and humour. Law is the expression of an authority more than human. We are not at liberty to make whatever statute-book we please, and choose for ourselves whether we will prohibit or encourage rapine, fraud and piracy. We can enact that only which is given us from above; which we are bound to obey ere to begin to enforce. In our legislation we are but secretaries of an auguster power ; to take down the suggestions of a Supreme rectitude, and post up the minutes of everlasting justice. The inner sense of Duty is presupposed in all outward definitions and enforcement of rights ; and the ultimate title and power to govern depend on the ability to interpret and declare with the voice of eternal majesty the verdicts and requisitions of the moral authority within.

This, however, is true of *all* States ; and assigns no reason why there should be a plurality of them. God's Moral Law is universal; man's conscience which feels and owns it is a gift, like Reason, intrinsically alike in all ; and if Law is only its interpreter, it seems consistent to demand a universal code and an all-comprehensive State. Whence then the division of tribes and nations ? By what right do they exist apart ? Is not their whole difference from each other an illusion and practical falsehood,—not a beauty, but a distortion of

the bustle of things ? May we not feel sure that
nothing is worthy save that in which the common
voice of the human race speaks in unison ; and that
whatever is special and exceptional, whatever we alone
possess and love, whatever vanishes from recognition
by change of latitude, is to be distrusted as a narrowness and let go ? And the aim of mere philanthropy
accordingly is to conquer these distinctions and remove
them, if not from outward fact, at least from human
feeling. If this view be correct, then all patriotism
must be wrong ; at best a concession to prejudice and
weakness ; and probably a surrender to temptation and
passion. Nay, all limited and preferential affections,
all at least founded on accidents of position, and not
on those moral grounds which make a difference to
God,—the ties of friendship, the attachment of family,
must be illusory sentiments, imposed upon us by
humiliating necessity, and having no validity in the
eye of higher reason.

It is evident, however, that God has not made our
world upon this plan. Not less certain than the unity
of mankind on the one hand are the ineradicable differences of race on the other,—differences which do not
lie upon the skin, but go deep into the heart of their
moral life, and regulate the manifestations of their
whole faculty. The negroes who sat for their portrait
to the father of history are still upon the African soil,
and though you take them to new climes, and set them

on the continent or islands of the west, their character-istics persevere through every experiment of slavery or freedom. The Hebrews, in universal dispersion and after centuries of money-changing and commerce, are the same as in the days of their intensest unity, amid the vineyards and olive-grounds of Palestine. The traveller who has not read the book of Genesis since he was a boy finds it brought back to him when he goes among the Arab Sheiks. And so it is through-out; the Chinese, the Hindoo, the Kelt, the Anglo-Saxon, preserve their lineaments distinct, and stamp them upon new centuries and new continents. Tribes vanish from the scene when their part is done; they are confounded with each other, as wave overtakes wave in the great tide to break indistinguishably on the shore; but while they remain their characteristics are upheld. Indeed, were it not so they would lose their very footing on this world; their distinction is their vitality; and a people with only the universal attributes of humanity would find on the civilized earth neither land nor sea to hold them more. Consider too how much is implied in that diversity of language which fanaticism esteems a curse, but with which you cannot tamper without bringing a fatal blight upon the nations. The vernacular tongue is the embodied shape of a people's thought and heart; not simply what they have happened to learn, but what it has been given them to create and fling off from their

D

mirth and sorrow, their passion and prayer ; it is their
spiritual life come out upon the air and light, and
looking out for a settlement in space and time.   Speak
for a people and it will live ; the hour it ceases to be
dumb, it first springs upon its feet and takes its stand
in history.   If no Dante had thrown aside the Latin
and broken into native song, Italy might never hope
to be more than " a geographical expression."   If
Luther had not translated the Bible and Hans Sachs
not shaped the people's lips to the very verse they fain
would speak, who can say what Germany would have
been ?   The sources of all healthful thought are
separate fountains, gushing forth and sparkling to the
day; you cannot conduct them far but they begin to
flow tepid and reluctant ; collect them into the huge
reservoir of a universal language, and distribute them
deftly as you may, they are flat and tasteless, and
disappoint any living thirst.   Every different speech
is the utterance and evidence of a naturally different
soul, intense and clear where others are dim, and empty
where some are full; and this it is that makes the
acquisition of a new language and literature little less
than the gain of a second life, and even a condition of
understanding the first.   For we die by self-repetition
and live by self-escape ; it is when natures unequal
and unlike meet upon their separate ways, and start
at the fire from each other's eyes, and feel the meanings
both noble yet not the same, that the blood quickens,

and the form of life dilates, and the divine spirit accomplishes its sacrament of thought and love. It is therefore evidently the scheme of Providence to place originally here variously contrasted types of human kind ; and far from making their differences accidental and evanescent, to establish them as the means of indefinite culture and development. Suppose them to chafe each other away and disappear ; and the world would become stupid as a country town, and history no better than an almanack. These differences then have a divine right to exist; they are here by ordination of heaven ; to love them and vindicate them is to fall in with its manifest design ; to disparage and scorn them is a vain attempt to be more catholic than God.

The physical constitution of this globe is not what its Author would have made it had he intended to constitute mankind into a single moral fraternity. In the distribution of sea and land, in the wanderings of the currents and the winds, in the flow of great rivers through the forests or the sands, in the allocation of mineral treasures and vegetable fruits, as well as in the scale of climates, he has determined the specific occupations of every region ; and thereby the habits, experience, and uppermost sentiments of its people. Each separate employment exposes to view a peculiar side of human life, demands peculiar qualities, involves peculiar temptations; and he whose horizon is determined by it will see what others miss, and ripen an order of tastes and admirations that remain crude elsewhere.   There arise class feelings and class moralities, all eccentric with regard to the balance point of perfect guidance, but so grouped around it as jointly to indicate its place.   The hard strength and fatalized will of the great manufacturer who is lord of huge forces, familiar with unerring mechanism, and carried out of routine only by the oscillations of economic law ; the flexible and dashing prudence of the merchant, schooled to freedom of hand if not presumption of calculation by vast contingencies ; the historic pride and loyal faith of the hereditary owner of the soil; the hardy self-reliance and uncertain self-restraint of the mariner who has to adapt himself to the weather or the port ; the indifferentism of the lawyer, the dogmatism of the divine ; the artisan's valuable aspirations, the labourer's dumb apathy; all constitute more or less permanent orders of interest and sentiment, and enter as factors into the country's character.   The aggregate nationality is the result furnished by all these, so far as they grow out of fixed causes inherent in the region or the race.   The individual citizens change and pass away ; persons and families shift their positions and modify their desires ; taken one by one and counted only as men, they present a mass of mutable relations unfit to be regarded as the constituents of an abiding State.   But

the great social classes of the country, being determined
by its physical features and its historic opportunities,
endure in perpetuity though with altering proportions.
These, with their peculiar moral physiognomy and
function, are the real elements and organs of the State.
As many as these classes are, so many types of desire
and opinion are sure to assert themselves from age to
age, and claim part and lot in the drama of the time.
Existing by Providential ordination, and endowed with
perpetuity, they have a right to their place; their
influence must be recognized and represented. But in
assigning its just proportions, the decision follows the
rule, not of numbers, but of social value, which may
often be greater with the smaller than with the larger
class. The persons in a country are thus grouped
according to its permanent functions ; these functions
compose the organs and give the contour to the national
life ; they are the natural units of legislative power,
whose presence and validity are essential to the vigour
and safety of the whole. The dramatist, holding the
mirror up to life, seizes not on individuals, but on
types of character for his representation ; and when he
has gone the round of our various society he has left a
perfect picture of·the English world. And so a Polity
is true to the conditions of national representation
when it sets upon its stage each generic form of want
and feeling, and permits it to speak in epic or act in
the tragedy of history.

The character then of each people has a right to self-assertion in the State, and the genius of each people to recognition in the world. They are strictly Providential trusts, which cannot be abdicated without guilt; and in the exercise of which we are not left to frigid conviction and sheer force of will, but sustained and impelled by intense natural affection. The disposition of religious people to disparage the love of one's country, not merely in its form of school-boy declamation, but in its gravest and most manly expression, is a deplorable and narrow-minded Puritanism. True, this affection is not wholly made up of rational conviction and moral preference, and has in it, with the glories, also the dangers, of all our unreflecting and disinterested passions. True, it is amenable to the higher tribunal of conscience, and can be allowed no hearing against the eternally just and true and good. But this holds equally of all our most innocent and noble inspirations, the love of home, of friends, of art, of knowledge. In their very nature they are mixed affections, half seeing and half blind, with negative concurrence and reason, but with positive force and love, with the chorus and Amen of ethical approval, but with the running melody flung out from the rhythm of the heart. Far be it from me to deny that there may be people whose love begins with esteem; probably in that case it ends there too. But with mankind in general, and especially with those whose nature is most healthy and complete, the order is reversed; and the assent of judgment is the passive condition, not the creative energy, of affection. In the dear thoughts you turn, in hours of weariness and exile, towards your own home, in the tears of joy with which you hear its merry voices ring through the silent halls of memory, you do not mean to maintain against the world that nowhere else is there such truth, such worth, such wisdom, and that our particular hearth is the real focus of God's approval. True, you know better than any other the beauty and the good that enrich and grace the sacred place; through the veil that is common and opaque to foreign eyes you pierce to whole galaxies of wonder and delight; but it is love that has couched your blindness, not sharp-sightedness that has opened the way to love. And, strange to say, attachment, though impossible without conditions of lovable character, does not positively dwell on these so much as on the neutral elements, the mere external scenes which are but the vehicles of expression; the very sign seems to touch you more nearly than the thing signified. It is not the virtues of your friend, or his wise counsels, or his steadfast will, that you bring before you when he is gone; but his image and his voice, the natural language of his form and step, even the eccentricities and characteristic imperfections that made him outwardly unique. You do not contend that they are

intrinsically beautiful and should be forced on the
world's admiration by a crusade of aggressive art. But
if they are derided and assailed, you feel that they had
a divine right *to be ;* that they had a thing to say for
themselves and for God in time and space ; that they
were inseparable parts of a lovable essence, which
else had not left its clear footprints upon reality ; and
you will not hear them rudely called in question. So
is it with the affection which men feel for their native
land. Their feeling is composed of mixed elements,
partly moral preference and insight, partly sympathy
towards features intrinsically neutral but full of
natural expressiveness. They discern and appreciate,
as no outward observer can, the particular portion
of sterling good which God has made the indi-
genous growth of their own soil. The great bases
of English character, for instance, its moderation
and veracity,—its firm hold of reality,—its reverence
for Law and right,—its historical tenacity and
aversion to speculative politics ;—these which appear
materialistic and unattractive when contemplated
from without, are the grounds of legitimate and
wholesome self-respect at home. We know them
better than we can any different good less intimate
with our own life ; and even our *blind* attachment to
them may be wiser than any precarious judgment of
understanding quickened by no love. At all events,
this attachment is the Providential guardian for the

world of the moral deposit which has been entrusted
to us, and which we are not to compromise through
indifference or to surrender to anything but indubitable
Right. And if patriotism is often quite unconscious
of its own grounds; if it does not reason on the
virtues and liberties of the national heritage, or
organize schemes for the future of the world; if its
imagination kindles chiefly at the mere mention of the
home name, or the sound of the native song; if the
mere shape of the island on the map, and the free line
of its shores should look up at our foolish eye with
unspeakable appeal; if the very hedgerows and dotted
trees, the sedgy streams and modest hills, though no
better than those of other lands, should rise into the
memory as pictures of untold beauty; this is but like
the recall of the sacred features of the absent or the
dead, not unique in loveliness themselves, but symbols
to us of a treasure consecrated and infinite.

The State then exists as the *Organ of Right;* to
define, to adjudge, to execute it, so far as the common
conscience is prepared to own, and the common arm
able to enforce it. And inasmuch as the Law of
Right is the Law of God, revealed to the heart of our
humanity, not voted into being by our self-will, there
is a deeper truth in the old religious reverence for
rightful authority than in the modern deference to
a mere collective human voice. Absurdly as the
doctrine of Divine right has been abused in favour of

forfeited and worthless claims, we do but fall into the converse absurdity if we seek the source of legitimate power below instead of above, in the accidents of popular desire, rather than the consistency of real righteousness.

This moral function, fundamental to all States, is never perfectly discharged by any. Each has its own richer vein of character, its special sense of obligation, and clears on some one side the manifold ideal of human life. This characteristic is its particular trust, to be protected by all just means; and the subsidiary affections that cluster round it, the natural ties of place and language, the heritage of historic admirations, the appeal of native poetry and music, are its living supports—the bodyguard of Immortals that ward off encroachment on the kingly genius of a Nation. This service is their justification and their glory. But for their perpetual play around the heart, no durable life, no determinate physiognomy, could belong to any human society. And the men who affect to be above them, who are too cosmopolitan to care for anything at home, who are critics and censors of all that is near them while taken by some alien fascination,—do they show any more comprehensive wisdom, or higher affection? Is not their disclaimer of a narrow prejudice of the heart usually the result of a narrower in the understanding? There is in truth a great responsibility on those who, in public life, put

themselves out of congeniality with the native Spirit
and past development of their country. And there is
a great **and** worthy service rendered by one who,
personating the better characteristics of a people, and
assuming **the** work they can best achieve, consolidates
their life, and suspends the forces that would else
divide them; especially if, like the statesman* just
removed, in his resolute war against the slave trade
he pays **his** steadfast sacrifice also to **the** principles
of universal human Right. The Unity of a people,
when at last attained by innumerable efforts, and
the struggles of a protracted history, is a grand and
sublime result,—the noblest fruit which the experience
of ages can ripen; and whoever contributes to it should
be admitted freely to his place of historic honour among
the benefactors of his time.

* Lord Palmerston.

LIVERPOOL, 1854.
LONDON, 1865.

IV.

The Mutual Duties of Nations.

—◆◆—

JER. x. 6, 7.

"There is none like unto thee, O Lord; thou art God, and thy name is great in might. Who would not fear thee, O King of Nations?"

It is obviously not the design of Providence to stock this world with a uniform humanity; but so to distribute both the endowments of nature and the gifts of opportunity as to variegate the globe with a diverse and unequal civilization. The play of contrast thus induced, the effort of one type of thought to apprehend another, the ferment of mutual admiration and repulsion, the check of each over-balancing tendency by its opposite, elicit the great forces of human progress, and save the earth from becoming a Chinese empire. Whether it will ever be otherwise; whether in some future kingdom of heaven unity of language is to attest the unity of race, and one literature, one law, one worship, will wipe out alien distinctions and leave nothing strange and new, may be left for prophets to determine.

Dazzling as such Catholic dreams may be, every approach to their realization has been marked by the spread of moral decay, and will be found at precisely the dreariest periods of history. And in the determination of present duties it would be not less criminal than visionary to ignore that constitution of the world to which, at all events, God has limited its hopes for indefinite centuries to come. To deduce a moral code from the assumptions of universal brotherhood, and ignore the fact of irreconcilable tendencies, to legislate for harmonies that only ought to be, and make no provision for conflicts that cannot fail to be, is to trifle with living obligation, and degrade conscience into a painter of romance.

Each nation, discriminated by its individuality from all the rest, forms a separate organism, and lives a distinct life ; and expressing its unity in some sovereign head, the symbol and embodiment of its being, claims and takes its place among the administrators of this world and the agents of history. It thus becomes invested with all the attributes of a *Person ;* performing responsible actions ; possessing indefeasible rights ; making binding engagements ; animated by a common consciousness ; maintaining its identity from age to age ; and gifted with indefinite life. To give intenser expression to this undying personality of the State, and cover over the very semblance of interruption, most nations have symbolized their life by *hereditary* servants, as the nearest human approach to perpetuity of aspect and of will.   Those who cannot conceive of a *person* apart from the corporeal shape of a man, may be inclined to treat this doctrine of the *personality of the State* as a mere legal fiction; yet without it they cannot advance a step in describing the simplest historic realities.   When they say, " England did this," or " France pledged herself to that," they mean neither the soil, the living inhabitants, nor the men in power, of these countries; for the first is not an agent; and the others will pass away, yet the act and pledge be visited on fresh generations.   This moral continuity of a State, whereby without offence to justice the sins of the fathers are visited on the children, and retribution strides by centuries yet finds the delinquent out at last, has in it something more than you can explain and justify by any mere individualism; it implies a collective life, and collective accountability, distinct from the cycle of private experience; a law between whose pulsations guilty generations may escape, but whose solemn throb is felt through history.   To me, I confess, there is something very mysterious in this personality of nations; nor can I persuade myself that it is a mere fiction of human thought.   Certain it is that God's government goes by it; and it is hard to think that he would conform himself in his facts to our empty tricks of abstraction.   He treats a nation *as if* it were a person; calling it to account as identical

when not a creature in it remains the same ; crowning
it with recompense when the heroes that earned it
have made way for degenerate heirs. If God acts upon
a fiction, who will tell me what is real ?

On what terms then are national personalities to
subsist side by side, and adjust their lodgment on this
earth ?

(1.) All are alike amenable to the universal moral
law ; and bound to act wholly within the limits of
justice and veracity. This is a condition into which
everything human, every will individual or collective,
is born, and from which no social partnership, no plea
of polity, will enable it to escape. The doctrine that
truth, honour, and magnanimity are good only for
private life, and have no place in the intercourse of
nations ; that self-interest is the single aim, and
chicanery and violence the allowable means, of action
in the State ; that history can be summoned before no
moral tribunal, but must have a character of its own
entitled to brand the noble and justify the guilty ; is
the creed, however common, of a shameless atheism
which believes in force and ends in tyranny. Between
State and State, as between person and person, the
right and true has eternal obligation, which no human
vote created, and no human vote annuls. It is in vain
that men in their lax tolerance and affected wisdom
pretend to slur a public crime or canonize mendacious
promises ; God abides the same, and only waits the

proper hour to show himself inexorably just; the false
race withers from the root, and proves to be no perennial in the field of time.

What then shall we say when a State starts up and
claims a new footing upon this world, for the express
purpose of giving unmolested contradiction to some
higher moral law; of laying the true foundations of
national existence in an institution like that of slavery?
We may not indeed reproach it with a crime which
not long ago was ours; we may have no potential
voice in an offence which is not international, but
domestic, and that remains the same whether poli-
tically severed or tainting a mixed and undivided
commonwealth; we may feel that the terrible experiment must be left to read its own lesson, which we
have no power to forestall; we may distrust the
solution by civil coercion as disastrous alike in its
failure and its success.   But we are not to let rational
abstinence be mistaken for moral indifference, much
less for gainful and guilty connivance.   We need not
disguise our belief that to the experiment with which
we have no call to interfere, the Providence of nations
will, in due time, have his word to say; that a social
State which exaggerates and perpetuates inferiority of
race, which denies the commonwealth, the family, and
even personality to the vast majority of its human
beings, which abrogates duties by cancelling rights,
and reduces religion to a sickly and a servile mockery,

can have no historic future before it; but, whatever be its economic expansion for a generation or two, must inevitably suffer the blight of moral barrenness which visits nations wanting other terms than God's.

(2.) With this reservation however of the universal rule of right, each nation is entitled to the free assertion and development of her own special genius. That genius is God's gift; the trust he commits to her for the benefit of the world; the distinctive essence which constitutes her personality, makes her what she is, and defines her place and function, the part she is to bear, in the great drama of humanity. To Greece, beauty and thought; to Rome, law and organization; to the Anglo-Saxon race, conquest over nature and themselves, are the talents providentially consigned; and to neglect or surrender them, at the bidding of any power or interest not higher than themselves, were not only pusillanimous, but unfaithful. The love of free institutions and of laws self-created from the justice of the commonwealth, belongs as much to the genius of England as the passion for colour or form to the artist's soul; and for any other country to look askance at this generous preference and dispute its place is no less absurd than for the merchant or the farmer to question the painter's right to be. The antipathies of prejudice and incapacity can have no authority against the trusts and endowments lent of God; and ere this truth can

clear itself to the reason, it feels its way to action in
the correct instinct of self-defence. The noble part
which this impulse plays in the economy of God's
government seems to be but little understood even by
those who allow it some authority. They concede the
right of *defensive* action ; but if you press them for
any exacter interpretation, they only mean that you
may protect your *body*, if it is attacked ! Is your
body then your definition of your all? and does
your defence of *it* exhaust your right of *self*-defence?
This surely would hold only if you were a brute, and
were known by nothing but the features of your noble
organism and your place in natural history.   But the
Self of a man is in his soul ; in his personal will, free
to take the evil or the good ; in his distinctive cast of
affection, making his latitude of temptation and opportunity different from others ; in his special insight
and faculty, demanding from him a work that shall be
his own.   These it is that make his essence, and
wield his body as their condition and their tool ; and
these it is which his instinct urges him to defend, the
moment they are wrongfully assailed, without sense-
lessly waiting till the aggression strikes a limb.   To
repel an interference with your responsible free will,
or an insult to your harmless tastes, or a censorship
over your peculiar endowments, is more truly an act
of self-defence than to ward off the blow impending
over your head.   And so is it of a nation ; whose *self*

is found not in her buildings, coasts and fields; not in her harvest, herds and stores; not even in the sinews of her peasants, and the lives of her children of to-day; but in the character she has stamped on history, the genius whose standard she has carried through time; in the type of her arts and litera-ture; in the spirit of her laws; in the pride and glory of her traditions. Whoever gratuitously tries to weaken or disparage her in any of these, as truly assails her and touches her to the quick as if he brought an armada to her coasts; and in the resistance he meets with encounters as truly her *self*-defence. In fact, this instinct is the inspiration by which each nation rises in protection of its own *essence*, and vindicates its right to be. And the moment when it most fitly starts into energy is not the last before impending physical death, but the first that announces moral danger, and hurts the integrity of the natural being. I do not say that this right is always to be exercised; much less that no proportion is to be observed between its occasion and its use. It is liable to be restrained, like other rights, by various moral cautions. It may have to give way before higher obligation or stern impossibility. But so far as it exists at all, it is valid for much more than the main-tenance of the physical life, and justly guards the whole nature that is assailed.

(3.) If, however, *each* nation is bound to vindicate a

E 2

place for her own genius, there can be none exempted from the duty of *respecting the claims of the rest.* The personalities of States subsist side by side with one another on the same terms recognized among individuals. It is not that all are really equal either in force or in excellence ; they may be in different stages of character and experience,—the boer and the sage, the neophyte and the apostle ; but as each is responsible and free, no one encroaches on the probationary experiment of the rest, diffusing, no doubt, influence by his presence, but abstaining from all interposition of his will. So among the co-existent civilizations of the world : there may be rational grounds for preferring one above another; but its higher position does not cancel its obligation to respect the independence of its neighbours, and let them work out their several problems in their own way. Nationality is to a people what free-will is to a man ; carrying with it a title to unconstrained action and development so long as no wrong is committed ; and finding a healthier discipline in its spontaneous efforts than in any imposed perfections or imitative admirations. Both in private life and in the history of States this rule of mutual forbearance and honour is perpetually violated by the egotism of mankind. Among individuals, not excepting the beneficent and good, it is not uncommon to find a narrow and rigid conception of excellence, as if it consisted of two or three prudences and charities, and all besides were spurious or questionable embellishments ; with a constant and necessarily vain striving to bring everybody into the likeness of this single type. Thus their very goodness, delightful in its place among the varieties of human love and conscience, they contrive to render disagreeable by deploring that it is not universal ; not perceiving that the world, however diligently stocked with this single form of grace, would be no longer rich as the prolific wilds of nature, but, like the nurseryman's enclosure, a garden ugly with the repetition of one flower. A certain portion of the virtues, paradox as it may seem, subsist as such only while they are exceptions. The charity by which the rich give succour to the poor becomes a curse where self-reliance ceases to be the rule, and would elsewhere make a world of the weak with no strong to help. The mercy which melts and subdues the guilty soul acts *by surprise*, and implies a steady background of retributive justice, and were it universal would simply dissolve all holy differences away. Still more unfortunate is the bigoted sympathy with some exclusive type of intellectual culture, which corrupts its admirations with partisanship, and turns its incapacities into censoriousness ; forgetting that human wants and human products are various as the climates of this world, and that souls are of every latitude, from tropic forests to the arctic moss ; and that if all were reduced, by the useful shears, to the formal hedgerows of common sense, we might have a mental world of trim roads and economic fields, but with no depth of glades, no flowing lines upon the landscape, no softening for the colour and glory of the sky. It is the same with nations. The patriot becomes the egotist, as soon as he shuts his heart against the genius of other lands, and establishes a propagandism for the peculiarities of his own. If they be really good and valid for the world, their silent presence, like the natural influence of wise and high-souled men, will better tell for their diffusion than the noisy pomp of self-esteem. The aggressive attempts of monarchs in the name of Order, of republics on the plea of Freedom, of priesthoods with the pretence of Religion, to drive back each other and coerce the world, are offences against the breadth and equipoise of God's government, which will not accept the formulas of any selfish and intolerant antipathies. There is a modesty possible for nations as for individuals; a moral and political tact, essentially one with nobleness and goodness, by which they feel, without exaggeration and without meanness, their proper place in the system of human things; firm to hold the good they have, and free from boasting where they have it yet to seek; quick to recognize the excellence foreign to the home soil, yet scorning the blind pedantry of alien admiration spoiled for the wholesome domestic love.

There is, however, a limit to the duty of mutual abstinence and respect among the collected masses of mankind. It is a restraining sentiment due between *person* and *person;* and is due wherever the personality is fully formed and still indubitably exercised; due therefore between nation and nation; due all over the morally constituted or civilized world. But between nation and *no-nation*, where one group is personal and the other is not, the obligation fails for want of the needful conditions of reciprocity. Hence, we feel it absurd to invest mere savage tribes with the rights of an organized and historical people ; and are conscious, whether we can answer him or not, of something unsound in the zeal of the philanthropist, who spends his affection on aboriginal heroism, and treats as wicked usurpation every encroachment of constituted States upon its territory. Where there is no *nationality*, but only a fortuitous concourse of individuals and families, *political* relations cannot exist, and political duty does not arise ; taken one by one, these human beings are personal existences ; taken as a whole, their aggregate is not ; they have, therefore, claims to humanity and tenderness as men, but not to recognition as a people ; and any State that has vindicated its moral personality possesses over them a natural advantage which that very fact makes rightful as well as necessary. Placed amid responsible nations, they are as the wild land of humanity, open, like the barren common amid cultured fields, to be reclaimed and annexed to a higher system; and I must think it would be an affectation, or a mistake of divine justice, were an historic Christian State to shrink from occupying this outlying margin of the earth, simply because it is not empty of human kind. Nor can we refuse to apply the same principle at the other end, where nationality, having once existed with its full prerogatives, is smitten with consumption and can discharge its responsibilities no more. As it loses its moral attributes, one by one, and from being a living person passes more and more into dead things, the moment must arrive, however difficult to fix, when other members of the great community of States must interpose to do its duties and assume its place. It is precisely at such moments that the temptation to egotism and arrogance are most felt and least resisted; and each nation, instead of owning its mere partnership of trust in the guardianship of the world, is apt to grasp for the gain of one what belongs to the equilibrium of all. But in itself this process of conquest and decay is not merely a fatal and lawless necessity to be abandoned by good men as an unmanageable devil's play; it is distinctly amenable to moral law, and reducible to just rule; not less so because the limits are often of delicate and difficult definition; for that is ever the character of right and wrong, of wise and foolish; they are never separated by hard and gaping opposition, which the knave and the fool can discern as well as the saintly and seeing eye; they are sure to be missed by sweeping affirmatives and negatives; and need for their discernment the tact of fine and living perception, the reverence for ethical differences logically slight, and the spirit of a divine consciousness ever ready to re-mould its forms.

If we have rightly interpreted the Providential order of the world, it is vain for any People to affect a policy of isolation from the great drama of its time;—to hug itself in the security of pacific gains; and look down upon the strife of justice from the window of cold neutrality. It is the glory of every civilized, especially every historic land, that its life ceases to be solitary; that its roots run through the very substance of the world; that it has pledges of honour to redeem, and conscious limits to the field of its desires. In the confederated family of nations, all own allegiance to the conscience of their common humanity, and are bound in a virtual league to guard its individual sanctities. When they have sat together round the council table of universal justice, each will retire to its place wiser and less selfish-hearted; struck with excellence other than its own, yet rendered by the very difference more faithful to the native heritage. To a nation, as to the individual, self-knowledge,—the right at once of humility and self-respect,—comes not in loneliness and seclusion, but in the testing of affection and the entanglements of sympathy. As the youth learns something of his secret temper when called to help a rival or give him the hand of congratulation ; as the old man discovers his real heart when younger faculties improve upon his work ; so may a People learn what spirit they are of, when a new nation is born before their eyes, with the promise of a fresher and kindred goodness. Is it with sullen disparagement or with frank welcome that the providential fact is met ? Is it with a tone of mean sorrow or of generous joy that the thought escapes, "He must increase, and I must decrease" ? From such appeals of Providence, the noblest discipline of humanity, may we never shrink in self-isolation ; yet in meeting them may we step without presumption, and remembering *whose* they are, take the words upon our lips, "Who would not fear thee, O God of Nations ?"

LIVERPOOL, 1854.
LONDON, 1866.

V.

Christian Resistance and Non-resistance.

ROM. xii. 19; xiii. 4, 5.

"Dearly beloved, avenge not yourselves; but rather give place unto wrath; for it is written, Vengeance is mine, I will repay, saith the Lord."

[The ruler] "beareth not the sword in vain: for he is the minister of God,—an Avenger to execute wrath upon him that doeth evil. Wherefore ye must needs be subject, not only for wrath, but also for conscience sake."

THESE two texts, within a few lines of each other, I have put together, in order to show how delusive it is to strain to the utmost detached precepts of Scripture, and allow nothing for the limiting conditions and peculiar applications silently present to the writer's mind. In the second of these passages St. Paul mentions with approval that "*avenging*" function which, in the first, he forbids the disciples to exercise; and consecrates as a divine trust and duty that *execution of wrath* to which before he had denied all place. No sooner has he exclaimed " recompense

to no man evil for evil,' than he tells civil governors
that it is their special service to " attend continually
upon this very thing,"—to do just this forbidden thing
and nothing else. Nor can it be contended that he
speaks only of the world as it is, and recommends to
the Roman Christians passive submission to its constituted authorities, without committing himself to any
sanction of their principle. On the contrary, he
distinctly identifies the *human law* which they
administer with the *divine law*, and calls them in their
representative character " *ministers of God;* " and that
which makes their office sacred, and constitutes its very
essence in his eyes is the exercise of *retributive* power,
the wielding of the penal sword against the life of guilt,
and of public honour for the faithful and the good.
Nay, he guards himself in express terms against the
imputation of giving the mere counsels of peace and
expediency ; it is " *not* for wrath only, but *for conscience sake*," that the disciples are to render their
civil obedience ;—not simply because it is prudent, not
even because it suits the unresisting character of
Christian love, but because it is no other than the
Moral Law itself that the code of States embodies ;
and to reverence it is an expression of the natural sense
of right.

Nothing then can be more certain than that the
apostle did not address to the State, or to the civil
magistrate as its representative, his injunctions to

repay evil with good. At the very moment when he condemns all vindictiveness, and entreats every tender offiee for the hungry and thirsty foe, and all the gentleness of Christ finds echo in his heart, he gives a different rule of duty to the commonwealth— viz., never to treat the evil as if they were the good, but to vindicate justice with the arm of force. If in Paul, surely in his Lord, there was no contradiction between these two things; and the utmost self-abnegation and placability of spirit between man and man could co-exist in his approval with free scope for retributive justice in the administration of the world. When therefore he said "Resist not evil, but whosoever shall smite thee on thy right cheek turn to him the other also"; he meant what Paul repeated when he told the disciples to "give place unto wrath,"— "to bless them that persecute"; and accordingly did *not* intend that punishment should cease and mercy rule alone; that public Right should lay down the sword, and the avenging arm of God's righteousness have no longer a symbol upon earth; that good-natured mutual allowance should melt away the distinctions of sanctity and sin, and proclaim universal amnesty for guilty license, and invite the insolence of unscrupulous power. Unless the words of Christ are restrained by the interpretation which Paul supplies, they must be taken to condemn all civil society whatever. For what is the whole end of legal government but simply this,—*the resistance of evil ;*—the repression of wild, destructive, selfish desires by the organized power of better principles ; the authoritative assertion of a Law which will not tolerate violence and wrong ? For a State to accept and obey the precept of Christ without qualification would be to abdicate its functions, and in reliance upon Christian love give place to universal anarchy. This undeniable consequence of their literal doctrine has actually perplexed the sects of Christian Quietists. They have not known what to make of political society and government ; have kept personally aloof from its functions ; have disowned its tribunals ; have merged its special duties in a general philanthropy ; have tried to substitute an aim at reformation for the infliction of retribution, or at least to conceal positive punishment under a negative disguise ; and in every way to sit loose from the civil ordinances of "the World" as belonging to a realm outside their own. Let us honour their efforts after an impossible consistency; but learn from its impossibility to suspect a tendency so hopelessly entangled with God's facts.

Still, the question must be asked, how are we to reconcile these two things, private forgiveness of injuries and public retribution on crime ? We see, you will say, that Paul approved of both; but what was the mediating thought by which sentiments so opposite were enabled to co-exist ? Did he, and does the religion which he taught, set up a different standard of Right for individuals and for nations? and while evangelizing the first, permit the other to remain unregenerate? Is the gospel all for private life, and the old law of nature perpetuated in public?

This reply, often avowed, oftener acted on without avowal, is the opprobrium of Protestantism. Far from admitting it, I would unreservedly maintain the unity and universality of the law of Right; which is the same for all persons, individual and collective; and speaks in the same tones to every responsible conscience. The enigma has its key in quite a different principle; and is resolved at once by this consideration; that Christianity demands the renunciation of revenge, which is personal, but does not interfere with the application of retribution, which is moral.

Surely this is no fanciful or unintelligible distinction. If the offender strikes me on the right cheek, I am to turn to him the other. But suppose he strikes my mother on the right cheek, am I to look on while he strikes her on the left? Does the precept contemplate any such case? Does it prohibit the generous interposition which flings back insults directed against the innocent, and stands between the defenceless and their oppressor? Not in the least; and if it did, no argument could be heard to prove that such a religion was divine. No; these are simply maxims of *self-*

renunciation; not renunciation of our brother's rights, of all struggle for the just and good, of all practical vindication of God's will. They suppose the case when only two persons are present on the scene—the *aggressor* and the *aggrieved;* and teach simply how to deal with the mere *hurt* inflicted on the sufferer's self-love; to suppress the resentment which promotes retaliation; to make no claim *on his own account* against the offender; but in the presence of higher ends to surrender himself to even further harm, and leave the award to a fitter tribunal than his own anger. In this solitude of relation, simply face to face with a personal foe, I may forego every title to withstand or even to protest; and if, like the first disciples, I am a lonely missionary, sent forth as a lamb among wolves, and seeking to win conquests with only the shield of faith and the sword of the spirit, it may be wise to ask no support from the sense of justice, but to disappoint insult by meekness, and break down the stubborn heart by unexpected love. But there is a third presence upon the stage in every scene of the great drama; usually in the shape of human beings, whose wrongs we witness, so that we have to play the part, not of sufferers, but of spectators, of injury; and if not, in the viewless form of God himself, whose Law demands our testimony and makes its repellant expostulation in our hearts. To confound this divine indignation at wrong with personal resentment, to see any resemblance, to miss the intense contrast, between the wrath of conscience and the petty spite of wrong, to look at the open countenance and free gesture of the one and not know it for a godly inspiration, to watch the pinched features and rigid shrinking of the other and not perceive it to be a devilish possession, is the mistake of a blindness without excuse. To quell **our** personal passion is Christian quietude; to stifle our moral indignation is sin against the Holy Ghost. There is a limit to what we have a right to surrender. We can renounce only *what is our own.* All that is really *mine,* my wishes, my pleasures, **my** property, my pride, my self-love,—these I may resign; in detaching my affections from these, and holding them ever at a higher disposal, in claiming nothing, asking nothing respecting them, and freely yielding myself, whether stripped of them or captive with them, into the hand of God to do with me as he will, constitutes the Christian's self-sacrifice; to overlook the hurts which these sustain is Christian forbearance. But our sense of right and wrong, our reverence for pure fidelity, our sympathy for struggling nobleness, our abhorrence of meanness and injustice, these are not ours to renounce; we are but their vehicle, not their possessors; they belong, not to our individuality, but to common trusts of the human race; they are the forms and media of God's life and presence in the soul,—the open court of his Law and proclama-

F

tion of his Will. To tamper with them, to let either
indolence or pity prevail over them, to refuse them the
willing service of all our natural force, is not the subjection of ourselves, but high treason against **Him.**
"Against thee, thee only, have I sinned," was the
cry of David unto God, though there was a human
plaintiff before him to reproach him with her shame
and agony. And it is the cry of all awakened penitence; which always knows the relations of its guilt to
be not human only, but divine, and sees the shadow
that scarce covers the crown of the head below, widen
as it shoots upward, till it darkens all the heaven.
Whoever, after wrong-doing, asks for human forgiveness, has no genuine penitence at heart; and if his
victim comes to him with pardoning words, he will
turn away, if his sorrow be but true, and say, "Who is
this that forgiveth sins also?" In short, the personal
affront or harm done to us we may overlook; but the
moral part of every offence it is not our prerogative to
forgive, or to treat as other than it is. We are to take our
part *against it,* as a defiance of eternal Right, which we
are forbidden to endure; which God marks out for retribution, and that chiefly through the indignation of our
hearts. Thus, the rule of Christian meekness requires
the entire relinquishment of merely individual claims;
the law of conscience and of civil society requires the
glorious vindication of that justice which is God's.

If however we are intrusted with the guardianship of

Right at all, we are bound to lend it all our resources, and to arm it with the weapons of force. Whether in defence against its own criminals, or in the repulse of external injury, a State has no other means of executing its mission. All Law rests on the principle of coercion, and is limited by the range of possible enforcement. It is a simple avowal of certain rules by which people ought to live ; with notice that if they do not put the restraint upon themselves, it will be put on *for* them. There is in some persons a sort of superstitious horror of all coercion, or application of force in the service of moral ends, which arises, as it seems to me, from a false spiritualism, and overlooks the relation between the divine life that penetrates this universe, and the material organism which manifests it. What *is* force, after all ?—the influence, of whatever kind, which procures actions not promising to arise spontaneously,—an influence varying in intensity according to the degree of reluctance it has to overcome. No doubt it were well,—nay, strictly speaking, the only thing absolutely and spiritually good, if all men were as angels, and did the will of God continually from the willing instincts of pure and fervent hearts ; if the inner fire of holy love were ever kindled and ever clear, neither damped and smouldering beneath the weight of temptation, nor fanned into intemperate heats. No doubt it is a poor substitute for the native power of divine affection and the freedom of glad choice

F 2

when in the individual, the family, the nation, the outward order of God's will is merely copied through constraint and fear. The soul that is simply *overawed* into right, whether by human opinion or by penal fires of earth or hell, rises no higher than mere prudence, and leaves the Christian standard far behind. If this be the comparison by which coercive influence be tried, we can hardly disparage it too much; and to introduce it while any nobler appeal remains untried, and free affection only waits a call, is to postpone the kingdom of heaven, and prefer a smaller sway. The real question however arises on comparing force, not with the purer order that stands as the term above it, but with the disorder that is the next step below it. Is it better to have compelled obedience, or none at all? the self-restraint of prudence, or a reckless anarchy? imitative habits of homage to divine Law, or a wild defiance of whatever is sacred? As we have to deal with an earth and not a heaven, with natures tempted and self-enthralled, not with emancipated Spirits, we cannot afford to dispense, in any department of life, with coercive influence, to support and eke out the defective energy of conscience. There may be in all men a latent reason and moral sense, a susceptibility to finer appeals, which infinite persuasion might reach and rouse. But meanwhile our resources fail, and rebel wills run riot; and we cannot afford to wait for their possible conversion. When we have exhausted our preventive resources, we have to deal with a remnant of realized iniquities; and to provide for a world in which there is ever a faction in revolt. What remains to us, in treating such a problem, but to imitate God and *enforce* the right which we fail spontaneously to produce. He, with boundless store of moving appeals and higher persuasion, does not refuse to govern us by a thousand coercions; visiting the body with the stripes of many a malady for its excesses, incarcerating the soul in darkness for her unfaithfulness; threatening the selfish negligence of nations with hideous decay or frightful revolution; and keeping open the gates of hell for wickedness that succeeds in flourishing on earth. Do you say, " God will repay, it is for man to let alone"; I reply, God acts, throughout his moral rule, not apart from man, but through him. Our nature it is that reflects his moral image, and is the organ of his moral empire; if we were swept away he would manifest but a physical life upon this planet; in proportion as we slumber, in passive reliance on some other agency than his, his living Word retreats, and his voice dies upon the heavy air; and were we all to break loose and play the carnival of fiends, our punishment would be that he would seem to be changed too, and we should take him for Satan instead of God. No; his Kingdom is realized in the approximating efforts of our communities and the highest wisdom of our laws; human society is the organism of his spirit; and his work is done no otherwise than through the energy of our noblest faculties and the persevering subjugation of everything lower to its higher.

If coercion be allowed at all for the attainment of moral order, there seems to be no reason, beyond the rational calculation of efficacy, for stopping short at one degree or form of it rather than another. All merely physical powers are at the rightful disposal of the ends, human and divine, that are higher than themselves; and *if* they can be made available for the enforcement of just restraints upon lawless passion, whether at home or abroad, I know of no principle which antecedently precludes resort to them. It is henceforth a question of gradation and detail alone. There is no intelligible ground of distinction between what is absurdly called "*moral* compulsion" and physical; between pain to the body and torture to the mind; between simple constraint and active infliction; between forfeiture of liberty and forfeiture of life; between the execution of national law by police, and of international by armies. This position we have shown to be untenable in natural reason, and unprotected by any gospel law. The Master himself and the chiefest of Apostles alike recognize the solemnity of public retribution and the obligation of private meekness; and feel no inconsistency between the self-assertion of Right and the self-abnegation of personal and passionate claims. On our own behalf we are taught to resist not evil; on God's, never to forego the righteous claims of the good. Force, no doubt, is a rude instrument, and by countless abuses has too well deserved its evil name. It has deserted the service of right, and set up for itself, in alliance with the wanton will it should restrain. Even in righteous hands it has mistaken its own limits,—and sought to control the inner thought, the fleeting word it could not reach, and many an outward act of conscience that looked down on it with scorn. It has buried prophets in its dungeons, and loaded patriots with its chains. It has armed priestly hands with stones to hurl at martyrs, and has lighted the pile of many a costly sacrifice. The more need is there not to surrender it to blind and selfish passion, while justice goes about as a suppliant unarmed. We are not yet among the saints in heaven where all goes by pure veneration and love; but in a mixed world of tempted, struggling, conquering and falling men; of sinking and rising nations; of plotting tyrannies and inexperienced freedom; of hoary-headed superstitions and an artless youth of thought; and so long as this strife remains it will be indispensable, after exhausting every appeal to the conscience and the heart of men, to make the acknowledged Law of God a terror to evil-doers; and where it cannot win them to spontaneous reverence, constraining them to reluctant obedience.

LIVERPOOL, 1855.
LONDON, 1866.

VI.

Right of War.

——◆◆——

REV. xix. 11, 13.

" And I saw heaven opened, and behold a white horse ; and he that rode upon him was called Faithful and True, and in righteousness he doth judge and make war. And he was clothed with a vesture dipped in blood ; and his name is called the Word of God."

It is worthy of remark that those sects which have most condemned all resort to coercion for the attainment or vindication of moral order in human affairs, have attributed to the Divine government the employment of force without stint. While trying to empty the natural realm of everything terrible, they have believed in a preternatural in which it occupies the greatest share. Proclaiming the principle of love to be the one heavenly sentiment which lifts us into affinity with the Highest, and forbidding in its name either retribution or constraint, they yet threaten us at the hand of God with the very wrath which it is wicked to allow, and draw pictures of penal judgments from which his forgiveness will never release. They denounce the intrinsic sinfulness of war; yet believe that under the Jewish dispensation the Holiest commanded it in its most exterminating form. They object to corporal chastisement; yet devoutly read that Paul was filled with the Holy Spirit when he struck Elymas the sorcerer blind. They disapprove of the punishment of death for even the most revolting crimes; yet in the case of Ananias and Sapphira, do not scruple to see Peter miraculously visit it upon a lie. They seek a kingdom of God which disowns every agency but the appeal to conscience and the pleading of affection; yet expect its realization in an Advent guarded with flaming swords, by a Son of God bringing "vengeance on them that know not God," and through the sentence of sweeping exile into an "everlasting fire prepared for the devil and his angels." Strange inconsistency! as if what were guilt on earth could be holiness in heaven; and the universe could be administered on principles, and in its final issues could express affections, which it would prove a man unregenerate to feel! It only proves how little the human mind can really dispense with the rule of retributory justice: how, if removed from one part of existence, it will assert itself in another; how love, when separated from it, though aiming to set itself forth as a divine perfection, turns out to be a human weakness; and how the stock of physical force and fiery terrors in this universe is felt, after all, to have its proper function and its ultimate destination in vindicating the Law of God, and securing to the good its final triumph over evil.

The Christian rule of " forgiveness " (it has been shown) does not enable us to pardon *moral guilt*, but only *personal affront*. It does not release us from the obligations of justice, which constrain us to deal with men according to their character, to hinder the wrong and help the right. It exempts no one of the resources at our disposal,—persuasion, discipline, power,—from free use in this service ; and if, by letting any of them lie idle, we permit an injustice we might prevent, we are in the sight of heaven accomplices in its perpetration. Bodily strength, and the skill which arms it with mechanical increase, are as much intrusted to us for this end as any faculty of thought and affection ; and to maintain that we may employ it in the service of our own convenience and luxury, but not in the defence of innocence and the repulse of guilt, is an incomprehensible and untenable paradox. Indeed everyone who puts his money in an iron safe, or a chain upon his house door, relinquishes his reliance on the appeal of reason and conscience, and accepts the aid of material power. And if, further, he has ever restrained the arm, or chastised the disobedience of a passionate child; if he has availed himself of the services of the police to arrest and the courts to try the offender against his person or goods; if, in short, he consents to have a place in civil society at all; he has engaged himself, by active coercion, in resistance to evil, and in his private capacity *gone to war* with the delinquencies he meets.

Nay, in the earlier stages of every historical community, the ends of justice, now so quietly obtained, were literally accomplished no otherwise than by *going to war*. Natural resentment, individual moral indignation, rising against the evil-doer and hurling him out, is the first protection which heaven provides against unjust aggression. The sympathy of observers prevents the strife remaining single, and soon supplies a law which the one combatant is glad to accept, and the other forced to obey. The neighbourhood however long continues small through which the same authority is acknowledged, and the weapons of personal defence laid down on its behalf. In the next village, or the next barony, another tribunal is obeyed; and a dispute between the two circles is settled by trial of local arms, adjoining districts often taking sides. A succession of such struggles disengages at last, and fixes in distinct form, the moral judgment of a wider circle, and erects a court of larger jurisdiction to interpret and enforce it. But while private feuds are thus banished between barony and barony, they may still break out between county and county, till by similar experience a common feeling is found which covers a broader area, and insists

on its verdict of right. With widening intercourse
and more settled relations the range of public law
extends; till at last province has no longer border-wars
with province, but settles its cause by Imperial appeal.
Throughout this process, what is the moving spring, the
real natural force, which conducts the march of security
and order ?—what but the human indignation at wrong,
—at first isolated and momentary; but gradually feeling its way to concurrence in expanding circles, till it
organizes itself into national law ?   Had that primitive
anger never struck a blow, no rudiment of social rights
would have appeared.   It is the arms of yesterday that
have won the field of justice for to-day; and the
fairest growths of peace have roots not unwatered by
blood.   And after all, Law in the last resort can but
economise force, and does not *dispense with it*.   It
transfers the weapon from the private to the public
hand, and stops the lavish violence of individual
passion.   But what would be the value of a judiciary
without an executive visible behind it ?   What else is
the whole penal administration of a country but its
perennial civil war against its own incorrigible
criminals ?

Far be it from me to say that the process of pacification
which replaces the warrior by the judge must necessarily
stop with the limits of each country.   As the barriers
disappear which hinder the sympathy of land with
land, the sense of a common justice and an eventual

common interest cannot fail to spread ; and already its beginnings are traced in the faint and uncertain outlines of International Law. But at present the group of European nations are in corresponding relative positions to baronies of the same county, ere yet there was any dominant power to summon them to its tribunal ; and as the struggle of castle with castle, and the alliances of chief with chief, were the means of ascertaining the common feeling, and working out the balance of a common right ; so, if States are ever to be brought into a court of general jurisdiction, they have yet to win by a like experience of conflict both the code which is to be there administered, and the cosmopolitian executive which shall enforce its decrees. Meanwhile, we are neighbours, each with his own trust, his own conscience, and his own force ; bound to keep what is committed to us, and not to stand by while wanton wrong is done. For these ends we have no guiding law but the sympathies of justice which bring States into generous alliance ; and no administrative power but those armed battalions which are the only police of nations. A people without an army is chargeable with more than folly. It refuses its fair contribution to the police of the world ; and if, while the power is there, it selfishly looks on, though murder it might prevent is passing before its eyes, its standard blazons forth a lie, and becomes the symbol, not of order, but of anarchy. As the feuds of individuals

and clans have been the parents of municipal law, so
the hostile collisions of nations are the necessary conditions under which, if at all, an authoritative code
can clear itself for the States of the civilized world.
The path to the court of justice lies, alas! through the
camp of war.

If this be so,—then there is no propriety in limiting
the right of using force to the case of self-defence.
Even using the word in its widest acceptation, and
understanding by the nation's *Self* not its territory
only, but its whole essence and genius, its children,
its arts, its honour, its place in the world, still it is
not this alone for which it holds its gift of strength.
To others as well as to itself it has to see that right is
done; and if with Cain-like sullenness it asks, "Am I
my brother's keeper?" the God of retributive history
replies, "Thy brother's blood calleth to me from the
ground." The justifying plea of war is not personal
danger, but moral equity; which indeed gives the title
to protect yourself, but also imposes the duty of
protecting others. There is an astounding meanness
in this doctrine of modern casuistry, that an injury
may be resisted if it be against yourself, but must be
let alone if it fall upon your neighbour; as if your
sacred person in particular were the turning point of
moral good and evil; and it were no rule that the
strong are to help the weak, but only that the strong
may help themselves! Defend yourself by all means;

but see to it that you defend yourself because it is right ; and not your right because it is your own. There is a curse upon selfishness in States, not less than in individuals. Often indeed a nation wins its first moral greatness in struggles for its own freedom, and from the sufferings and heroisms of that time makes up the earliest crown of brilliants that history puts upon its brow. But it can preserve no enduring nobleness if the power it has vindicated be used in no service but its own, and amid the ferment of humanity it cares for nothing but its securities and gains. Generous sympathy and self-denying action are just as indispensable a discipline for a collective people as for each man among the mass ; if you despise the wealthy recluse who shuts himself up in his country house, without a thought that disturbs his ease, whether for the worthy enterprises of his equals, or for the sins and miseries of the village at his Park-gate, how can you praise a State that never listens to the groans of oppression, or spares its cruse of oil to feed any lamp of foreign liberty ? And what common action can a nation have, what magnanimous sacrifices can it make for others' good as well as God's justice, unless it takes its responsible place in the council chamber of the world, and causes its voice to be respected for faithfulness and resolution ? It is only foreign matters, problems starting up in the great commonwealth of States, that can ever call a nation out of itself, and by directing an enthusiasm abroad, clasp it in genuine unity at home. Every other influence is either personal, sectional, or world-wide; this alone finds expression for the country's heart, and opens for it its distinctive place in history. Boast is made of commerce, as knitting the bonds of sympathy between land and land. It may link the sea-board of many a latitude, but it unites the hearts of none; it is rich in geographical distribution, but not in historical creation; it is the expression of self-interest, not of self-forgetfulness; it is the speculation of individuals, not the enterprise of the State. And if anyone thinks that its grandest scale and hugest capital can constitute the life of a great people, let him ask the muse of history what she has to tell of Phœnicia, but stupid traditions of monster ships and universal factories, and vile idolatries and Cornish tin; what also of Carthage, except her one military effort, and her one great hero whom her merchant princes hated and disgraced; and what, in comparison, of sterile Attica, which, in the name of Europe to this hour, denied its earth and water to Asiatic despotism, and not only earned a glorious existence for herself, but on the field of the world substituted for Oriental monotony the priceless example of Hellenic beauty, simplicity, strength and wisdom. It is the sympathy of person for person that puts a soul into private life, and makes it human with pity and love; of class for class, that gives to a nation manly vigour and a fearless brow; of nation with nation, that touches the world with moral nobleness, and turns history from a statistic almanac or a volume of price-currents into the Epic of humanity,—nay, the very biography of God. What makes the sixteenth century so rich a page in British and European annals? Do you suppose it was the mere dogma of Wittenberg or Geneva? When the dogma triumphed the glory was gone. No! it was the fellow feeling of one struggling Church through many nations; the flash of pity and the cry of shame that darted on the Netherlands, crushed and tortured by the tyranny of Spain; the eye kindling with sympathy towards the young life and faith of the time, watchful against sacerdotal conspiracy, and eager for openings to help against oppression. The torpor of selfish ease was broken; foreign ideas stirred the intellect; foreign admirations moved the heart; foreign persecutions quickened the pulse with generous resolve; and the high consciousness of a responsible place in the family of nations and the courses of time gave to England a dignity of mien and thought which she has scarce known since.

No doubt, this openness, on adequate occasion, to mingle in moral struggles of the world involves a readiness for war; and must be regulated by the clear sense how dreadful is the scourge of war. On its miseries and horrors I will not dwell; they are such

as to render a selfish, a rash, an ill-ordered war the
greatest of crimes; but they are *not* such as to justify
us in preferring, when we can prevent, the triumph of
wrong.   Those who in this argument draw in detail
the picture of the battlefield, the siege, the hospital,
the mourning homes, the crippled bodies, the wasted
treasures, involved in the conflict of great nations,
practise deception on themselves and contribute little
to the solution of the moral problem.   In such painting
both the spirit and the scale of these things are falsely
presented, because falsely compared.   Wounds inflicted, wounds received by men acting as the organs
of a higher personality, and inspired by a sense of
fidelity and honour to a power that has a right to
wield them at its will, are not the same things as cuts
in the private flesh made upon their own account; not
debasing the giver, and glorifying the suffering to the
receiver.   And however awful the dimensions of this
evil measured by the standard of the individual
observer, taking himself as the unit, and multiplying
that unit in imagination till it covers the statistics of
privation and death, their magnitude is very different
when estimated by their fractional relation to the unity
of a people's life.   Even to decimate one of its generations, what would this be as the price of that self-
respect and faithfulness without which the very terms
of existence are ignoble, and the most comfortable of
populations is nothing but a blot upon the world?

Where God embodies great principles in historic forms, and makes mighty nations the organs and medium of moral conflict, it cannot be expected that the arbitrament should take place without a piercing shriek of the hour, wailing and dying down the winds of time. There is no chloroform for earthquakes; the giant mountain heaves and cracks with its throes; but when the equilibrium returns, the villages rise again, the plough cleaves again the resting soil, the vine-trellice reappears upon the slope, and the Spring field smiles beneath the sun once more.

The objection is often brought against the morality of war, that the soldier is not the principal in the quarrel, but hires himself to kill, without regard to the rectitude of the cause. The remark appears to me essentially unjust in two respects. He does not hire himself out to kill; killing is not the end of an armed force, but only the possible means by which it may enforce its defence of right. As well might you say that the surgeon exists for the sake of *wounding;* or that the apprehension and incarceration of a culprit by the police was kidnapping a man into slavery. And that he is agent of a higher authority, obliged to act without option of his own, is equally true of every public servant. The Judge engages in like manner to award punishment, not excepting the alternative of life or death, according to the law as he finds it, be it according to his private estimate of equity or

not. Nor as a general rule is there anything
degrading in *this* surrender of individual judgment.
To go into the hands of a *lower* authority than ourselves is indeed debasing ; but to act as the vehicles of
a higher personality, whose decisions have natural
right over us, is an ennobling sacrifice of self-will ; it
quiets the egotism of the part, in presence of the Duty
of the whole. To what extent precisely this renunciation of individual judgment may go, is no doubt a
delicate question, which comes back upon us in a
hundred forms, and has to be practically answered
every day by the Statesman, the advocate, the
ecclesiastic,—in truth by all who have to act in a
representative as well as a personal capacity. And
cases cannot fail to arise in which the private conscience is at positive variance with the public,—is
preoccupied,— like the mind of the early Friends,—
with intense convictions clashing with recognized
national obligations. For such a conjuncture what
solution shall we find ? Is the Christian citizen to
violate his sense of Right ?—Or is the Commonwealth
to resign its claim upon him ? Neither the one nor the
other ; it is the Duty of the State to enforce ; it is the
duty of the individual to resist ; till out of the moral
struggle between them the disputed problem clears
itself, and the appeal to the judicial conscience of
humanity has been adequately heard and answered.
Like the pleas of two suitors in court, such con-

troversies may quite well be honourable on both sides; and only by the trial of spiritual strength which they involve can the rude public conception of Right be purified of tyranny, and the scruples of individuals discover their eccentricity. But these are exceptional collisions. In the usual course of national history we are not to presume on any such contrariety between personal and social obligation; and where they are in that healthy degree of accordance which a State like ours secures, there is nothing unworthy of a noble mind in becoming the executive organ of national resolve.

Even the terrible right—or rather the stern trust—of Arms, I do not hesitate to claim for every righteous State. With that last arbitrament, however, all questions cease. It is the confession of something irresolvable by Reason, irresolvable by Right; it is a solemn appeal to the collective forces, spiritual no less than material, which God has shut up in our humanity. Here, therefore, the Christian moralist comes to the end of his theme; owns that his principles avail to settle nothing more; that all beyond is indeterminate except in the counsels of eternal Providence. In surveying the great natural relations of the civilized world, I have endeavoured to draw them within the lines of a Divine order; to make them unconditionally amenable to universal Moral Law, which holds all races, times, and latitudes; to vindicate (on these terms) the conditional right of each people to its special genius and forms of good; to find a place, in this view, for the varieties and inequalities of men, their local love, their alien languages, their inherited traditions; to insist on the responsible personality of nations, binding them to veracity and honour, and making selfish isolation shameful; and to show that not the will and word alone, but the force also, of a people must be held at the disposal of those high trusts for which it has a life given to it in history.

When, in the light of these thoughts, we look at the great features of our time, signs of promise meet us everywhere, which the shadows of war and the cloud in the west are insufficient to eclipse. There is a temper abroad,—a league of silent sympathy, a consciousness of mutual duty, among the directing minds and earnest classes of many European countries, in the presence of which even tyrannies have to rest upon their *character*, and Superstition to make terms with Reason. The resurrection of a great nation,—its sudden entrance among us with the seals of its sleep broken and its infirmities left behind, is naturally followed by a political Pentecost, which pours out a new spirit on us all. Its marvellous examples, of heroic resolve, of wisdom in counsel, of moderation in act, have been upon a scale which forbids despondency even under irreparable loss, and fills us again with living faith in the future of the world. What form that future may assume it is not ours to see. But we may be sure it will harmonize with the progressiveness of God's ways; and so fair is its first gleam that the young may well rejoice to enter, the old regret to leave, the stage on which it will appear.

LIVERPOOL, 1855.
LONDON, 1870.

VII.

The Sphere and Spirit of Faith.

HEB. xii. 2.

"Looking unto Jesus, the author and finisher of Faith."

IF we were called upon to state the leading characteristic of modern religion, it might be said, without any
wide departure from the truth, that ours is an age fond
of *trying to believe*. It is not uncommon to meet, in
the same person, with the head prone to doubt and the
heart averse from it. The struggle between the two is
often sad to witness; though not half so humiliating
as the unfaithful determination to throw it off, and
close it by dishonourable capitulation; to put it out of
sight by a mock triumph of one of the contending
powers; involving thenceforth either a real slight of
that which is suspected to be noble, or a false homage
to that which is secretly despised. This is a thing
which, in spite of fashion and the show of pietism,
Christ, were he among us, would denounce as he did a
Pharisee; for it was on this very ground that, while

he never inveighed against the sceptic Sadducees, he set himself completely against the high religious party of his day, and so was crucified by the saints and popular preachers of Jerusalem. But on the sincere and secret conflict between the intellect and the affections, so long as it was truthfully conducted and patiently endured, he would surely look with a divine pity, and help it to a harmonizing faith. Often, I am persuaded, it is a natural cross, which God himself puts upon his children to bear with meekness unto the hour when they are received up. Oftener it is the result of the ill-proportioned culture so prevalent in complicated societies. An understanding, requiring to *know* before it will believe, cannot adjust itself to affections ever longing to believe what they cannot know; and as we have lost the art of mediating between the opposite tendencies, and blending into one healthy nature the elements of thought and feeling, we have nothing but a devotion that is irrational, and a reason that is undevout. The mind's demand for proof impertinently interrupts the heart's disposition to trust; and whichever gains the victory is conscious of being frowned or laughed at by the other. And so we find nor faith nor doubt that is not ill at ease; without courage, without freedom, without hope. The religions of our time are full of fears, and shrinking with antipathies; charged with holy horrors; drawn hither and thither by pious repulsions; trimming their course for the avoidance of evil, and flying from shadows that dart around them from lights beyond their reach. Their trembling security in the present is evident from their antiquarian propensity to reproduce the past. A nation ever emigrating to foreign lands is suffering uneasiness at home; and an age eager for historical revivals betrays a living unbelief. Distant countries lie quiet on the map for those who have domestic liberty and content; and distant times will keep their far perspective for those who have a God at hand. Why go back with so much learned reverence, and scrape up the soil of centuries for a few old seeds and exotic roots to be forced on the hot-bed of our faith's decay, as if we dwelt in a desert where heaven clothes no grass with beauty, and permits no tree of life to grow? Depend upon it, the true soul of faith is ever trustful and prospective; with no moping and monastic face bent downward to peer into the abyss where the giant shadows of departed ages lie; but with features uplifted to the morning light, and kindled with the blushing heavens of the opening time. It loves the young spirit of every earnest period. It has no fear of the world lapsing into decrepitude and living into incorrigible superannuation, so that there is no hope but in putting back the shadow on the dial to its middle-age career; but remembers that every soul that is born is as fresh and new as the first life in Paradise; as open to the mellow breath of creation; as quick to answer the tones of human love ; as ready to listen to the whispers of the warning and inspiring God. Far different from this is the frightened and fluctuating religion of the present day, which exhibits to us the last effort of exhausted creeds to uphold the glorious fabric of human worship, like old Atlas, fainting beneath the weight of heaven. No man can suppose that Reason and Faith, the two highest distinctions of our nature, are really at variance with each other. It must be some false representation of one or both of them which gives them such temporary appearance. And in hope of finding the point of their real harmony and their seeming discrepancy, we may endeavour to determine their respective limits.

Faith, according to all latitudinarian churches, is nothing else than *imperfect knowledge*. It is *opinion*, resulting from the operation of preponderating evidence. Knowledge is that of which we are assured by our own senses or consciousness ; Faith, that of which we are assured by the testimony of others, by general reasoning, or by any *indirect* means. They differ only as truth at first hand differs from truth at second hand. No further than within the sphere of our personal perception can we be said to *know* ; all beyond this is the object of *belief;* and the process of inference, by which we extend our thoughts further than our individual experience, is in all cases the same ; so that whether we are determining the reality of Hannibal, or the existence of God,—the boundaries of the antarctic continent or the outlines of the immortal life,—the crown rights of the Stuarts, or the divine authority of Christ, we must pursue the same method of procedure, and apply like rules of argument. Faith, therefore, is not at all peculiar to heavenly things ; it has the nearest and the lowest objects, as well as the furthest and the highest; the divine has no more to do with it than the human. Natural religion is only an extension of science, the Creator being known to us precisely in the same way as the law of gravitation ; and revealed religion is a branch of history, Providence and futurity being reported to us by the testimony of Jesus, just as the history of Solon and the theology of Egypt by the evidence of Herodotus. All alike lie within the range of the understanding, and are amenable to the maxims of the inductive logic.   Religion has no more mystery in it than mechanics ; and though its doctrines have general value, when ascertained, their discovery is an affair of the mere intellect ; and faith in them is as little a moral act as belief in the nebular hypothesis or the Copernican system.

In order to show the real character of this rationalistic theory of faith, it is only necessary to point out a few of the consequences which it plainly involves.

(1.) If all that we *know* is that which is present to Sense and Consciousness, then the whole of human knowledge must be possessed by the brutes; for these are precisely the powers which they possess in common with ourselves. Our senses have no wider range and no exacter discrimination than those of the creatures below us. What can our eye boast of that the vulture's does not surpass? or our ear, which can compete with the listening antelope? Let perceptions of this class be dignified with the exclusive name of knowledge, and all creatures that can hear and see possess the requisites of knowledge, and no man is wiser than the beasts of the field.

(2.) If the moment we leave the range of the senses and consciousness we quit the domain of knowledge, and enter that of faith, then the whole body of human science is handed over from the denomination of knowledge to that of faith. For scientific truths, it is evident, are no objects of sight or hearing; they present us with a series of laws deduced by processes often exceedingly circuitous, and always removing us by several steps from the contemplation of particular facts. Make immediate perception the characteristic of knowledge, and we can no longer be said to know the composition of the atmosphere, or the orbit of the planet Mars, or the solidity of the Sun, or the existence of the Antipodes; we must profess our *faith* (as in things unknown) that there was once such a people as the Athenians, and is now such a country as China. Nothing can well be more perverse than this appropriation of the term Knowledge to the animal consciousness, and denial of it to the rational thought.

(3.) If conviction obtained by testimony and inference constitute *faith*, then, being gained by an act of pure reasoning, it is open to all intelligent beings alike. It sustains no relation, in its origin, to the natural feelings and conscience, and may be possessed in perfection by a mind entirely destitute of the moral sentiments and affections. In short, it is the mere triumph of *Intellect over Sense;* so long as a cold impartiality is maintained for the sifting of evidence, the process is neither helped nor hindered by the presence of a Will, be it of angel or of reprobate ; and the promise to the "pure in heart" that they " shall see God," means that they will give a candid hearing to the evidence of his Being !

(4.) Revelation, according to this view, is a simple case of external testimony. Christ reports things physically known to him, and informs us what has been presented to his observation. He has been told that there is another life, and he comes and tells us. He has heard it said that the hairs of our head are all numbered, and he telegraphs it on to us. So far as can be learned from the language of the theologians to whom I refer, they actually suppose that the Infinite Spirit talked (in Syro-Chaldaic) to the ear of Jesus, and showed off proof miracles before his eye to satisfy his doubts, and sent him with a literal " message," or set of grammatical propositions, to be repeated in Galilee and Jerusalem ; and if they were to discover that to the Redeemer's senses, no less than to their own, God never broke his everlasting silence ; that the solitudes of Nazareth were only deep and awful, and left the prophet's meditations free ; that the midnights on the mount were fanned only by the breath of nature, and roofed only with the speechless stars ; if they were to be assured that Jesus saw no unaccountable phantasmagoria, and was startled by no audible voice, they would renounce him as an impostor, and hold themselves deceived. Tell them that it was Thought and Love and Sanctity that filled Christ with divine and imperishable truth, and they will feel sadly disappointed, and say, " Is that all ? we fancied it was sight and hearing ; we will walk with him no more." Yet, if all this materialism were true, Christ would be revealed to us in a manner infinitely below the reality ; he would be merely a discoverer, telling his excursions to his people at home ; or a witness entering our court. What he has done is simply to increase our information, and contribute something to our science. And he himself has shown *no faith.* He knew it all as an affair of perception, and was secured against having to take anything on trust. In the very act of being our teacher he ceased to be our model ; and in proportion as he became qualified to instruct us by his lips he was unfitted for inspiring us by his life.

So ends the theory of those who apply the physical notions of the heathen oracles to the interpretation of the scheme of Christianity.   Thinking to keep their judicious foot upon the earth, they grope they know not whither ; and become blind leaders of the blind, both falling into the ditch !

In fact, it is in vain that liberal divines endeavour to strip faith of that *moral* character, which Christ, and Paul, and John, and every age of the Christian Church, and the unperverted feelings of every pious mind, ascribe to it.   It is, and in spite of the babblings of false philosophy, will remain to be, first-hand belief, not second-hand belief; and yet in all respects as reasonable and as indispensable as belief upon the strongest proof.   It is the interpretation which pure affections, and awakened conscience, and ideal apprehensions are constrained to put on the invisible ground and realities of our existence.   Of the whole realm of things open to our conceptions, there is a portion within the reach of our discovery by Sense or Inference, and an infinite remainder beyond.   The one is the field of Science ; the other is the sphere of Faith.   Through the one we are guided by our intellectual light, and move with the careful steps of number along the traces of constant law.   In the other, these vestiges of everlasting order soon vanish from our perspective ; and though knowledge is ever pushing on her lines of observation, and making straight in the desert this highway for our God, the unreclaimed region is still boundless after every successive reduction. There it lies, brooding around our thought, impenetrable to our perceptions; haunting us as an infinite night, into an inch or two of which our rushlight shoots its tiny bunch of rays; and how shall we deal with a presence so awful, which may be the hiding place of thunder and destruction, or the nest where the morning light of godly order awaits its birth? We believe that all is well; we make the darkness the secret dwelling of our God; we are sure that no terror lurks therein; we put forth an un-trembling foot, assured that it will find a sufficient ground, and lift a waiting hand, persuaded that we shall be led; we do not doubt that if in the twinkling of an eye a new sun were to be kindled in the midst, it would show no skulking horrors, no retreating fiends, but only some unlooked for apparition of steady order and silent loveliness. This is *Faith*—this taking of the hidden universe *on trust;* this tranquil belief in good without evidence, except the internal evidence of beauty and excellence in the thing itself. And may we not then say in a word, that as *in science* the intellect inhabits the *known*, so *in faith* the moral sentiments and affections take occupancy of the *unknown?*

If this be a true account of the matter, we shall find the sphere of things differently divided between science and religion in every age, ever changing with

H

the shifting boundaries of knowledge. And no fact is
more plainly marked in the history of human progress than this. The frontier line of religion has
constantly receded, as discovery has advanced; and
has abandoned province after province once consti-
tuting a portion of its holy land. Where Homer's
awful ocean-stream nightly floated the sun from West
to East, the sea-captain will show you the soundings on
his map ; the approaches to Tartarus now swarm with
colliers; the Titans groaning beneath Ætna have been
stifled by modern chemistry and lie dead. The
demons of madness have become inflammation of the
brain. The telescope has burst through the old
windows of heaven, pushed the survey of our senses
past the primeval throne of God, and sent us forward
in search of Him amid a forest of worlds, of whose
shadow there was not the faintest mark on the most
distant horizon of ancient genius. And geology spreads
before us mighty cycles, whose expansion has burst and
shivered the old creation week, turned its six days'
wonders into boundless ages of order more wondrous
far, and driven chaos sheer away into fabulous chrono-
logy. And yet, with all this, though we have the
more to know, we have no less to trust; the proportion
is constant, and remains quite unchanged, between our
bounded science and our infinite religion ; as our range
of vision opens, our sphere of conception also grows ;
and the highest angel must have as large a realm of

faith as the simplest child. If means of physical transit from planet to planet were ever to be found out in the progress of human art; and if, in a voyage of discovery through the skies, some explorer were to land on a world where he met with the departed generations of our race, and conversed with Abraham and Socrates and Christ; from that moment the future life of man would be transferred from our Religion to our Science, and would have a chapter to itself in every subsequent treatise on astronomy. And those who already occupy that life, find it a reality present to their perceptions; and send forth their sweet hymn of faith into the ages yet dark to them, and the secrets yet invisible, from their station of glorious advance.

It is not, however, *every* conception or persuasion about the unknown, not the mere consciousness of its existence and conjecture of its contents, that constitute faith. Every man is aware that there are things beyond his ken; every man makes some sort of representation to himself of how they may be; but we do not call all these notions indiscriminately by a religious name. He who fills the abyss of Death with annihilation; he who takes the unseen Rule of the world to be a dead Fate; he who expects an inevitable declension, or a hopeless periodicity, in human affairs; is regarded as *destitute of faith*, though, after a fashion, his imagination dwells upon realms of mystery. And why is this? Because Faith denotes a belief in the *beauty and excellence* of what we cannot see,—a repose upon it as all right,—better even than we can know. It is a persuasion of *the reality of perfect knowledge,*—an assurance that if a thing is *good,* that thing will surely *be.* And hence a man that *sees* a higher than he can *believe,* that loves a divine order and goodness in his soul of which he thinks the real universe quite empty, is the genuine and only *infidel.* He has no *trust;* he cannot worship, for the single thing that he reveres is to him a fiction, —a vain delusive shadow of his own heart. And this unreliance on what is felt to be noblest and best is just to live without God in the world.

And why do we, in spite of the most charitable reasonings, look upon this state of mind with repugnance? Because it implies a weakness and poverty of the moral nature, and is utterly inconsistent with noble and great affections. Every faculty of the soul necessarily has faith in its own objects; the senses, in material things; the understanding, in law and order; the imagination, in beauty; the affections, in love; the conscience, in goodness; and where there is no trust in perfection there can be small aspiring towards it. It has been well and truly said, that any man may readily make himself an atheist, by simple neglect of things divine. Selfish affections, impure imagination, relaxed or abandoned duties, will speedily penetrate the whole nature with the canker of unbelief, and leave it to sink into bottomless depths of a reprobate mind.

And so it is impossible to divest religion of its moral character; a devout trust shows a heart that habitually communes with its own highest, and approaches its own God. As to external aids to the attainment of this state of mind, there is but one of deep and almost resistless efficacy; the presence of a soul filled with like absolute trust and living a divine life which glorifies all earthly things. Place me beside a brother man of high capacious spirit, and let me watch his uplifted eye, and overhear his low-breathed prayer, and I cannot but catch the influence of a temper so lofty and holy; and instantly I not only love what he loves, but by an ineffable agency I believe what he believes, and assimilate my poorer nature to his. And if *faith only* can awaken faith, then Christ, who has so perfected it in us, must be its supreme example in himself. His inspiration was one not of knowledge to the intellect (which were paltry in comparison), but of spiritual insight to the soul. He occupied the region unknown to the perceptions of us all, with a moral perfection never conceived of before. He created a higher highest, and so revealed a truer God. There can be no other revelation that deserves to be called Religion. And though otherwise he might give us *information,* thus only could he become the Author and Perfecter of *Faith.*

LIVERPOOL, 1845.
LONDON, 1868.

VIII.

Faith the Symbolic Aspect of Truth.

———✦———

DAN. iv. 3.

" How great are his signs ! How mighty his wonders ! "

MANY English writers have maintained that Natural
Religion differs in no essential point from physical
philosophy; inasmuch as both rest upon the same
logical principles, and it is the office of both to infer
the character of an unknown cause from the observation
of known effects. No one can fail to be struck with
one important difference between theology and science;
that while the speculations of the latter steadily tend
towards certainty and general consent, those of the
former make no visible approach to such an issue.
Philosophy, the historian of her own debates, records
innumerable disputes, now at rest and obsolete, and
exhibits to us the precise fruit of truth which each
has yielded; but age seems never to antiquate the
controversies of religion; if for a while they are
abandoned through weariness and exhaustion, the

world takes time to be refreshed and then returns to them again ; so that after an interval of centuries the same doubts and difficulties reappear, and produce again the same solution; the very same texts are marshalled to do battle in the same cause; and old forms of thought become as familiar to our minds as antique shapes of art to our dwellings; and a practised theologian of the present day would find himself as much at home in one of the ancient councils of the Church as would the accomplished antiquary amid the streets and villas of Athens and Pompeii. Even where new topics of discussion occupy men's attention, they do not appear to be steps of direct advance upon their predecessors, positions gained by some previous advantages; but questions so like those which have been agitated before them, that though they have followed, no one can say why they might not have preceded. I do not know of any existing controversy in dogmatic theology, which might not as well have been in the hands of the scholastic doctors of the Middle Ages; but of extant speculations in science there is not one which they could have touched.

This absence of all speculative improvement in religion, in the midst of increasing diversity of opinion, and assiduity of debate, is the more remarkable when contrasted with that progressive development of the practical Spirit of Christianity which has perpetually widened the distance between ancient civilization and modern.   That it does not arise from dearth of intellectual power in the disputants must be evident ; for in every Christian country the Church has always engaged in its service a vast proportion of the acuteness and learning and genius of the age.   The fact would seem to depend, not on the mind of the advocate, but on the subject-matter of the debate ; for the very same men who, like Newton and Priestley, have agitated without bringing nearer to a close difficult questions in theology, have ripened some of the richest fruits of philosophy.   We could almost suspect the assertion of the sceptic to be well founded, that the truths of religion are incapable of exact determination, and that this subject on which the world has always dogmatized the most, is precisely that of which it understands the least.

If this statement be made by way of taunt, if it be meant to imply that a mind empty of religion is more free from delusion than the mind full of it, nothing, I conceive, can well be more false.   But if it be simply affirmed that the objects of scientific inquiry are widely different from the objects of religious contemplation, that the method for conceiving truly of the one (that is knowledge) is unlike the method of conceiving truly of the other (which is faith), the remark is both just and profound.   The ceaseless endeavour in this country to systematize religion, to compress it into a series of well-defined propositions, implies, I believe, a total misconception of its nature, and inflicts a deadly wound upon its power. To expound fully the distinction between knowledge and faith would require discussions inappropriate to this place; and I will content myself with the notice of one or two characters by which they are discriminated.

(1.) The objects of all knowledge are either things or events, either what exists, or what happens, in nature. The naturalist takes an inventory of the world's treasures, and prepares a well-arranged list of its mineral, vegetable, and animal productions; the man of science makes a similar catalogue of its various changes, and ascertains the rules by which their order is regulated. Neither of them has occasion to pass beyond the limits of experience; to state anything for which there is not sensible evidence; to use any vague or figurative terms. Every object they describe either exists or it does not; every phenomenon either occurs or it does not; every arrangement and succession are precisely such as they represent, or different; and all this can be ascertained with such exactitude that their statements must always be definitely true or false. On the other hand, the objects of religion, so far as we learn them by any process of strict inference, are certain abstract qualities of mind, invention, power, benignity, which we justly deem essential to explain the structure, the scale, and the happiness of creation. The countless adaptations of beings and laws to each

other, force upon us the idea of design; the movements and majesty of the system, that of irresistible
volition; the evidently general tendency of all known
adjustment to the enjoyment or improvement of
sentient creatures, that of goodness; and with the
proof of these attributes, as causes of what we see, all
the philosophy of natural religion ends. But the
propensities of our nature absolutely forbid our stopping here; for how can any mind rest upon a conception so indistinct as that of three or four qualities,
apart from a Being in whom they reside? How avoid
filling up the faint but grand outline, and adding
whatever is needful to make up the mighty image of
that awful Cause? The human mind finds it difficult
to dwell upon any abstract idea,—to think of colour
without something coloured, of weight without something heavy, of wisdom without someone wise, of love
without someone affectionate. The conception of any
individual familiar to me presents itself easily and
vividly; I imagine his features, his gestures, his voice,
his manner of thinking and feeling, and all that dis-
tinguishes him from others. Ask me to reflect upon
the notion, not of any particular person, but of the
human being; and being obliged to drop from view all
the characteristics of any individual, I am conscious
that the idea of the whole class is feeble and obscure.
Bid me call upon the thoughts, not of the entire
human being, but of his mind alone; and with the

further loss of the corporeal image, the conception becomes fainter still. And, if I am to meditate, not upon the mental and moral conception as a whole, but to insulate certain properties of it, without adverting to the rest, the phantom thought seems to pass away in shadow. Yet such would be our idea of God, did we confine ourselves rigidly to what we can be said to know. But our nature grows impatient at this dimness; the affections refuse to embrace anything so cold; the will evades the force of so thin a power; and we involuntarily clothe this abstraction with personality; and surround the attributes we have proved with others, purely ideal perhaps, but without which the real ones (like certain musical notes, said to be inaudible by themselves, but heard in chords) would be imperceptible. All these additional parts of the great conception are supplementary to the bare truth; the shape with which our minds spontaneously invest it; the comparison by which we strive to comprehend the unsearchable reality. Were they changed, it would only be that one metaphor would give way to another; and the fit inquiry would be, not which is most true, but which is most beautiful and noble. We cannot speak of God without the use of these ideas; our faith in him is chiefly composed of them; and that faith is therefore at best not so much the truth itself, as the vehicle of a small portion of the truth, and the symbol of the rest.

The same remark applies, with little variation, to the other great object of religious belief; the doctrine of human immortality. This truth, whether taught by nature or by scripture, furnishes us with the conception of immense time, prepared as a vast blank, for unknown events; we are in knowledge of the duration, and in ignorance of all its successions; we discern the outline of an unbounded ascent shooting into the heavenly light, but with all its steps invisible. But our minds cannot dwell upon this mere film of expectation; while they are intent upon it, insensibly it seems to fill with life. Untrained to think of time except as the depository of occurrences, we cannot contemplate the great future without peopling it with events; any more than we can look at the vacant place where some friend has always sat without his image rising upon the inward vision. Every conception we can form of the eternal state may be false; and yet to lose it would be to sink into a state of mind far falser. It is at least the token of a truth, which represents it to us till we can exchange it for the reality. The philosopher who thinks of heaven as the elysium of science, and with Plato speaks of the Creator as the great geometer; the busy and uninstructed trader, who, finding in the excitement of worship his most refined refreshment, imagines the life to come a sabbath of melody and prayer, may each enjoy unmolested his own conception; all the forms of thought may be erroneous alike; yet each the truest which its possessor can attain. A controversy respecting their relative merits would evidently be a controversy not about any ascertainable truth, but about the fitness of the imagery which we substitute for the truth; and must be determined by an appeal, not to the rules of logic but to those of feeling and of taste. Of this nature I conceive to be a large number of the disputes which have agitated Christendom.

(2.) Another character belonging to the objects of faith, by which they are distinguished from the objects of knowledge, is, that they are infinite. Science indeed, by discovering no limit, goes far to assure us of the boundlessness of creation; but it is only with its finite changes that philosophy has any concern; it takes us to the gates of Infinitude, but leaves us there; and it is faith that passes with us the awful threshold, and becomes our guide. Now it is clear that we can have no adequate idea of what is infinite; we cannot define to ourselves that which, in its nature, is indefinite; we cannot by any force of thought measure the unmeasurable, and know the unknowable. To say indeed that anything is infinite is only a way of affirming that it transcends our conceptions, that our ideas of it come to an end before the object is fully understood; that there is a little which we know connected with a great deal of which we are ignorant. We cannot think of such an object except by cutting out from contemplation the known parts and regarding them as merely a species; by taking the visible edge of the inscrutable, and remembering that it is only an edge. The very terms by which we strive to express our reverence for God are but confessions of the littleness of our minds; we say that he is omnipotent, and mean that we are ignorant of any effect beyond his power; that he is omniscient, and mean that we know of no relations or events of which he can be unaware. Strange to say, this very language, which has no meaning if it is not a confession of ignorance, is used by men inflated with all the confidence of knowledge; this, which has no use but to cover the dark and undefinable, is employed as if it contained the essence of light and certainty; this, which should simply be received reverently to represent a blank, is uttered with a positive voice in creeds which propose to define the composition of the Divine Spirit, and expound the psychology of heaven. Our duty, did we know it, is of a humbler kind; to accept the little experience which God may give us, as a sign of undiscoverable things beyond. Our lot of life in the immense ocean of Providence is like that of the coral insect in the deep; which feels over it the alternate pressure of a deeper or a shallower wave, but knows nothing of the great tidal laws which agitate the element in which it lives, and connect its changes with the revolution of distant worlds. And like that little creature too, it is our task to build while the current favours, and deposit patiently our tiny grains of toil; and at length it may be given us to see a portion of the deep filled up with structures curious and firm, and islands of new life rise up amid the sea of things.

The truest attainable notion then of things infinite must be partial and erroneous. The scale of Deity is altogether beyond our grasp; and however correctly we may conceive of His operations in spirit and in kind, their dimensions, when discovered, will never fail to astonish us; they will often tear asunder, and distribute at incredible distances of time and space, objects and events which, for want of so vast a field, had co-existed in our conception. Often indeed has God disclosed to us great truths in this way; explicit respecting their nature, but silent for a while respecting their magnitude; suggesting their essence, but leaving us gradually to rectify the form; delighting our hearts with the idea of the greater events of his Providence, but regardless of their temporary misplacement in the accidents of time and space. And then when the nucleus has expanded itself, when the object of our faith becomes known in its magnitude as well as its character, how gloriously does God disappoint us by its majesty! We find that that which was written in our faith was but a symbol of the reality; a wondrous sign of a mightier wonder signified. An instance or two of this will show "how great are his signs, but how mighty his wonders!"

All that is essential in the doctrine of the creation of all things by one divine Will, is contained in the Mosaic record, and has always existed in the faith of Christians. That the architecture of the heavens and the earth was designed and executed by a single Mind, that the last species created was the human, that all our race are of one blood and one brotherhood, are the grand ideas conveyed in that narrative, and to this day confirmed by every appeal to nature. But the shape which these notions have assumed in our faith has developed itself anew in modern times. For ages creation was conceived to be almost a momentary act, from which the universe, with its throngs of living beings, instantaneously sprang; or at least that the process was so short as to vanish into a point compared with the centuries that have since elapsed. But now we know that this conception is too mean for the reality. In the rocks of our globe we have found the cemetery of departed races of creatures; in its strata, their tomb-stones, inscribed with intelligible notices of their successive disappearances from the earth or sea. And hence we have learned that the whole duration of the human race, which before we had imagined to comprise the whole history of our system, is only like the most recent hour of our world's longevity, that we are but the latest born of an immense series of tribes, which, one after another, have found upon this planet a residence and a grave; that the line of their accumulated lives would reach, if uncoiled, into the deepest darkness of the past eternity; so that creation is to be regarded, not as a solitary deed, but as an immeasurable process of infinite energy and sustained inventiveness of beneficence. Once the imagination of men conceived of the heavenly bodies as crowded into one convex plate not far above the clouds; and science interposed, multiplied their numbers, transmuted them from brilliants into worlds, and distributed them variously throughout the infinite fields of space. And in like manner, the creative activity of God, which had been crowded into a moment, burst open, and spread itself over the infinite stretch of time. Our former faith was good and noble; but it was only the symbol of the marvels of the Creator which we now behold. Great was the sign; but greater the wonder!

The doctrine of the reunion of friends after death grew, I believe, in like manner, out of a small point of faith at first. In the beginning of their independent career, the apostles, looking for the speedy return of their Lord from heaven, do not seem to have expected that any of his disciples would die; but to have thought that all would remain to hail him when in glory he came to reign, and would be invested with immortality without death. When at length this friend or that was called away, they learned that these wanderers from the fold on earth were gone to the Shepherd of souls in heaven; and it was believed that, having been sequestered there awhile with Christ, they would be found among his companions and attendants when he came, and thus be restored to their Christian compatriots below. It was but a slight departure from the anticipated plan ; a short separation and delay, ere the whole family in heaven and earth were finally united. Doubtless the conception served to keep alive the union of heart and sympathy between the two spheres, until the tie of association was firmly fixed. Meanwhile, time passed on ; and while Jesus returned not, more and more of the faithful went away from the mortal life ; as each one dropped, another set of home affections lingered around and followed his ascent, till at length human love became more and more habituated to take the upward direction ; and the path from earth to heaven has become the beaten track of humanity, smoothed afresh by every pilgrim's feet. And surely we see now that the *way* of reunion with Christ and with each other mattereth nothing. He will not indeed come to us, but we shall go to him ; and *there*, instead of here, we hope to be for ever with the Lord.

By a method perfectly similar, the faith which we entertain in the universal and ultimate supremacy of Christianity grows out of the expectation to which I have alluded, of its author's personal return to reign. It is perhaps impossible for us to realize the feeling with which Paul contemplated the world in which his lot was cast. Never was political power apparently more solid and compact, never any external civilization more vast and magnificent, than that with which Rome swayed its subject world. And yet the apostle, even while walking the streets of the Imperial city, and in the presence of its palaces, believed that its principality tottered to its fall ; that it rested on a thin crust of time, or one of those volcanoes of Providence by which thrones are wrecked and nations convulsed. He looked for the speedy and exulting dominion of Christ, as the commissioned spirit of God's government, and for the ascendancy of his power over all that should oppose itself. And was he wrong ? Not by any means, in the spirit of his hope. Rome has crumbled away, with its splendours and corruptions, into the dust. Its priesthoods have collapsed ; its temples are gone. And Jesus, though not in person, now rules the people in augmented righteousness. Had he been actually here, it would have been his mind that must have wielded dominion ; and has not that mind dominion as it is ? It has still indeed further triumphs to win. But this only shows that the purposes of God are progressive, not momentary ; and that the end of all things, like their creation, is not concentrated upon an instant, but led on by successive development of events through protracted ages. Over these ages let the spirit of Paul's expectation be distributed, and who will say that the anticipation is not true ?

The greatest truths then have often been developed from unquestionable errors; and the miscalculations of men have given birth to the noblest and most transforming agencies of God. The wisest, in questions of faith, cannot reach the divine reality; and the most erring may find its glorious symbol. Providence has evolved the sublimest of faiths,—the conceptions most sanctifying to our inner nature and most ripening to his great designs,—not by triumphs of reason and discovery, not by logical detection of fallacies and skill in thought and inference, but by historical and accidental methods; compelling the enthusiastic mistakes of one age to yield up some healing and mighty truth for many. Surely it becomes us, the subjects of such a Providence, to hold our own portion of apparent truth with modesty, and to treat the seeming errors of others with forbearance at least, not to say with reverence, as the possible sources of some consecrating power unseen as yet. Amid the apparent discouragement of meek and thoughtful wisdom and the spread of unsocial superstitions, trust in the Providence of humanity and the Guardian of truth is the cheerful lesson which experience teaches. The mighty tide of human improvement sweeps so majestically on, and with such various ebb and flow, that our own life, and even that of many generations, can no more mark and measure its advance than the froth on the retiring wave. Let us only yield ourselves up with perfect trust to the faith which God has given us for our guidance ; and meekly go with it to that world where its errors will fall away, and its elements of good be visible in the clear and heavenly light.

LIVERPOOL, 1838.
LONDON, 1869.

IX.

Moral Influence of Reliance upon Faith.

JAMES ii. 14.

" What doth it profit, my brethren, though a man say he hath faith, and have not works? Can faith save him? "

No sooner was the great truth of human Immortality published by the first missionaries of Christianity, than its professors, with the perversity of mastery, drew from it an occasion of controversy, instead of the principles of consolation. In this sublime hope, so fitted, one would think, to give to Duty a new fortitude, and to suffering a conscious dignity, the world would seem, on a first view, to have acquired the fuel of passion rather than the conditions of peace. The question, which if doubtful must be admitted to be tremendous, " on what terms does the Giver of Immortality bestow its blessings," still vehemently agitates the churches of Christendom. They are divided between two opposite systems ; of which one, founded mainly on certain misapprehensions of the writings of Paul, insists upon faith in Christ, and especially upon implicit trust in the vicarious merits of his righteousness and suffering, as indispensable to salvation ; the other, supported by the writings of James, and the natural dictates of reason, represent the moral character and conduct of this life, with whatever belief they may be accompanied, as alone determining the condition of the agent hereafter ; so that " *in every nation,* he that feareth God and worketh righteousness will be accepted of him." Doubtless these antagonist notions will seldom be found in their natural and consistent separation from each other ; they are variously blended and compromised in the actual sentiments of men ; but the predominance of the one over the other marks out the two great schools of Christianity, whose respective symbols are Justification by faith, and Justification by works.

Were any impartial and reflecting man asked to anticipate the probable moral fruits of these opposite views, it would not be difficult to conjecture his reply. He would at once assign the superiority to the system which staked everything on character, which made the attainment of eternal peace contingent, not on an act of judgment, but on efforts of the conscience. It would appear impossible to conceive of a more solemn and stimulating position than that of a responsible being invited to toil up the ascent of an immortal life by the forces of his inward will,—to wake and win the height—or sleep and perish ! What adjustment of motives can be so commanding and penetrating as that which immediately connects all that is peaceful and glorious in our hopes with purity in the heart, the order of sanctity in our homes, and uprightness and beneficence in the world?—which makes every lapse from our best aims cancel a blessing from the future, and every triumph of high resolve bring us nearer to the heavenly Mind. Duty, in short, would appear likely to be best performed, when it is best rewarded. On the other hand, consequences the most dangerous would seem to be inseparable from the idea, that salvation, instead of being contingent upon the future conduct, is already secured upon a particular belief. Must not he who has an entail in the inheritance hereafter, be tempted to become a spendthrift in morals here? What worse economy of motives can be conceived, than to withdraw the awful sanctions of futurity from morality, and to append them to the involuntary operations of the understanding; to annihilate them as forces of duty, and use them as a dead weight upon inquiry? If a malignant being were to desire a scheme for the demoralization of men, it would appear difficult to devise a surer method than to persuade them that eternal happiness awaited them on conditions perfectly independent of their will; that no act of theirs could either secure or forfeit it; that to a certain talismanic faith the gates of heaven were ever open, and against all who from ignorance or doubt

were without the charm, inexorably closed. Let a
church be unhappily possessed by such a system of
ideas, and we should expect to find *within its pale*
relaxed moral obligation, a slight estimate of the sin
which, as they suppose, cannot harm, and the virtues
which cannot benefit them ; a careless life and slippery
integrity ; and, in its *external relations*, the inflation
of pride and the propensity to persecute.

Yet everyone would acknowledge this to be at least
a very exaggerated description of those Christians who
hold Luther's great doctrine of Justification by Faith.
Whatever may be said of their exclusive and intolerant
spirit towards those who do not enter their sacred circle,
no one can affirm that they are marked out from the
rest of society by neglect of the great moralities of
life, by the Epicurean licence of their habits, and the
coldness of their sympathies. Nay, justice requires a
much larger admission than this. History and experience appear to me completely to reverse our natural
anticipations ; and to prove that the purest morals,
the profoundest sentiments of Duty, the promptest
self-denial, have always appeared among sects whose
favourite symbol was salvation by faith ; their fault being
indeed that, by an extreme of rigour they have failed
to carry with them the permanent convictions of the
human conscience, and after a generation of enthusiastic austerity have provoked a fatal revolt into
reactionary licence. Whatever advantage the civiliza-

tion of Protestantism possesses over that of Catholic
countries (and this it is impossible to deny) has been
gained concurrently with the spread of this doctrine and
the extinction of its rival.   If the Reformation has been
a blessing to Europe, if it has not only roused its
understanding, but shaken off many a corruption from
its conscience; if its delay was marked by the growth
of servility and sloth, and its establishment by improved
industry, sobriety and order, by a more elevated
estimate of human rights, and a more energetic
sympathy with the oppressed and outcast, it must be
remembered that on the very front of this great social
Revolution was inscribed the very tenet which we
conceive to be so full of danger.   And among the
churches to which the Reformation has given birth,
those which have distinguished themselves by their
powerful and beneficent effects, by their determined
resistance to some social crime, by their dauntless
protests against the corruption of a court or the
oppression of a people, will be found to have been
characterized by their attachment to the same notion.
The Huguenot, the Covenanter, the Puritan,—names
representative of the strictest manifestation of moral
principle, and handed down in the traditions of
Conscience, reposed trust not in their virtue but in
their faith.   Heathenism and slavery abroad, ignorance
and depravity in our population at home, have been
grappled with most strenuously by Christians of the

same class.   And if you look into the interior spirit
and working of their system, the fierce or contemptuous
aspect which they bore towards you disappears;
the tones of polemic rancour mellow instantly into
those of Christian love ; all offensive sanctimoniousness
is exchanged for severe self-vigilance ; and a temper
meek and merciful, a pure pity for the sad and lost, a
heart scrupulously faithful to the little band of comrades
in hope, and a life reverently transcribed from the
image of Christ within the mind (O that that image
were truer to the reality!) will surprise you into
admiration of an opponent and a bigot.   Believing that
Christianity has never manifested itself in so affectionate,
disinterested, and energetic a spirit as in churches
which, like the evangelical, lay great stress on the
doctrine of justification by faith, I propose to attempt
some explanation of so singular a fact.

A very simple reflection will convince us that a
delusion lurks in the technical language of this system ;
and that in the *faith* to which an efficacy so great is
ascribed, much more is implied than a simple process
of belief.   If God really made the eternal happiness of
men depend upon their assent to any truth, we should
naturally expect that he would select one of the most
obvious and intelligible of truths for this end ; some
certainty which would find an unobstructed admission
to every understanding to which it was presented.   To
propose to save them by a conviction, and then offer to

their acceptance something against which the nature which he had given them necessarily rebelled, would be a cruel mockery.   But it cannot fail to be observed that no sect has ever rested salvation upon an easy and welcome faith; the moment the creed ceases to be mysterious, all reliance on belief disappears, and is transferred to the practical obedience of the life.   The very essence of the saving views is thought to reside in their bold defiance of human reason; their advocate exults in the vehement repugnance felt towards them by the natural mind; and esteeming that mind to be corrupt in its judgments and feelings, deliberately measures the sanctity of these ideas by their repulsiveness to the unconverted understanding, and places their power in their unexpectedness.   And is he not right? Not indeed in the imagination that there is anything acceptable to the Parent Mind in the prostration of that intelligence by which we call ourselves his children.   But is not the unreasonableness of a doctrine a kind of rude test of the force of religious sentiment in its sincere believers?   If the understanding have struggled against it and yet it has found entrance, it must have been befriended by some vigorous agency, and that agency can be no other than the devout affections.   How acute and of what ethereal temper must be those weapons of the heart which can thus cleave asunder the adamant of proof, and pass through unharmed!   Whenever the dictates of obvious reason are discarded, it is evidence that some passion is at work; the wider the departure from common sense, the more vehement must be the deflecting force of emotion. We acknowledge this principle in the world, and cannot refuse to recognize it in the church. Nothing short of the intensity of religious feeling could consecrate the follies of religious creeds; so that the absurdity of a system may be regarded as a resistance, arbitrarily set up for the affections to close with and overcome; and it becomes a measure and proof of the forces of piety in the mind, just as some idle feat of athleticism may attest the muscular power of the frame. Thus the very irrationality of the belief imposed as the condition of salvation operates as a safeguard against the natural consequences of this doctrine of faith; it is a guarantee for the existence of a powerful principle of religion; and if once the demand on assent were lowered to something simple and true, the appropriate effects of this scheme of justification would break forth, and an instant demoralisation ensue.

The mere vividness of the feelings of veneration would however be but a poor security for virtue; for their direction may be so perverted as to render them the associates and apologists of vice. But when we look narrowly into the ideas which Christian Churches consider to be essential to salvation, we find among them some moral ingredients so pure that the quality of the devout feeling involved in this system seems to be as safe as its intensity. In speaking of the doctrine of Atonement theologically, I should maintain that such an illogical and monstrous congeries of ideas could with difficulty be found; but in speaking of it morally I must admit that an absolute reliance on the merits of Christ implies two sentiments of a very high order of worth, and capable of becoming the source of all the sanctities of duty; I mean, the deep sense of personal imperfection; and an appreciation of the disinterestedness and holiness of Christ. He who has within him so pure a conception of excellence that he can see nothing comely in his own life,—whose vision of the right is so undisturbed that self-flattery is disarmed,—who so feels his dignity as a child of God that he must weep over the frailties of the tempted man; he whom no respect and admiration from friends, no conscious superiority to others, no repeated victories over self, can beguile from the quiet conviction of his weakness and the intense thirst after a holier and wiser life, cannot but exhibit the instincts of a heavenly mind. I know that the excessive self-depreciation, the language of which this system adopts, easily passes into self-deception and insincerity, and always borders upon abjectness; but the effort to attain to it can scarcely fail to fill the heart with the sense of its own wants; nor can the intensity of an artificial self-annihilation be maintained, but by drawing largely upon the feelings of a genuine humility. But the true power of this scheme will be found in the sentiment which it incidentally awakens towards Christ. Not of course in the terrific ideas entertained of his cross, not in the savage conception that Hell then emptied its agonies upon his head, not in any of the sacrificial images by which the scene on Calvary is deformed rather than illustrated; but in that entire recognition of the holiness of his Mind which lies at the root of what is called the repose upon his merits. His absolute moral perfection is the fundamental principle of this theory ; and to its professors he becomes the very image of whatever is pure and great and merciful, the impersonation of a Divine goodness, the effusion of celestial moral beauty upon the earth. Whatever fanciful and mysterious offices their imaginations may attribute to him are expressive of qualities of soul which he really possessed ; and perhaps his disinterestedness, his tender and versatile sympathies, his tranquil dignity of aim might not have been distinctly perceived by the common mind, or have occupied a space broad enough in its field of vision, had they not been viewed through the magnifying medium of the marvellous. Within the details of a life so brief and humble, in the dimness of an antiquity so great, in the fields of a peasant's history, the manifestation of perfected humanity might scarcely have been dis-

covered.   The error in theology kindles the attention
to the historic truth; and the sense of an infinite
personal benefit concentrates on Jesus an affection
which, without being one iota too intense, might not
have been awakened by the mere force of moral
admiration.   To those who conceive themselves
redeemed by his sufferings from eternal woe, he is the
object of unutterable gratitude and veneration; his
image lives unforgotten in their hearts; his spirit is
the very light and atmosphere of their minds ; gives
audience to their tenderest prayers ; is the divine
recipient of their griefs; is at their side in struggle
and temptation; and stands as the affectionate centre
of their hopes, when they think of heaven.   Now it is
precisely by this sympathy with great and holy minds,
and not by the operation of hope and fear, that the
world's wisdom and virtue are most powerfully
advanced.   These hearts lose no useful and available
motive, by feeling sure of their salvation.   Rather are
they benefited by being set at liberty from the
constraint and anxiety of so awful a contingency ;
untroubled about themselves, they are the freer to
put forth a profuse spontaneity of goodness, and to
originate deeds from the heart instead of suppressing
tendencies within the will.   Salvation hereafter, like
happiness here, is best secured by those who do not
incessantly strive after it.   There are two very
different classes of men that never aim directly at the

rewards of futurity; there are the slaves of gross interests and mean desires, who never rise so high; and there are the inspired by vivid instincts and disinterested affections of goodness, that never need descend so low; that are occupied by the secret conceptions of character which their life is a perpetual but unlaboured attempt to embody; that do gentle and generous deeds because there is nothing else in their imagination; that do battle for truth and rectitude, because it is the only spirit of combat in their hearts; that bear up against suffering nobly because they discern in every trial more purifying love than grief; that think with a placid joy of the immortality of goodness, yet would embrace that goodness still, though it were mortal. This spirit is of greater excellence and power than that which is eternally concerned with its salvation, and makes its religion only a system of far-seeing prudence. And to this the doctrine of works inevitably reduces itself; it does more harm by impeding the growth of generous affections than it does good by sharpening the sense of self-interest. Its essential and leading idea is that of *obedience.* If by saving works you understand merely the outward acts of the life, an uneasy scrupulosity, a nice weighing out of virtue by quantity, an excessive reverence for the bare forms and means of goodness are created. If you extend the idea to the internal dispositions and feelings from which the conduct flows, this cannot be directly produced by efforts of obedience; the heart is no day-labourer, and cannot work for wages; nor is there any other way of exciting a new affection than by bringing the object of it before the mind, in any aspect attractive to its sympathy. It is by its use of this principle, by the courage with which it abandons the superficial anxieties of fear, remounts to those sympathetic affections which are the purest sources of action, and trusts to their disinterestedness alone, that the doctrine of **justification** by faith proves itself a better moral instrument than its competitor.

Perhaps too there is a cause, not obvious at first sight, which determines the most practical of religious men to this doctrine, and the most enthusiastic to the other. This suggestion is, I am aware, in direct contradiction to our natural expectations, which would lead us to suppose that the most imaginative minds would seize most eagerly on the promise of faith. This expectation however takes for granted that in choosing their religion men are guided by their natural temperament, and select for themselves the scheme which gives greatest encouragement to their prevailing feelings. This may be the case with those whose religion is assumed as a convenience and with indolent formality; but where it is earnestly embraced and powerfully felt, a rule the very reverse may be observed to prevail; and the heart seizes on its faith by a principle not of unison with its predominant propensities, but of contrariety to them ; it betakes itself to the system which is in the most direct opposition to the common tenor of their emotions and their life. It would seem that the mind, when touched with spiritual fervour, is intuitively aware of the great function of religion, and is conscious that it is to act as the great corrective power in our nature ; and is therefore impelled to choose for itself that faith which is the natural antagonist of its prevailing habits, which grapples most closely with its favourite sins, and infuses most copiously into the life the thoughts and excitements most certain to be needed. With whom do the most enthusiastic views of Christianity find the readiest acceptance ? Precisely with the pure drudges of toil, who wear away their years in the secularities of existence, and would never rise from the dust of this weary world, but for their religion. The afflicted understand best the cheerful peace of devotion and the tranquillity of holy trust. The most sensitive and dreamy will give you the most solemn and melting representations of the obligations of practical duty. And on the same principle it is that the doctrine of salvation by faith has found its chief retreat in the North of Europe, and especially in England and in Holland, where the plainest, the most laborious and thrifty population of modern times is to be found ; while in the South, among the excitable inhabitants of Italy and Spain, the chief importance is still attached to works. It is not therefore merely that the doctrine of faith is favourable to the production of the practical moralities ; but that those who are most distinguished by an antecedent tendency to their performance naturally embrace this system, because it infuses a higher spirit into their material life.

From this analysis of the popular creed in one of its most important points, who will disdain to derive a lesson of forbearance and gratitude ? Who will be unwilling to see in forms of intellectual error a compensating element of moral good ? Surely it is befitting an hour of Christian worship to seek the peace of Christian charity ; and yet more fitting to learn how to transplant the germs of truth and good-ness from another creed into our own ; that, springing there, they may blossom in better beauty, and shelter us by their shades. The moral vitality of the scheme which we reject is derived from the unhesitating reverence it inspires for the mind of Christ, and the disinterested aspiration after its similitude. In us let the same reverence arise, not from the ascription to him of marvellous and mystic attributes, but from a wise and entire appreciation of his spirit. Often let that sacred image of Jesus visit our hearts, as a historic conscience consecrated by God himself ; refreshing us in our griefs, and giving victory in our temptations, and inviting us to his sainted rest.

LIVERPOOL, 1837.
LONDON, 1869.

X.

𝔉𝔞𝔦𝔱𝔥 𝔦𝔫 ℭ𝔥𝔯𝔦𝔰𝔱 𝔣𝔬𝔯 𝔥𝔦𝔰 𝔬𝔴𝔫 𝔖𝔞𝔨𝔢.

——◆——

JOHN x. 38.

"But if I do, [the works of my Father], though ye believe not *me*, believe the *works*."

THESE words render it certain that the Author of our religion regarded himself as a proper object of belief, independently of his works. They even mark the direct and immediate reception of Christ as at once the natural and most excellent course, and advert to the miracles as inferior sources of faith, fitted to startle those who had closed up the purer ways of access to their minds. Here, as elsewhere, Jesus addresses his hearers, not as incapables, disqualified for judging of the true or the false, the heavenly or the earthly character of his religion; not as creatures without power to appreciate what is intrinsically holy and divine, when fairly presented to their acceptance; not as beings requiring, in their dulness, some outward seal or label to be put upon a sentiment, before their conscience could say "this is good," and "this is evil"; but rather as men who might be called upon (by any voice skilled to reach the heart) to judge even of themselves what is right, and to whom it was a just reproach that "except they saw signs and wonders they would not believe." Christ everywhere assumes, in the minds with which he reasons, a capacity, not indeed of spontaneously discovering, but of recognizing and venerating God and his truth; conversing with them, he does not so much contribute wisdom for their memory to acquire, as evolve it from their own hearts for them to attest and revere. He speaks as to a portion of the Holy Spirit latent within them, and ready to answer, if the appeal be true enough and pure.

In conformity with this disposition to treat human nature with reverence rather than with scorn, Christ did not begin his teachings, like some of his modern disciples, by showing how totally destitute of all religious knowledge mankind must have been without him; how futile all the devout faith of those who had never seen his mighty works; how foolish and delusive the hopes of heaven already in the hearts of men; how sceptic and profane were all the teachings of the universe and the soul, and how the natural whispers that repeated to the spirit some notice of infinite and invisible realities were such as no wise man would heed. We should be much nearer the fact if we said

that Jesus began from the beginning with no one
department of human faith; that he assumed, without labouring to prove, all the principles which he has
commended to our reception; and that, so far from
announcing them as novelties, he rather treats them
as ancient and everlasting certainties, that needed but
a true interpreter to speak and echo from heart to
heart. Revelation, thus regarded, is not so much a
set of doctrines, deposited by force of outward
authority on societies of men, as the development of
their germs from within the mind, the production of
that genial condition of the conscience and affections in
which religion spontaneously lives. It was the office
of Christ's inspiration to hush the voice of passion,
and quiet the thrill of sense, and clear away the bab-
bling of disputation, till he reached the divine silence
of the deeper spirit, in which God and Eternity *reveal
themselves,* and stray tones as of an infinite music for
ever wander. Hence he distinctly assumes *that the
mind faithful to itself can intuitively discern a divine
voice addressing it, and spiritual truth suggested to it;*
that it is almost useless to assail with external proofs
men in whom this power has been benumbed by the
overgrowth of the animal, the selfish, the merely
intellectual nature; and that his truest disciples are
drawn to him by the simple and unconditionating
force of moral and heavenly sympathy. "If God
were your Father," he exclaimed to his objectors,

" ye would love me " ; " why do ye not understand
my speech ?—because ye cannot apprehend my sentiments." " Every one that is of God heareth God's
words " ; " my sheep hear my voice, and I know them,
and they follow me " ; upon all others, he declares,
even the greatest miracles are thrown away ; " the
works that I do in my Father's name, they bear
witness of me ; but ye believe not, because ye are not
my sheep."

Christ then, with the majesty of inspiration,
claimed for his religion an obvious accordance with
the highest attainable perceptions of human intelligence and affection ; and laid the deepest foundations
of his system in the secret consciousness of every good
mind ; and appears to have accepted many as disciples
who were attached by the unquestioning allegiance of
a penetrated conscience, and felt his divine mission
to be one of many things which are too true to admit
of proof. It is important to recall attention to this
real basis of Christianity, because to destroy it has
been and still is one of the objects of that scepticism
which produces all books of Evidences, and all anxious
definitions and exclusive fencing round of the Christian name. The first symptom of a " heart of
unbelief" in a society is an apparent eagerness to
strengthen the grounds of belief; a discontent with
the simple and natural sources of faith, with the
heartiness of its moral and religious results, together

with a wish to intellectualize it; and the disposition to limit the title or the credit of genuine discipleship to those who consent to believe according to argument. Thus it was anciently sufficient for us to believe in Christ on his own account; but now we must believe in him on account of his miracles; all faith in him which is underived from these, and would have stability enough to remain though these were gone, is strongly denounced, in a tone of alarm which would seem itself to betoken doubt, as virtual unbelief. This rationalistic chain by which men think to hang from a distant heaven the sphere of belief on which they live is indeed well for those who would else not feel secure against falling into some outer darkness; but is needless for others whose world of faith, like this planet of ours, already *is* in heaven, swimming alone and by mysterious attractions through the infinite, and any way nearing the everlasting stars. I do not by any means question the powerful agency, in certain relations, of the Christian miracles; nor am I able to sympathize with the repugnance of many inquirers even to consider the testimony on which they rest; but seeing that by wavering minds they are quite as often felt to be difficulties as admitted to be proofs, I do lament (to use the words of Coleridge) that "fashion of modern theologists which would convert miracles from a motive to attention and solicitous examination, and at best from a negative condition of

Revelation, into the positive foundation of Christian faith."* The truth is, I apprehend, that you *cannot* establish them in this position; that men do not, in fact, erect their belief on the historical certainty of the miracles; that the recognition of the divinity of Christianity, supposed always to *follow* from admission, usually *precedes*, and renders them credible. At all events, those are not to be excluded from the Christian name who accept the gospel on its internal or self-evidence, and to whom Christ would have had no occasion to address his somewhat reproachful words, " if ye believe not me, believe the works "; for they would eagerly answer, " Yes, but indeed we do believe thee ! " Divines may open their straight and level road of argument across the plain of history, and we will thank them for their worthy toil ; but let them not stop the old mountain by-paths, which however incommodious to them, may yet tempt the feet of many a pilgrim that delights in the purer air and wilder solitudes of God.

The power of the human mind intuitively to discern the teachings of a divine truth, and consequently to accept Christ himself without necessary reference to his works, appears to me to follow from several considerations; to some of which I will now briefly advert.

This power seems to be implied in the very idea of revelation, and actually to lie at its fountain-head. For

* Lit. Rem., Vol. III., 72.

before a single Christian miracle was wrought, the religion of Christ existed, and his divine mission was an object of the most devout and effectual belief; inasmuch as he must have known his own mission, apprehended his own faith, become his own disciple. It was this state of mind out of which the first miracles must be conceived to have arisen, and without the pre-existence of which no impulse towards supernatural acts can be supposed. If they were necessary to impart conviction to others, there is yet a prior question, what was it imparted the conviction to himself? When the ideas which constituted his inspiration first stole in upon him, how did he recognize them as divine? How know them to be no dreams of imagination, but constraining realities, bringing with them responsibilities the most awful? He had no earlier Messiah to demonstrate his errand to him by a show of mighty works; to discriminate for him between the false impressions derived from Jewish education and a natural childhood, and the true conceptions which made him the man of sorrows and the Son of God. The supposition of any system of external miracle for *his* instruction would be wholly unwarrantable; and no one can entertain the notion without being aware that it is a mere invention. And whoever sends a thought back to the time when the prophet of Nazareth was still an uninspired man; whoever adverts to the moment when the first celestial conception rose within him, and then asks how did he perceive the real character, the sanctity, the authority of this conception, must acknowledge some intuitive discernment, by which the human and the divine could be separated. And if, in the first instance, his inspiration took him up as a human being, this faculty, enabling him to welcome a heavenly idea, must have belonged to his humanity, as an element of his and of our nature; nor is the denial of it anything else than a declaration of the impossibility of all inspiration. If an idea, when primarily presented to a human mind, can be recognized as intrinsically divine, so may it equally when readministered to others; and by the same immediate and self-persuasion which rendered him the disciple of his own inspired thought, may listening followers find a pure and perfect faith. We may surely be content if men believe Christ on the very grounds that made him believe himself!

In truth, miracles themselves would be totally devoid of persuasive efficacy, were it not for that primitive religious sentiment which is supposed to detract from their value; and the moment we suppose them left to themselves, abandoned to their mere logical operation on the understanding, and unsupported by the intuitive religion of the heart, we perceive their inadequacy to the work which divines would intrust to them. Before displays of supernatural power can address us with the least authority, we must already have a conviction of the greatest of sacred truths which indeed comprehends all others, the moral perfection of God. In vain would miracles appeal to one who unhappily doubted or denied this great certainty; what matters it, he would say, even though you prove this message to come from God? If indeed I knew him to be true and good, I should then rely upon its tidings; and if I were assured that he was Holy, I should feel the sanctity of its authority; but alas! if these should be the very points on which I long for revelation, what help have I in these works of might, by which creative benignity might doubtless enlighten, but cruelty might also deceive? Unless there is some method of which I am not aware of meeting this objection, we must admit that in every argument from miracle we necessarily assume the moral perfection of God; that by the external miraculous method his character,—the sublimest topic of revelation, and indeed the sum total of all,—could never be disclosed; that our faith in this, implied in the very existence and operation of miraculous evidence, has a natural origin within us;—not, I believe, in any frail process of intellectual proof, but in those intuitive perceptions of the deeper reason, these primitive and indestructible beliefs, which the understanding vainly strives either to strengthen or destroy. We may put the case in another light, by observing that there are two meanings in which a doctrine or a mission may be termed *divine*; with reference *to its origin,* as derived from a superhuman source, it may be spoken of as *genealogically divine ;* and with respect to *its intrinsic character and quality* as infinitely pure and sacred, it may be regarded as *morally divine.* At best, it is in the first of these senses only that miracles can prove its divinity, as having a birth beyond the powers of this world ; and it is from the second aspect, which no mighty works can portray, that all its authority descends; for God himself, with all that issues from his will, is venerable simply inasmuch as he is Holy ; and celestial things themselves would lose their title to command, if they insulted the supreme sanctity of conscience. Supposing, therefore, that miracles had shown a command to be *God-descended ;* still, before its legitimate power over us can be established, one of two things remains for our natural mind to ascertain ; either the *morally true and divine character of the Being* who has sent us the heavenly message ; or *the morally true and divine character of the message itself.* In both cases the vital and influential element of our faith is contributed by the light within us ; the authoritative revelation is developed from our own consciousness ; and outward sign and wonder are but a challenge to attention,— an appeal to the verifying faculties of our own nature. Seeing then, how much is presupposed in every argument from the supernatural, what are we to infer from the general disposition of men to ascribe great

force to it? This, and this only; that they unconsciously bring to it a belief in divine perfection, and
that such faith is not only competent to our minds,
but natural, intuitive, and necessary.

Our own private experience appears to me to confirm
this doctrine, to show how little any reasoning process
can avail to establish the authority of moral and
religious truth; and at the same time to convince us
that it has a deeper, not a shallower seat within our
nature than any scientific knowledge, and like all self-
evident things, comes out false as a deduction, simply
because dislodged from its place among primitive
certainties. Show me a tenet which mankind have in
every age been labouring to demonstrate; in behalf of
which genius has piled up structure after structure of
massy argument; in reference to which each period
has been conscious of the failure of the preceding, and
yet set itself to try another turn of skill; let me see
that this untiring industry has applied itself to the
proof by opposite and distinctive methods, and after
exploring in vain every road of thought is fresh and
unexhausted still; and I at once recognize in that
doctrine the very happiest order of truth, and precisely
because, all men trying, no man can prove it. No
amount, no duration of failure sufficing to throw it off,
what shall I infer but that it is one of those things, not
which the mind must believe because it has proved, but
which it would prove because it must believe. Futile

defences are enough to ruin whatever is weak and
doubtful; and can leave unharmed nothing but the
indestructible.   In truth we must all be conscious that
it is not the clear understanding, but the pure heart,
that beholdeth God; and in spite of every persuasion
of a false philosophy, we are compelled by the force of
nature to feel that the states of mind in which we
worship are higher, truer, than those in which we
reason.   Nay, does not even scepticism tacitly admit
this, and look up with tearful eye of reverence to the
tranquil faith of others, and confess to itself that
though it may be acuter it is ignobler too?   We can
have observed others and ourselves to little purpose if
we have not discovered that the strength of religious
conviction depends much less on the power or the
culture of the understanding, than on the depth of
the affections and the clearness and brilliancy of the
conscience.   The eye of devout faith opens most fully,
not necessarily in the hour of mere intellectual activity,
but rather in the moment of strenuous resolve and
moral victory, or perchance of melted sorrow and
bereaved hope ; and it closes, not with the obscuration
of the worldly judgment, but with the retirement and
death of our higher aspirations, and the declining
delicacy of our moral perceptions.   Indeed, faith is a
birth of the affections and central reason, far more
truly than of the judgment ; and to prove by a display
of evidence and supernatural force the reality of things

divine, is like working a miracle to establish the sublimity of the heavens or the immensity of the sea ; or like recommending by proprieties of argument the caresses of a mother and the reliance of a child. That which we have truly to deprecate is, not the understanding, but the heart of unbelief.

LIVERPOOL, 1840.
LONDON, 1870.

XI

The Religion of Assurance and the Religion of Desire.

"The publican, standing afar off, would not lift up so much as his eyes even to heaven; but smote upon his breast, saying, God be merciful to me a sinner. I tell you, this man went down to his house justified rather than the other."

THE sentiments of religion, it is evident, can belong only to a nature which is intermediate between the highest and the lowest order of beings. A mere animal is beneath them; God is above them. A creature without capacity for knowledge cannot attain to this form of truth; without imagination, cannot frame this idea of beauty; without the sense of Duty, cannot yearn to the perfectly good. And on the other hand He who sustains no relations but to the beings he has made, who has nothing external to his nature but the effects of his own volition, whose ideas of power, and truth, and excellence are but conceptions of himself, must be a stranger to anything like those blessed emotions with which the remembrance of him refreshes our hearts. Whatever the range of his mighty thought, it cannot pass beyond the limits of his own infinitude; and the laws of right which he observes and loves are the internal sentiments of his own pure nature. Absolute impotence and unlimited power, total ignorance and finished knowledge, moral incapacity and perfect holiness are then alike disqualified for the exercise of religion; and it springs up only in a nature like the human, which has affinities with both the animal and the divine; which combines their contrarieties; which knows much, and is ignorant of more; which has enjoyments in its possession, but more in its desire; which wields a noble power, and sinks in melancholy weakness; which loves the good, and is tempted to the evil. If our minds were perfectly dark and depraved, they would furnish us with no notions of intellectual and moral qualities, no hints and materials for the formation of the idea of Deity; if they were perfectly discerning and good, they would leave no unsatisfied desire to pant for ampler forms of spiritual life. In the one case the ingredients, in the other the impulses, of worship would be wanting; and the sources of devotion would be dry. Religion starts up on the collision of opposite elements in our nature; when the love of life encounters the impressions of death, and the perceptions of conscience are sickened by the spectacle of sin, and the joyousness of human affection is checked by sudden bereavement. It is the visible suggesting the invisible, the ideal healing the actual; the known driving us to the thought of the unknown ; the greatness of our capabilities revealing to us the depth of our wants. Two classes of feeling must therefore meet, in order to give origin to the sentiment of piety,—positive and privative ideas,—the thought of what we are and of what we are not,—of what we have and of what we need ; nor can any mind be the seat of devotion without the conception of some absent good. To be grateful for present enjoyments, we must imagine our condition without them ; to desire a future peace, we must be depressed by some anxiety ; to aspire to a nobler virtue, we must be conscious of moral infirmities ; to venerate the infinite Mind of God, we must be sensible of our own insignificance, and beat against the barriers of our finite nature. Every unchangeable condition of feeling, whether of happiness or of misery, would effectually suppress the possibilities of religion ; it is not, in fact, during the protracted continuance of any single state of mind, but in the transitions of emotion, that the affections most earnestly look to God ; and the most impassioned utterance of devotion will burst from the happy on the first terror of anxiety, from the wretched on the first gleams of hope. The hour of mental twilight, either in the awe of a darkness every moment deeper, or the silent return of peace to the vigils of sorrow, is the period of most spontaneous piety; and as if in symbol of this truth, and in consciousness of analogy, the outward forms of prayer have always been felt to have their fittest season at the passage of the external world from day to night and from night to day; and the matin vow and vesper hymn have been the natural expression of a heart sympathising by the access and recess of emotion with the transitions of nature, and disposed to plant itself on the confines of its light and darkness, to float between the visible and the invisible, to look round on the little circle that it knows, and above into the unbounded expanse of which it can only wonder and imagine.

While the two opposite feelings, of possession and of want, are both essential to the existence of religion, they may be mingled in various proportions, and thus give rise to different modifications of devotional sentiment. From the predominance of the one or the other arise two contrasted forms of character, which, though no names present themselves by which to discriminate them, have always existed, and constitute two great natural classes of minds; the one betraying in all its movements the vigour of assurance, the other the aspirations of desire; the one taking a cheerful and solid stand upon the actual, the other haunted by shadowy visions of the possible; the one looking on the positive side of all that exists, and treating its

own portion of what is true and good as if there were
no other truth and goodness,—the other looking at
the negative side, and conscious that what it has is but
a dubious encroachment on the margin of what it has
not. In the parable of the Pharisee and the Publican,
Christ, I conceive, intended to give preference to the
latter of these; and beautifully illustrated the moral
tendencies of their opposite modes of thinking. He
did not perhaps design, as is commonly supposed, to
hold up the Pharisee to unqualified contempt and
reprobation, to insinuate any charge of hypocrisy, or
even to deny all worth to his piety; but simply to
recommend the devotion of want as nobler than the
devotion, possibly equally sincere, of assurance.

In the Pharisee will be instantly recognized the
representation of a class not confined to that age and
country, but familiar to everyone even in our own
land and at the present day; those who are deeply
impressed with the advantages of their religious and
moral condition; and whose piety is one prolonged,
it may be very affectionate and grateful, expression of
self-satisfaction. They may conceal this personal complacency from themselves by many ingenuities; they
may save their humility by subtle distinctions between
their original and their acquired state; they may revile
their own proper nature, and utter the language of penitence for its corruptions, and declare that it can produce
nothing good; they may disown all merit, and ascribe

to Deity every blessing recounted in their prayer; and at times you might suppose them dissolved in actual grief and fear from their infirmities; but penetrate to the real fact, and you find that they hold their own condition to be eminently desirable. Hear them confess their ignorance, their vanity of heart, their propensity to do evil continually, and you conclude irresistibly that these things are matters of profound sorrow; but on explanation it appears that there is no just subject of regret; for the knowledge which they do not possess, and the good work which they fail to perform are after all of no worth; their absence signifies not at all; they are replaced by a divine illumination and a saving faith which give all that is glorious in earth or heaven, and render their possessor wiser than the wisest, and holier than the best. So that they are assured of their possession of all that an immortal can desire; and deplore their deficiency in that which they do not value. In these men the tones of tender, distant, and moral veneration are exchanged for those of confident intimacy with God; they believe in the power of devotional persuasion, and hold it to be the Christian's supreme accomplishment; and they are fond of declaring, in language which we cannot repeat without a shudder, that they will give the Lord no rest till he sends them what they want.

Nothing however can be further from my wish than to attribute the dogmatic temper of which I speak to any

one class of doctrinists in particular. Intellect as well
as faith has its Pharisees; and philosophy has been
heard in the temple, thanking God that it is not as
others are, superstitious, idolaters, and Calvinists, and
telling him with what invariable correctness it has
learned to think of him and his government. There is
a complacency of disbelief no less than of belief; a
pride in detecting the fallacies of other men's creeds; a
piety that never prays without hinting at the highly
rational nature of its worship; a knowledge that seems
content with discovering what kind of being God is not,
and having laid in a store of truisms respecting popular
errors, men and sects may repeat them with pragmati-
cal perseverance, to the annoyance of many persons
faith   and   the   animation   of   nobody's   religion;
obstructing improvement the moment it threatens to
pass them by; pleased with the task of drawing off the
life from ancient forms of thought without inspiring any
vitality into new ones. This disposition of mind may
indeed present itself in total separation from all religion;
connected with particular qualities of the intellect, and
thrown upon certain combinations of circumstances,
it may assume the shape of total unbelief; if so
however it is still dogmatic and confident, less from any
over-trust in its own processes of reasoning than from
contemptuous discovery of the weakness of others.

Christ however speaks of this form of character
only so far as it occurs in conjunction with religion;

and it is to be observed that he by no means insinuates
that there is anything false in the Pharisee's enumera-
tion of his advantages, anything insincere in his
expression of thanks, or anything absolutely wrong
in his indulgence of such feelings. And the truth is
that this mode of thinking is not necessarily either
delusive or worthless ; it is simply one-sided and
imperfect. The qualities which excite complacency
may truly exist; they may be really excellent, and
constitute a just ground of comfort and theme for
gratitude. This feeling too may enter the mind with
unaffected vividness. It may and continually does
pour itself forth in action ; in benevolent efforts to
confer on others the blessings which it values so highly
in itself ; in strenuous and unhesitating aggression
upon evil, and deep and operative compassion for those
who are its victims. No religion can exist, I have said,
without a sense of **deficiency**, the idea of some absent
good ; and the class I **am** describing, not obtaining
this feeling from themselves, with whose condition they
are satisfied, gain it by looking around them; by
comparing their own advantages with others' wants,
the springs of their pity are powerfully touched; and
they go forth, in happy unconsciousness of any misgiving, resolved to impart their faith, their knowledge,
their hope, their peace, as the only cure for the sins
and sorrows of the world. They do not shrink from
constructing the most gigantic institutions, and

spending immense resources for the sole purpose of
carrying their own private views to the extremities
of the earth, as the only means of saving a wretched
race ; nor do they ever seem to think of the responsibility of rearing so stupendous a monument of
benevolence on so slender a foundation as their
own uncertain logic on the most uncertain of subjects.
This capability of benevolent activity, admirable as it
is, has however its weak side ; it is a desire of self-
multiplication ; it adopts its own state of mind as the
standard, and proposes to repeat it by reproduction in
every human being. And from this state of feeling it
inevitably follows that there must be failure in respect
for others, and a stationary condition of personal
character ; compassion, instead of honour, is rendered
to all men ; no ready reverence springs forth to bow
before purity and wisdom, wherever found ; no patient
toil to gather up the fragments of truth, that nothing
be lost ; no dignified docility, willing to seize the
simplest element of good, and feel itself blessed in
the accession whencesoever it come. Never looking
beyond its possessions which are small, and those of
others which seem less, such a soul dwells in a sphere
miserably contracted, and mistakes it for the universe ;
moving about a little way with its inch measure, it
thinks it learns the size of all things ; unconscious of
the heavens which spread their brilliant infinitude above,
and laugh at the puny ambition of the child of earth.

In the Publican is delineated the form of character which has been mentioned as precisely opposite, and which may be best understood by simply reversing the foregoing picture. Whatever is omitted from the view of the mind we have been contemplating, is present to this man's thought. He is heedless of his possessions, and haunted by his wants. He looks with no eye of gratulation on his intellectual or moral or religious attainments ; not that he is ignorant of them, and practises any self-deception, as others dream ; but because his soul is gone forwards, and felt the immensity there ; the unexplored puts contempt upon his wisdom ; the unattained overshadows his virtue ; the invisible has secret rebukes for his creations of the beautiful ; the future veils within it a thousand corrections of his meditations on life, and humanity, and God. However humbling and sometimes melancholy may be the emotions of such a one, his position is yet dignified and solemn. He stands between the two worlds of the known and the unknown, on the outer border between the human and the divine ; his left hand grasping the familiar and the finite ; his right hand put forth into the spaces of the infinite, and feeling for the touch of its mysteries. It is easy to see what will be the effect of this moral attitude on his affections with reference both to God and man. His piety dwells too little on present good to be distinguished by the bursts of gratitude; it is one perpetual aspiration of desire; it is prospective, looking less to the march of Providence than to its issues; it praises little, trusts much; pretends not to know the motives of the Eternal Mind, or expound the order of his policy, but waits the great issue with a faith serene; and renders the thought of him the vast receptacle for all its imaginations of the fair, the holy, the tender, the majestic. God rises up before him as his own ideal of moral beauty and excellence, invested with reality and life and power, dwelling near as his protector, moving within him as his conscience, going before him as the everlasting aim and reward of his affections. In relation to men, it may be admitted that this temper is less practically vigorous than its antagonist. It does not feel itself sufficiently lifted up in superiority to others to think that heaven depends on their being assimilated to itself; it is therefore less boldly aggressive upon error, and is roused chiefly against sin and wrong; its sympathies are those of equal with equal, the respectful mercy of a kindred sufferer; and its exertions, not the passionate precipitation of enthusiasm or despair, but the tranquil effort of a heart which, though without exaggerated expectations of good in the present, has no dread alarm in its vision of the future. In the abasement of a soul like this there is no meanness; its lofty sense of the divine and the immortal is a sufficient security against that; the consciousness of imperfection that never quits it serves but as the incentive to new effort, and the attraction to unresting progress. Flying from the infirmities that chase it, and bending towards the good that moves before it, its step acquires an involuntary speed, and it visibly bounds up the ascent of excellence.

This is the type of mind which Christ prefers as the basis for the religious affections. In our days its moral peculiarities are sometimes attended by an intellectual tendency which popular prejudice would little lead us to expect in any character praised by Christ. Never losing the sense of what it does not know it must continually expect accessions of truth. Its possessor cannot regard his opinions as final, but must be ready to resign them in favour of other and ulterior views, whenever fresh evidence shall recommend a change. He can never therefore take a stand of absolute and unhesitating confidence upon his existing convictions, but must feel some degree of contingency to attach to them. In other words, he will experience a tendency towards the spirit of doubt. I do not mean the spirit of *disbelief;* the positive believer and the positive unbeliever belong to the same class with each other and with the Pharisee; but I mean the spirit of modest, humble, open-hearted doubt; which in its sublimest form, of trust in spite of darkness, borders close upon faith. There can scarcely be a prejudice more mischievous and cruel than to suppose that this spirit is necessarily indevout. Certainly it *may* be so; and so may dogmatism. But the most earnest cries of piety are always the outpouring of doubt. Why are men irresistibly religions in grief, in danger, in transition of faith, but that there is an element of new uncertainty introduced into their minds? An affectionate spirit does not need any broad basis of certainty as the foundation of its trust; give it but the simple faith in God above it and immortality before it, and it will frame from these a lofty and profound and operative devotion. Nay; an affectionate mind not only does not need, but it does not desire the feeling of positive assurance. For the most favourable position for the human being for the exercise of piety is his actual position; a station as on a narrow footing of security in the midst of a vast ocean of uncertainty. Extend the solid space on which he stands far around him, and he forgets the fluctuating deep. Contract his circle and bring the billows near, and the awe creeps back upon his heart; he looks around and prays; he looks above, and trusts; the rock on which he stands is no other than the Rock of Ages.

LIVERPOOL, 1836.
LONDON, 1869.

XII.

The Unjust Steward.

———•◦•———

LUKE xvi. 9.

"Make to yourselves friends of the mammon of unrighteousness; that when ye fail, they may receive you into everlasting habitations."

THE parable of the unjust steward, being full of local allusions, and designed to extract from a momentary position of parties in Palestine a great lesson of political morality, cannot be understood without a sketch of the condition of that province at the time.

It had been better for Rome if the ancient city of the Hebrew tribes had never attracted the cupidity of her rulers; for the possession cost more bloodshed to her sons than it brought of tribute to her treasury. It is not indeed to be wondered at, that when the Nile had become one of her provincial rivers, and her sovereignty was acknowledged from the snows of Taurus to the Tyrian shore, she should be impatient to sketch upon her map of empire the intervening inch or two of coast, and thus sweep with her galleys the whole circuit of the Mediterranean. The petty independence of Judæa, breaking the line of so vast a sway, was like a peasant's field between the lawns of the great man's estate; and it was not to be supposed that a power like Rome, which was in a position to gratify every refinement of desire, would abstain from an encroachment so essential to the symmetry of its possessions. The awful city of the Tiber, which had made the Alps a highway for its arms, and quieted the factious Greek, and brought into servitude the free commerce of Phœnicia, and forced the hierarchy of Egypt to bend the knee, was not likely to think twice about an obscure corner of territory, which the mere show and shadow of its name was enough to win. That the Hebrews had religious objections to becoming subjects would but excite a smile; to set aside the scruples of a vile superstition it was enough that the slopes of Lebanon and the plains of Jezreel were pleasant and fertile, and that the terraces of Judæa that faced the breezes of the western sea would be as a fruit garden to the banquet halls at Rome.

The Empire, which plumed itself on being frugal and benign in the expenditure of its immense force, often found its approach to new lands welcomed as the steps of a protector. But the Jew watched them with hate and terror, like the viper waiting the crushing

tramp of the near giant, with intent slippery and
venomous at once. His feelings were purely Oriental,
purely national. He lived in a region that had a vast
memory, and that could count with centuries where
others numbered generations. The East, which was
the birth-place of the earth's earliest monarchies, and
gave to man the first idea of Majesty ; whose pedigree
of empires reached back to the era of creation in two
or three huge strides ; whose very deserts were strewed
with the wrecks of an immemorial magnificence; whose
history, moreover, looked fairer and greater through the
mists of tradition and the sunlight of the world's
dawn ;—the East regarded the upstart powers of
Europe with incredulity and contempt ; its tribes could
not yet believe that they had lost the heritage of
sovereignty; their dreams, like those of an exiled
monarch, were of thrones and conquest; and with
indolent superstition they fancied it their destiny still
to rule, and expected some Restorer to arise, who should
bring back the age of glory. Such however was the
decrepitude of most Eastern populations, that these
ideas were connected with no generous aspirations after
liberty, no true feeling of nationality; they were but
voluptuous images of thought, never interfering with
abject submission to the first tyrant that should bid
them kneel. But with the Hebrew these conceptions
were blended with a deep religious sentiment, which
freshens everything that it may touch; and that kindled

M

a fire of passion upon his heart; the intense flame of whose piety evolved continually black and massive clouds of vengeance. Though for centuries he and his fathers had licked the feet of despots, he nursed a mystic ambition unabated still; for once, the habits of subjection had failed to touch the sentiments of the slave; and it was still believed that submission to a foreign power was domestic High Treason to the King of Kings. Old as was the Hebrew servitude, there were prophecies of freedom and of greatness yet older; and these had kept awake the people's heart through the tedious night of tyranny, by haunting it with the ideas of emancipation, and singing to the sad the songs of happy days. A nation's mind may live long on glorious recollections of the past, and maintain itself above utter degradation by the mere force of its ancestral virtue; but when the vision of liberty is in the future instead of in the past, not receding but approaching, watched with an eye not of regret but of exultation, it inspires an intenser vigour; it privately consoles, instead of publicly shaming, the present ignominy; and yet maintains a spirit of preparation, and an eagerness for revolution, which no despotism less ponderous than that of Rome would be adequate to crush. The impatient Jew had already waited too long for the golden age which his prophets seemed to have foretold. The Assyrian, the Persian, and the Greek, had planted a foot upon his neck; and must he now lie down again beneath the heavy heel that was marching still further from the West? Hemmed in on every side, except where God's pure sea protected him, by nations foul in their idolatry, he grew sick at the insufferable contamination, and burned for the avenging hour, when he should wash it out in proselytism or in blood. Yet all this he was obliged to keep within his teeth; for the civil officers of Rome came round the villages, taking the census of the people, and though they said nothing, he knew, when he gave the names of himself and his house, that the next thing would be the tax; and as he turned in at his door, he taught his children a curse on the Gentile dogs. A few years of forbearance passed, and then the tax fell upon the land; an organized body of collectors were soon distributing themselves through the towns and hamlets, and the soldiery were not far off. A sigh went forth from the land, when Israel's hopes were again deferred.

The sway of Rome over its provinces, so far as the central authority could control it, was mild, and what is called *paternal;* though that word is greatly misapplied where self-government is so much excluded. Small and powerless tribes might, without dishonour, regard it as a payment of tribute in return for protection. So long as the revenue was punctually raised, and the garrisons encountered no turbulence or sedition, national usages were not interfered with;

Roman law was very partially and gradually introduced into the tribunals, and the popular worship was sanctioned,—perhaps even imported into Italy, and honoured with a new shrine in the imperial city itself· A power so gigantic could afford to be gentle ; and a religion so populous with Gods might as well open another niche for a new Deity in its pantheon. This was the Roman's tolerance ; nor did he dream that any people could object to return the politeness of his devotion, and invite Jupiter or Apollo to receive the incense which he did not refuse to burn to Jehovah. Never, till he entered Palestine, had he, throughout his amazing dominions, come into collision with the true religious sentiment,—the undivided allegiance, the jealous conscience, the faithful veneration, which the heart cherished towards an object of pure and earnest worship. It was nothing strange to him to be for awhile detested by barbarians who had felt the weight of his sword. But it was a new thing to find himself scorned by his own slaves, and regarded as the refuse of the earth in a province that obeyed him ; his touch held to be defilement, his tribute sacrilege, his piety inexpiable sin. He stood among his subjects in Judæa, at once the invader of their rights and the violator of their conscience,—their seducer no less than their oppressor ; and he was hated with the twofold intensity of disappointment and remorse.

The real rulers however were placed, either by

distance or by rank, far beyond the reach of these fierce
feelings ; the emperor was cut off from them by the
Mediterranean, the local governor at Cæsarea by the
flatteries and corruptions of a provincial court. The
objects on whom the storm of national passion actually
spent itself were the officers of the revenue, or
publicans. Distributed throughout the country, and
in contact with the people at every point, they were
the visible representatives of the power so deeply
abhorred. And the enmity towards them was the
more implacable because they were, for the most part,
native Jews, who were regarded as having sold themselves for gain to administer an unholy and anti-
national system; like all men that thrive upon their
country's shame, they were execrated as extortioners
and apostates. And since men speedily become what
they are assumed to be, and the despised, losing their
self-respect, sink into the despicable, the character of
this class could scarcely be very elevated, and realized
in frequent instances, no doubt, that compound of
recklessness and cruelty which popular prejudice
ascribed to them all. In their wretched position it
could not be otherwise; Hebrews, without the Hebrew
hopes,—Romans, without the Roman pride,—re-
pudiated by one nation and tools of the other, they lived
without a sympathy. Thwarted and deceived at every
turn, they grew familiar with the severities that ground
down reluctant wills. Outlaws from all that is genial

in life, they must need contract the slyness and the daring of those against whom society proclaims war. The very coin in which all their transactions with their country people were conducted bore Cæsar's odious image and superscription, and the nation, compelled to touch it, revolted at the unclean thing. In short, this unhappy class was like the people's evil conscience, always chafing and never healing; they were the visible mementoes of slavery, corrupters of faith, and tempters to seduction and blood.

The religion of the Jews, however, while it exasperated them against the oppressors, consoled them under the oppression. It persuaded them that the Messiah, promised of God, was ready to bring in the last days; and that with all her children and plenitude of power, the city, vainly called eternal, was already tottering to her fall. In the secret councils of Omnipotence, there was a thick darkness and confusion preparing to fall on Pagan thrones and nations, and a morning light of everlasting peace to envelop the towers and hills of Israel. A wild revenge on past humiliation was to fill the first hours of that eternal day;—a clearing off of defiled nations, for the solitary sway of God's vicegerent over his ancient and approved people. This faith in the Hebrew was vivid and unconquerable; every rumour, every tumult confirmed it; the earthquake and the pestilence were omens of its fulfilment; the shooting star at midnight might be the angel of its coming; or the noonday rack bring it on a car of storm. As the Roman eagle hovered in majesty above him, he watched for the sudden flash of heaven to strike it to the earth; but alas! while the lightning of **Jehovah** tarried, the bird of Jove hastened to fall on him, and made a dreadful prey. But to the last the deluded Israelite had the comfort of his hope. He paid every tribute, as a man commits every sin, persuaded that it will be the last. The work of the hated publicans would fail them soon; and he would clap his hands to see them shut out from the everlasting habitations.

Such was the relative position, and such were the mutual feelings, of the parties concerned in the religious politics of Palestine. Not indeed that passions so vehement were universal. Doubtless there were many observers who regarded the Roman ascendancy with milder feelings, and saw no sin in a payment that purchased security and peace, and indulged no merciless hostility against the officers of revenue. But the spot on which Jesus stood when he spoke the parable from which my text is taken was near the centre of the fiercest fanaticism against Rome and all her representatives. He was near the southern extremity of the Galilean sea; whence recently a turbulent enthusiast, Judas the Gaulonite, had gone forth among the excitable people, proclaiming the unlawfulness of tribute, and sword in hand preaching the high doctrine, "none is our Lord but God"; proposing to sweep the whole tribe of publicans away, and raise the banner of religious insurrection. The man had perished and his followers dispersed; but his spirit animated all the fiercer zealots of the law; it was cunningly fostered by the officious Pharisees; it prowled about the land, watching its opportunity, and spreading the explosive materials of revolt; which when they burst in after years proved too strong for the social frame that held them, and shattered the nation into ruins. In the story of the unjust steward, Jesus enters into this controversy respecting the tribute and the collectors, and defines the real duties of the several parties. The debtors are the tributary Jews; the rich creditor, the Roman government; the steward, the public officers of the revenue, whose hard position was appreciated and pitied by Christ, and in this parable drew forth his gentle and generous wisdom in their instruction and defence. They were never safe from the malignity which their office brought upon them. If they exacted the Pagan impost to the full, they were execrated for extortion; if they relaxed its severity, some ungrateful enemy who profited by the indulgence, accused them to the government for "wasting its goods." It is probable that, in this precarious position, the publican resorted for self-defence to an artful system of arrears; and kept all possible accusers in his power, by registering a state debt against them, which on the first show of hostility he could either affright them by exacting, or conciliate them by remitting. This latter and more generous course is recommended to him by our Lord, who assures him that in the end he will thus make friends; that no bigotry can for ever withstand the appeal which forbearance and mercy makes to the better feelings of the heart; that even in the administration of an unpopular office, even in the collection of a tax which, being imposed by foreign force and not by free consent, may well be called the mammon of injustice, and he will find it not impossible to recover the social sympathy of his countrymen; they will gradually recall the outcast publican from excommunication, embrace him as a true Hebrew again, permit him to share in the national hope,—and when his occupation is gone by the downfall of Rome, and the empire flies before the Messiah, will concede to him a participation in the glory, and a shelter in the perpetual abodes of that heavenly reign. Thus, where it might be least expected, out of the very mammon of injustice,—from the system of foreign exaction,—a loving and patriotic spirit will find the means of making friends;—friends who, when all commission from Gentile states shall fail, will receive an Israelite so true into everlasting habitations. Having with loss and danger to himself been faithful to his country, in the management of an unfair tax, having been severely tested by the transitory and trivial interest of the present age, he will be intrusted with the true riches, the imperishable treasures, of the kingdom and the age to come. Placed between two masters, the selfish gains of his own commission and the mammon of a foreign exchequer on the one side, and the faith and sympathy of his native land upon the other, he boldly gave the preference to the latter, wherever the interests clashed ; and in thus abjuring mammon, he served his people, and thereby his God.

Nor could the Romans in their hearts avoid praising this mild policy in their agents.   There was, no doubt, a semblance of injustice to their interests in the collection of a mere percentage upon their dues, instead of the full tribute, and allowing a nation of debtors to come to an easy composition with the imperial creditor. But where, as in this case, a tax is hopelessly unpopular, and the people on whom it presses are inflammable and vindictive, there is no wisdom and no true loyalty in straining the forces of the law, till they threaten to give way beneath the tension. A prudent government, like that of Rome, will deem eighty measures of wheat, obtained with content, better than a hundred wrested by the sword. The precise and greedy Jew, judging all things by the letter rather than the spirit, and boasting that he is one of the children of light, might in like circumstances

madly treat this conduct as a deceit ; but the children
of this world are wiser than the children of light ; the
Romans will connive at it, and approve so honest and
merciful a fraud. They know the cost of sedition and
war ; and prefer a peaceful and contented people to a
rich but insecure exchequer.

This view of this celebrated and obscure parable
appears to me to remove all its chief difficulties. It
relieves Christ from the revolting imputation of
approving for its quality of prudence an act which has
the additional quality of genuine fraud ; an act, moreover, in which, as it is commonly conceived, the
prudence consists merely in the fraud. Can anyone
truly believe that Jesus, in selecting an example by
which to recommend discretion to his followers, would
dwell on the adroitness of the clever cheat ? Away
with an interpretation so ignorant and shameless ! But
the lesson which I have represented him as adminis-
tering seems full of penetrating and noble wisdom.
He vindicates the most despised of men, and shows
them that they have grave and solemn responsibilities.
He forbids them to return evil for evil, and exhorts them
to bear all for their native land, and wear down calumny
by mercy and fidelity. He proclaims the blessing of
social peace, and esteems the happiness of a nation
worth any sacrifice of gain. He pronounces the
enlightened and disinterested love of country to be
identical with the obligations due to God. He bids all

who have to discharge unpopular duties maintain with faith and patience a steady course of forbearing uprightness; consoles them under scorn and public insult by the tender of his own pure sympathy; and assures them that, however calumnious may be the present, the future will be just in its awards, and open to the good an everlasting dwelling in the remembrance of men on earth and the peace of God in heaven.

LIVERPOOL, 1837.
LONDON, 1870.

XIII.

Christ's Definition of "Neighbour."

——◆◆——

LUKE x. 36, 37.

"Which now of these three, thinkest thou, was *neighbour* unto him that fell among the thieves? And he said, he that shewed mercy on him."

IT is little wonder that Jesus thought the road "from Jerusalem to Jericho" the fittest locality for the lawless violence of bandits. No sovereign less prosperous, and no merchant less enterprising, than Solomon, would ever have thought of opening a highway of traffic towards the tribes of Jordan, and the remoter plains of the Euphrates through the calcined heights of Judæa; heights that seem like the scattered links of a mountain chain; as if an earthquake had peeled off the vegetation to the bone and split them in wreck upon the land; or a volcano had boiled up through the desert sands, and its blisters had burst and hardened into Alps. The traveller who has once left behind the Mount of Olives, plunges into the silence of this waste; on whose summits there is nothing to invite even the shriek of the bird of prey, and whose hollows have never heard the trickling of a stream. The eye has as little to relieve it as the ear; peak after peak is reached in vain; nothing is discovered but the dreary expanse of the Dead Lake, sleeping amid hills of iron,—except when the wind whiffs up an ashy dust, and spreads over everything a dingy shroud. During the eight or ten hours' journey not a human habitation appears, except the one little inn or caravanserai, with whose host the good Samaritan left his wounded charge;—a house whose site is permanently fixed by a scanty water spring, and on the walls of which the words of Mahomet are now engraven, as if to remind one of the world's vicissitudes, since the place was immortalized by Christ. Even the bold Arab shouts for joy, as he descends from these dread hills; and his noble horse, that has felt their sultriness though not their fears, snuffs the first moisture of the breeze, darts forward, like an arrow, over the sandy plain, and never stops till he stands under the willows of a distant stream. To turn round and look back on the way which has been passed by no means lessens the impression of its wildness; and those battlements of rock, these black ravines opening their jaws upon the plain, and disgorging the lazy mists, which are but intruders where there is not a moss to be refreshed,—have excited many a shudder in the careless traveller, and drawn many a thanksgiving from the devout.

This scene, which nature has blasted with sterility, Christ has refreshed with a tale of the most delicious humanity. That tale, if regarded merely as a picture of the time,—as painting with a few strokes its most marked forms of character, and distributing their genuine colours over its peculiar prejudices, vices and miseries, possesses inimitable beauty. There is the Priest, whom we are accustomed to see amid the stir of Jerusalem,—the very model of pompous piety, the master of sanctimonious ceremonies, beating his breast in the market-place, and stretching forth his hands at the corners of the streets, the scrupulous adviser of the people's conscience, and idol of their stolen peace; we are invited to see him on the solitary ride; his back turned to the metropolis, he is a saint no more; he performs no charities among the hills; delivered from the public eye, he breaks loose from the moralities of life and the reverence of God. There is the Levite, a kind of menial of the Sacerdotal order, whose conduct towards " him that fell among thieves " is true to his usual mimicry of the priests, with whose interests his own are interwoven, and whose habits and hypocrisy he copies to the life. And there is the Samaritan,—half foreigner, half apostate, and more wholly outcast than if he had been idolater downright,—the object of irritating historical recollection,—the living memorial of captivity and schism,—the centre of a hate both national and religious ;—with no offiee, or dignified caste, like the others, to protect him from peril by their sanctity, but traversing a hostile country, he stops to bind the wounds of a stranger, and tarries with him in a house where, while he tenders the cup of cold water, bigotry forbids his blaspheming lips to share the draft. Thanks to Christ, time and the human heart have retorted on that intolerance; for, since this tale was told, what age has refused to call the Samaritan good?

And this shows that the parable is something more than a picture of the time, and envelops it in some permanent and universal principle of morality. To this higher view of it, to which indeed the very occasion of its delivery points, let us then turn. It contains Christ's definition of the word *neighbour*, and forms his conception of the rule, Thou shalt love thy neighbour as thyself. Except in the practical commentary afforded in his life, the spirit of his morality received no such distinct elucidation. I fear, however, that to most readers much of the point of the illustration is lost through mistaken interpretation.

Were I to ask you to state, from your own impressions, what was Christ's definition of a neighbour,— every one would, I believe, be ready to answer in the spirit of the old psalm,

> "Our neighbour is the *suffering man*,
> Though at the furthest pole."

Jesus is supposed to teach here the lesson of universal philanthropy, to vindicate the ties of a common brotherhood, to claim for oppressed and insulted humanity that respect which, even in the most ignorant and debased, is due to a thinking, feeling, responsible and immortal mind. The affection which is thought to be recommended is that general tenderness which is independent of all personal qualities, of all particular relations of kindred, friendship, or country, and contemplates only the indestructible elements of our nature, and venerates it as a child of God, and the heir of a perpetual progress. A heart filled with such a spirit will have a sympathy ready for every woe that needs it.

That such a lesson as this would be in perfect consonance with the character of Christian morality, and is in fact nowhere so completely in its natural place, I admit; but that a very different principle is incorporated in the parable before us the following reasons will perhaps make evident.

If Christ had intended to assert the claims of suffering, he would surely have fixed the title of *neighbour* upon the wounded man; his distresses would have been represented as having earned the name; and the concluding question of Jesus would have been, Which now of these three loved his neighbour as himself? Instead of this, the relative position of the actors is reversed; the lawyer is not allowed to apply the term " neighbour " to the bleeding way-farer, but is required to attach it to one of the three

N

travellers; " Which now of these three, thinkest thou, was *neighbour?* " And the qualification which settled the appellation on the Samaritan was, that " he shewed mercy." Everyone therefore is our neighbour, it would appear, in proportion as he manifests beneficent and holy dispositions. It is goodness, and not sorrow, that wins the name.

Were it otherwise indeed, the rule that we are to love our neighbour as ourselves would be chargeable with great moral exaggeration. No one can love another as himself simply because he suffers pain; much less can he feel the same emotion,—an emotion always equal to his self-love,—towards every member of the miscellaneous class of human sufferers. The various kinds of human suffering *must* excite in us affections equally various in their nature and intensity. How different the feeling must ever be towards the meek and self-forgetful victim of disease, amid the wasting of nature lifting up from his own cheerfulness the shaded spirits of his friends, and the fretful, requiring temper that adds to physical pain a moral torment incomparably worse;—towards the frenzy that fires a brain overtasked in the service of science or liberty or love, and the idiocy that creeps upon besotted sin;—towards the despondency of baffled beneficence, and that of detected and trembling crime! To say that all these are to carry the same appeal to our affections, that the wailing of a child and the tears of a Milton are to be visited with emotion of like intensity, is to confound all moral distinctions, and insult the natural perceptions of the human heart. Christ well knew that love is an emotion awakened by moral qualities, incapable of subsisting where they are not, and proportioned to the degree in which they are observed; that it has no relation to mere suffering, and could undergo no worse profanation than to be withdrawn from excellence to be given to pain. The pure and gentle spirit, the clear and prompt conscience, the adamantine will which sophistries cannot bewilder nor interest bribe, the profound and reverential sense of right, the self-oblivious and affectionate heart, the aspiring and holy mind sensibly enveloped within the infinity of God,—these are the attributes to which alone the admiration, the confidence, the attachment of our souls may be awarded. To mere suffering the far lower feeling of compassion is appropriate; and I suppose it is upon this emotion that Christ's precept is usually thought to prefer a claim. But that by the love of our neighbour he could not mean mere pity, or any of the acts due peculiarly to the " suffering man," is evident from its being the same affection which just before he required to be directed towards God. It is past all dispute, that the class of feelings which Jesus enjoined in the first commandment are those of moral veneration; he would penetrate us, not merely with instinctive awe of God's power, and the imagination of his immensity and the impression of his duration; for in this sense of physical sublimity the desires may be unenflamed and the conscience cold; but he would inspire us with that love of God which is the love of perfect excellence; it is as the Original of all moral distinctions, who has devised the peace of virtue and the woes of sin; as the Revealer of the idea of duty, and the ineffable sanctities of conscience; as the inventor of the humanities of life; as the archetype of whatever is beautiful and noble and tender; it is as the voluntary parent of the life with which Creation teems, and overflows with good; it is as the ever-acting Mind whose Providence is perfect alike in comprehension and in minuteness,—walking the zones of the universe and shaping the petals of a flower,—conducting unerring evolutions of systems, and threading the mazes of the most private thought;—when a world is made, organizing its fresh pleasures, and, when it is crushed, measuring the sensations of every fibre of its sentient life; it is as the Designer of immortal existence to the great family of minds, that their faculties may dilate for ever into a nobler similitude of his; it is in such characters as these which exhibit the *moral* nature of the Infinite Spirit, that we are called on to render him the love of our whole minds. And in the second commandment the very same term describes the affection due to our neighbour; and how can we doubt that the affection is the same in kind;—founded on a perception of *moral qualities*, and having for its object that excellence which, in the Divine nature, we acknowledge to be the only just foundation of our love.

It seems, then, that we may accept *literally* Christ's construction of his own parable; that we are to regard the Samaritan as the intended model of a neighbour, and the Priest and the Levite as representing those who are excluded from that relation; and that we should not consider Christ as imposing upon men the obligation of loving as themselves any but those who, like the Samaritan, win the title of neighbour by the dispositions of a beneficent and good heart. This gives so new a turn to the morality of the whole passage, that it must be useful to glance at the principles which, according to this view, are enveloped in it.

Since it is goodness that places a man in the position of our neighbour, and we are required to love our neighbour as ourselves, it follows that the feelings towards virtue ought to equal our feelings towards self. The perfect state of mind is that in which our moral sympathies are no less intense than our self-love; and the contemplation of a noble sacrifice, a firm resistance of wrong, a patient fidelity to unostentatious duty, or the silent deed of mercy can move us not less than the pleasures of personal prosperity and success. To one who reaches this elevation of conscience nothing has any attraction which is purchased by an insult to his sense of right; if by his ease others suffer, he takes the path of toil; if for his opulence others must live in chains and tears, he loves rather the content of poverty; if for his distinction a people must be less well served, he takes the unambitious course. And in thus requiring that the selfish desires should operate only within the limits allowed by a perfect morality, Christ demands nothing repugnant to the laws of our nature. For what does this describe but the character of Jesus himself? in whom the passion for excellence was checked by no personal desire; who most expressed himself when he yielded to the highest convictions of duty; with whom negligence, and unkindness, and the sleep of indulgence, and the insensibility to wrong, and exclusion from the spectacle of sorrow, and life itself at the price of compromise, would have been the utmost torture of self-denial, the crushing of his most craving desires; who held the escape from duty to be an exile from the peace of God; and who would have sunk beneath the intolerable sacrifice, had he not toiled and taught and suffered, and stolen into the heart of poverty to refresh it, and placed himself by bereavement to banish it, and brought sin to his feet that he might raise it to a better life. Those who, in following their love of moral excellence, follow their own warmest personal passion, are true subjects to the rule of loving their neighbour as themselves.

Since it is goodness that renders a man our neighbour, it follows that we are under no obligation to love as ourselves the selfish, the malignant, the depraved. Such are not our neighbours, but occupy the same position with respect to us as the Priest and the Levite in the parable, from whom, it is plain, Jesus withheld the appellation. That Christian morality is hostile to personal resentment, that it softens the irritations of natural passion by the memory of our common nature and common immortality, that it so lifts the eye above the little orbit of our earthly life that we may serenely study its seeming disorders, that it so enfolds us in consciousness of universal providence that nothing can seem totally deranged in the affairs of men, is perfectly true; but it does not stifle, it rather quickens our moral indignation and aversion against wrong; and while it disposes us to patient and practical exertion for the debased, while it creates for us new moral obligations towards them, which no other religion ever recognized,—it yet renders the sentiment of interior affection for them more unattainable than ever. In spite of all the refinements of a sentimental morality, it is impossible to separate in our regards the agent and the act; disgust at intemperance is disgust at the intemperate; aversion to hypocrisy is aversion to the hypocrite; indignation at tyranny is indignation at the tyrant. That honour, which, for the sake of our universal Father, is due to all men, that respect which, in consideration of its great futurity, is to be rendered to every human soul, that promptitude of beneficent effort which, in hope of abating misery, must be ready for every occasion, are never to be withheld from natures the most lost; but the emotion of love like that which springs upward to God, the affection which even our self-respect must not be permitted to exceed, is too holy to be squandered on any but those who bear on them the signature of Divine approval.

Finally; if goodness and that only renders a man our neighbour, it follows that we must find it out, as did the wounded Jew in the good Samaritan, though it lurks amid opinions, feelings, prejudices, perfectly opposite to our own. A clergyman wrote to me, "I am a Calvinist; belief in the Incarnation appears to me indispensable to salvation, and to my recognition of any one as a child of God. But I confess that the enormous difficulty of at least apparent facts staggers me; one of the most perfect characters I know is an aged Unitarian lady; but then are there not most exemplary people to be found who deny *all* Christianity in every shape and form? The more I think of it the more perplexed I am." "I should *welcome a Revelation from heaven* to tell me that I might acknowledge as a child of God anyone who seems to love Him, and his brother, believe or disbelieve what he might."—And *here,* my friend, you have the Revelation you desire. It is given indeed already in your prayer for it, and your perplexity without it ; for these, you must inwardly know, are higher and truer to the spirit of God, than your textual disbelief of it. But, if you need the authority of the outward word of Christ, here it is in the parable which commends all goodness to our love, and takes the brotherhood away from the cold sanctities of orthodox decorum. What is it that we here learn ? No party ties are to be put into a competition with the sympathies of good hearts; no similarity of creed to vie with the congenialities of virtue ; no dislike of doctrines to blunt the pure and quick sensibility to the presence of qualities great and excellent. To call those of different faith our neigh-bours, and yet to be blind to their virtues, is an act which our interpretation of Christ's parable brands as an hypocrisy. To withhold our veneration from goodness because it is not conformed to our own type, or derived from our favourite notions, to sneer at religion which gives forth good fruits,—which touches the conscience, and inspires the affections, and strengthens the will, of its possessors, because we discern an error in its logic, betrays a narrowness of heart, a sterility of moral sympathy, an absence of the genuine perceptions of holiness, a preference of resemblance to ourselves to the traces of loftier similitude to perfection and to God, entirely at variance with the generous mind of Christ. The immortality which will terminate our errors, will perpetuate every element of goodness ;

and those who have the most irresistible passion for every form into which the soul of excellence can be thrown are the most ready to breathe the air of the eternal world.

LIVERPOOL, 1836.
LONDON, 1870.

XIV.

The moral power of Christianity evinced in its corruptions.

---◆---

MATT. xiii. 37.

"He that soweth the good seed is the Son of Man."

THAT a religion must be judged by its fruits is a favourite doctrine of the school of practical men. With habit averse to speculative inquiry, and unused to the toil of collecting and balancing evidence, they have recourse to their familiar oracle, experience, and deem it easiest to determine their assent or dissent with respect to matters of faith by the apparent good or evil of the system proposed. On this principle the Christian controversy itself has been reduced to a question of fact; and the magnificent circle of gospel evidence is narrowed to a point of historic research. The trial of a prophesied revelation for eighteen centuries is thought to be sufficient to unfold its character, and through its character its origin. During that period it has passed through every conceivable vicissitude

requisite for the development of its resources; it
has been brought into contact with every variety of
human character, and made the companion of every
human fate ; reposing on the seat of royalty, or swept
into the desert by persecution ; familiar alike with the
camp and with the market ; dwelling in the soul of
ignorance, or allied to the genius of philosophy and
poetry ; passing in short from age to age, and
migrating from land to land, it must have visited every
form of mind which is to be found in human populations, and presented every phase which it is destined
to exhibit.   The preponderance of good or ill which
the history of its influence shows may be taken as the
test of its value and the mark of its derivation.

This criterion of Christianity, however plausible an
air of practical simplicity it may assume, involves in
truth one of the most complicated processes of
speculation, and the profoundest labour of research.
In order to apply it faithfully, it is necessary to know,
not merely what society has been with Christianity,
but what it would have been without ; to lift the gospel
and all its effects out of the line of history, and calculate
the progress of the world under the remaining causes ;
to conceive those portions of human nature laid asleep
which Christianity has peculiarly stimulated, and others
brought forward which it may be thought to have
repressed ; and when our conjectural history has been
brought down to the present day, it must be placed

side by side with the reality, and the verdict of preference be awarded after cautious comparison. Of the difficulty of such a task anyone may be convinced by the most cursory glance along the chain of events in which Christianity has had the most unquestionable share. Suppose Christianity not to have been, and the alteration goes deeper than might at first have been supposed. It is not merely that instead of the churches that now stud the land and overshadow every village with their protection, we might have had Pagan groves inviting our population to rites that may well hide themselves from the eye of day; nor that, where the cathedral aisle now spreads its perspective, the monument of the dim and mystic piety of other days, the worshippers of our cities might have bent the knee to the marbles of a Grecian shrine. It is not merely that the long line of Sabbaths must be struck from the calendar of the past, and two centuries and a half of rest and prayer, with all the peace that has been imparted, the fervour that has been kindled, the awe, the love, the vivid faith that have burst from within the soul of Christendom beneath the powers of that holy time, must be wrenched from the history of Christian nations. Had Christ not come into the world, the whole literature, law, philosophy, and institutions of modern times, would have been different; the genius of Dante and of Milton must have sought another inspiration, the prophet of Arabia another foe, and the enterprise of the Crusader some different glory; the warm spirit of the East, without the chain of religious sympathy, would not have been transfused into our Northern mind; the productions of ancient genius, destitute of the monastic shelter which preserved them, would have perished in the wreck of war; Europe would not have witnessed the sleep of its mind beneath the opiates of Papal influence, nor its awakening at the voice of the Reformation; and where the new world has been gloriously peopled by the persecutions of the old, the forests might still have been uncut. I do not mention these events to prove the benefits, but merely to exhibit the extent of the gospel influence; to show how deeply it has been wrought into the whole fabric of our history; how impossible, even in imagination, to dislocate it from its position and its connection there; and consequently how intricate instead of simple a problem it is, to determine its character by its effects.

The more complicated the problem, however, the better does it answer the purpose of the partisan. If it be difficult to embrace in one comprehensive view, and to discriminate by one piercing glance, all the effects of the gospel, there is the greater temptation to drop out of sight some part of the calculation, to look at some fragment of its agency, and on this partial estimate to pass a sweeping sentence on the whole religion. Judge Christianity by its fruits, is the favourite cry of its modern critics; and then the history of fanaticism is ransacked, and every absurdity that has broken forth from the delirium of ignorance, every delusion that has ever linked itself with Christian faith, every unsocial passion that has put on the stole of piety, every horror that has been devised beneath a mitred brow, has been called out and held up in mockery of the cross. The objector points out to us certain remarkable forms of character, certain peculiar types of mind, which have proceeded from the school of Christianity; he reminds us of the spontaneous martyrdom of the early church, of the anchorite wasting his life in the desert, of the ascetic morality of the monk, of the chimerical beneficence of many a missionary, of the cold ferocity of the persecutor; he compares all these complicated mischiefs with the Christian's repre-sentations of the regenerating power of the gospel; infers that all such representations are deceptive, and that to rely for the improvement of human character on the agency of Christianity is to lean upon a broken reed.

It is useless to deny that the history of religion in general, without excepting Christianity, presents us with a melancholy catalogue of human errors, follies, and crimes. Devotional sentiment would seem capable of allying itself with the lowest as well as the loftiest passions of mankind. There would appear to be scarcely any contradiction too revolting, any rite too unmeaning, any cruelty too barbarous, to find admittance into the mind under the sanction of its faith; and so great is the versatility of evil, that the most opposite forms of superstition and immorality are to be found preferring their claims to sanctity. Dependence on personal merits and dependence on implicit belief, the vices of asceticism and those of voluptuousness, have attempted to shelter themselves under the same great and sacred name, which equally disowns them all. And there are those who take a malignant and unsocial delight in dragging forth these sad sins of humanity, and who would avail themselves of the disgust which they awaken, to persuade us that the religious principle with which they are associated is worthy of all contempt, and must be discarded by the maturer mind of society, as a prejudice of infancy. The inference is false as it is insidious. These intellectual and moral extravagances do but prove the tenacity and indestructibility of the religious sentiment in the mind of man; odious as they are in their own nature, they could never have retained a hold on the human heart, had they not entwined themselves around some instinct which is an indissoluble part of its structure. Why should they have been so obstinate but that they have fastened themselves to an essential portion of our being? and thus, temporary and factitious as they are, have secured (for a while) a participation in its stability? Why should they have been so various, but that the religious principle possesses a universality which gives it place in every mind,—that it is not like an accident of our constitution which may exist here and there, and blend itself with some peculiar caste of understanding, but like a pervading tendency which runs through every diversity assumed by our multiform nature? What must be the tenacity of that faith which clings to the mind which has lost every other truth? What must be its power, to reconcile the soul to absurdities which no other persuasion could introduce, and to render its authority permanent in opposition to the dictates of taste, of reason, and of natural affection?

But the mental and moral eccentricities which have distinguished the Christian history possess a peculiar character, illustrative of the spirit of the religion from which, in one sense, they may be said to have sprung. At the root of each of them there has been the intense appreciation of some one moral excellence; each has been a contrivance for perfecting or expressing that excellence, whatever it might happen to be; and the evil of each has mainly arisen from the partial view which has been taken of moral perfection, from an exclusive attention to some solitary virtue, often subordinate in its value and useless in its isolation, and from the mistaken and pernicious means adopted for its nurture and display.

First in the train of Christian fanatics comes the

Eremite, condemning himself to voluntary exile from the activities of life, and thereby assuredly absconding from all its duties. Living beneath the placid skies of Asia or of Egypt, the clime of sultry days and brilliant nights, with constitutional tendency to the dreamy spirit of Eastern reverie, he was struck with the meditative glories of Christianity, and his fancy seized upon its spirituality as its idol. The vision of its sublime truths, the consciousness of its infinite Spirit, whose presence spread beyond the solar radiance, whose finger wheeled the concave of the heavens, the unapproachable centre of whose glory was buried somewhere amid the stellar light; the remembrance of that Saviour who had passed from the shadows of his human life to the invisible receptacle of the blessed; the clear and unimpeded thought of that immortality before whose immensity even those cycles of the universe which affright the imagination by their vastness, dwindled to a point of time,—all this could ill be realized amid the grosser elements, the trivial concerns, the distracting turmoil, of a worldly life. To mingle with the throng of men, to stoop to the supply of animal wants, to be harassed with the competition of commerce, or the pressure of domestic cares, was beneath the dignity of a soul appointed to harbour the conceptions of infinitude and eternity; solitude was the fitting home for such a mind, that it might gaze for ever on the undimmed effulgence of Deity, and feel the divine similitude silently burn and brighten.

Such was the delusion which led the solitary to the desert. It was a miserable miscalculation of the elements of devotion; as if the mind were not its own place; as if locality were piety, and the rock or the grove were nearer heaven than the city or the field. It was a feeble misinterpretation of human life; as if its energies were not the most effective stimulants to the soul, its vicissitudes the purest discipline for the affections, and the sacred ties of nature the best link of earth to heaven. It was a grievous reflection on the government of God; as if he had planted man in a world ill suited to his needs, set him at enmity with his own futurity, and made his position jar with his obligations. And the effect was such as every wise man would expect; a wretched dwindling of the intellect, and a total withering of the heart; he whose pride towers above his nature, will end by being below it; and by aiming at the position of the angel, he inevitably sinks towards the level of the brute.

But Christianity, my friends, is not concerned in the defence of the anchorite's absurdities. Let them pass with the full sentence of condemnation. I only say that they show the strong impulse which Christianity can give to the contemplative faculties, the unrivalled sympathy there is between its truths and the profounder exercises of thought and emotion.

Take next the religious Ascetic.   His interpretation of
the gospel is different.   He remembers that its author
was a man of sorrows and acquainted with griefs ; had
not where to lay his head, and called on his disciples
to take up their cross and follow him.   He is smitten
with the Stoicism of Christianity ; his imagination
dwells on that sublime spectacle of meekness which his
faith presents to him, Deity melting at the sight of
human suffering, disrobing himself of his ineffable
glories, taking on him the woes of mortality, dwelling
amid human infirmities, and yielding to the bitterest
of human fates.   Self-denial becomes the centre of his
Christianity.   He loves the mild but stern sway of
inflexible determination over the versatility of impulse ;
his spirit is at home in the elemental war of passion,
and glories in keeping down its bursting winds by the
intense pressure of resolve ; he abjures his body ; he sets
a foot of scorn on the uprisings of rebellious nature ; he
welcomes pain, and deems endurance the mission of
his being ; his mind is fascinated by the contrast of
solemnity within, and poverty without, of peace in the
thoughts, and suffering in the frame, and of conscious
immortality bending to the menial offices of life.
Here too is a visionary and a mischievous piety ; a
piety which represents God as a lover of misery, and as
demanding, not the sacrifice of lesser good for greater,
or of personal ease for others' sake, but the absolute
annihilation of enjoyment ; a piety which inflates with

the vapour of spiritual pride, and makes up in self-flattery the deficiency of self-indulgence ; a piety, too, which, like all fictitious systems of duty, must soon retire before the returning energies of nature, and leave the conscience void and dead. But with all its faults, it proves how deeply the self-denying character is stamped into the ethics of Christianity; it evinces the restless power with which it can seize and subject the lower to the higher desires of human nature; it exhibits what mastery of will it can impart; what contempt for present evil, what enthusiasm for future good, it can inspire.

The crusader affords an anomalous exhibition of an armed and aggressive Christianity. In studying him it is difficult to believe that we are witnessing an outbreak of the very same religion which in the Eremite had displayed itself in the spirit of contemplation, and in the ascetic in humble self-denial. The central sentiment of the Christian warrior was one of deep local veneration. The land of sacred story, whose airs had vibrated with the voice of God, the land of miracle and prophecy, whose river had witnessed the consecration, whose deserts the temptation, whose homes the mercy of the Saviour, whose mountains had seen his converse with visitants from heaven, whose seas and storms had felt the impress of his power; the very spot where he had commended to his Father his agonized and expiring life, the holy ground where the weeping Mary stood and the vision of angels had been seen, the place of the cross, the sepulchre, the ascension, were held by the scoffing infidel, and overshadowed by the crescent of Arabian imposture.　The innocent pilgrim, who had traversed seas and continents that he might but breathe a prayer where Jesus had been, was injured and insulted ; he was not permitted to bend the knee upon the rock of Calvary till he had first done homage to the unbelieving prince.　He brought home the tale to Europe, and Europe vowed that the land of Christ should be the land of Christendom ; its population rushed to the mad enterprise ; their motley hordes were wasted dreadfully, cut down by the scourge of war, and want, and pestilence, and a track of dead was spread from Jerusalem to Rome ; but on they moved, with dauntless ardour, till the red cross was planted on the hills of Judæa, and on the spot where Jesus had breathed his last petition of forgiveness, thousands uplifted their blood-stained hands and sent forth a chorus of savage prayer.　Wretched infatuation !　Well might the Lord in heaven seek for his followers the boon which in his anguish he had implored for his foes, " Father ! forgive them, for they know not what they do."

No judicious Christian would ever dream of defending this wild and woeful scene.　By whatever test it be tried it must be unsparingly condemned.　And the condemnation of the act involves condemnation of the character of the actors. Christianity has seldom allied itself with a form of human nature more melancholy or degrading. And yet it must be allowed to show the sway exercised over human feelings by the character of Christ; its power to summon forth all the deep and affectionate veneration of the heart; the generous heroism which that veneration can inspire, and the incredible hardships to the endurance of which it may prompt. We may read in these events a matchless homage to the power of Christ's character.

Another form of enthusiasm which excites the derision of scepticism is the missionary. Himself enjoying the sublime solace of pure worship, and the ineffable peace of an immortal hope, he views the distant spectacle of idolatry, its servile fears, its inhuman cruelties, its mental imbecility, its moral impurity, with irrepressible compassion. The cry of its victims travels to him across the ocean and their image stands over him by night and whispers to his pity, "Come over and help us." He construes the pleading of mercy into the voice of God; and thinks that he who will have a home in heaven may well abandon the hope of a rest and home on earth, and dedicate himself "a living sacrifice" at the shrine of human good. Could he but plant the rose of Sharon on the icy plain of Greenland, or cause the fountain of living water to roll over the sands of India, what toil, what sickness, what tears, what contempt, what

exile might not be endured! With apostolic self-
devotedness he takes up his resolve; goes forth on the
embassage of salvation; denies himself any lingering
look at kindred and at country; shrouds himself
within the impenetrable protection of God's spirit,
spread, like a cloud of light around him, and lives and
dies apart from every human sympathy that he may
convert the barbarians into citizens of heaven. Year
after year he labours on in love and faith; nurtures his
meek courage on prayer; is not daunted by the contrast
of his own untiring energy, and its feeble and languid
fruits; but waits humbly for the display of God's spirit,
when the lips of a divine persuasion shall be given him,
and thousands shall be converted in a day. Let it be
granted, my friends, that there are fallacies here; that
there is some miscalculation of the evil to be cured,
and more of the remedy to be applied; that resources
have been wasted, and lives sacrificed without need.
Still, I would not desire a purer exhibition of the
philanthropy of the gospel. There is clearly a strong
power at work upon the disinterested affections; and
a proof that Christianity can convert the mere sympathies of nature into a principle of impassioned yet
patient beneficence.

Now, my friends, let us see what is the real
experience with which the extravagances of Christian
faith supply us; what the real inference to which they
lead. Do they justify contempt and condemnation of

the gospel? or do they furnish us with a principle of profoundest reverence for it? Each of them is derived from an exclusive perception of some one moral glory; each of them pleads that its favourite quality is superlative in the ethics of Christianity; and each of them proves that Christianity can produce it in the highest degree. Put then all this testimony together; to what conclusion does it lead? Does it not show that there are various departments of the human soul, various degrees of strength and sanctity, which the gospel has the power of developing to intensity? The narrow mind of ignorance is indeed unable to embrace the grand proportions of lofty and symmetrical goodness; it contracts its attention to some one part, and so exhibits it in caricature, distorted from its position, and destitute of the reflected light from the surrounding glow of the spirit. But if the gospel can produce and perfect every moral grace in turn, there is nothing to prevent its maturing them all together, except the narrowness of the field on which its good seed may fall. Give it ampler scope, spread beneath it minds of wide and genial capacity, and what shall hinder their apprehensive sympathies from fostering all its germs of good, and covering the ground with every tree of life which has a leaf for the healing of the nations? And what a soul would that be, which, on the common ground-work of the private and civic virtues, should blend besides in one the ideal enthusiasm of the recluse, the self-abnegation of the ascetic, the heroic devotion of the soldier of the cross, and the tender beneficence of the missionary! And for this glorious result, nothing is wanting but natures capacious enough to give it place. The vital power is there; the seeds have already been scattered broadcast by the Son of Man. Let but the human faculties lie broadly open to the sunshine and the mellowing breath of the world's ripening seasons, and the creative energy of the religion is equal to all demands; and will produce ever new forms of spiritual life, and nobler growths of moral power.

LIVERPOOL, 1832.
LONDON, 1871.

XV.

Historical elements of Christian Faith.

---

1 JOHN v. 4, 5.

"This is the victory that overcometh the world, even our faith; who is he that overcometh the world, but he that believeth that Jesus is the Son of God?"

THAT every class of believers has eagerly defended its right to the appellation of "*Christian*," and that even unbelievers have not been willing to let it go, can surprise no one who reflects on the religious necessities of the human heart. This tenacity is no selfish pretension to the benefits appended to a name; for persecution has never weakened it, and it has proclaimed itself most in the face of danger and of death. It is no device of spiritual pride, anxious for exclusive possession, as against more plain and modest natures, of the world's most honoured designation; for it is chiefly seen in the meekest and most generous, who had rather kneel unseen in the Church of nations, than take the chief seat in the closet of the saints.

Rather does it arise from the feeling that to recede
from this word is to stand alone in life, and that he who
ceases to be the disciple of Jesus can be the disciple
of none.   It is no light thing to cast ourselves loose
from a community like that of Christendom,—to feel
that that truest and mightiest of brotherhoods is
nothing to us; to become estranged from a society
which gathers into it the highest greatness and glory
of history, and inherits the memorials of the world's
noblest heroism and loftiest thought; to stand erect
and cold amid the prostrate worship of dead and living
generations, and preserve a sceptic silence amid the
anthem of inspired tribes and ages; to be of different
faith from Pascal and Newton and Luther and Paul.
For he who quits the association of Christendom fiuds
no other historical community that he can join; the
Prophet of Nazareth has spoiled him for any other
guide of soul and faith, and left him to the forlorn
exclamation, Lord, to whom should I go, unless thou
hast the words of eternal life ?   To retreat back within
any of the elder religions of the earth, or to retire
laterally from the school of Christ into that of
Confucius or Mahomet, is admitted to be impossible;
if the voice of Jesus be lowered to the human,
assuredly nothing remains that can be called divine;
and the earth, whose spiritual heights had seemed,
with Alpine grandeur, to pierce the clouds of mystery
and find the upper light of God, sinks into the dullest

flat, disenchanted of the beauty which was but a painting of its atmosphere, and with no spot nearer to heaven than the hot places of chaffering and toil. Christ being confessedly at the summit of humanity, to disavow allegiance to him is to be without superior ; to proclaim self-subsistence and stand aloof from all communion ; to abscond from the household of faith only to become an exile and a wanderer. And this is a lot, however conceivable by the human head in no way tenable by the human heart. Solitary religion is quite impossible ; it is a light from other souls, a revelation from nobler natures ; heaven is first seen reflected in the clear depth of another's eyes ; God is first heard in the mellow tones of grief or prayer ; and though we may walk alone in the sharp daylight of finite things, we do not even discover the infinite till we make confession and hold sweet converse together, and must knit our hands in fast embrace ere we can enter this solemn darkness, and steal into its fields, vast and still as midnight. Man will always be either a leader or a follower in religion ; and if he have not the prophet's power, it will be sad for him to be without the people's faith ; his attempt to maintain an equal, independent, uncommunicated, lonely devotion, must end in a lifeless, unproductive conformity to an outward law ; in a morality, exact it may be and true in action, but without grandeur and glory in the soul ; in a blindness to one half the universe visible from our human station, and a mechanical rather than ideal survey of the rest.

Yet such minds there will always be, occupying especially the transition states of society, between the submersion of an old world and the disposition of a new. They are numerous without example in our day ; and present us with a large and increasing class who cannot with propriety be termed Christians in their belief, and yet with still less propriety can be called anything else ; and who, on this account, retain the name longer than would be possible if they receded towards anything positive instead of a mere negation. This loose and confused appropriation of such a term, though it often foils the inquisitor and the bigot, often also protects the disingenuous, and encourages the self-deceptive professor ; and as there must be a range beyond which the word cannot fitly be given, I propose to mark the limits of historical belief within which it should be confined.

(1.) *Belief in the historical personality of Jesus* is surely a necessary element of Christian faith. This proposition, evident enough, one would think, by its own nature, is an immediate consequence of the true idea of a revelation. If religious truth reveals itself to us only through the divine action of a sublimer soul, if there is no medium by which God holds converse with us except the sanctifying operation of higher upon lower minds, then he who denies the real existence, in the case of Christianity, of any such mediatorial spirit, takes away the prime condition of the system, and leaves the religion impossible. Trust in a person, not admiration of a scheme, is the essential sentiment of every faith; and where the person is supposed to be unreal, the faith cannot be real. To the relation between Master and disciple both parties are indispensable; and if the Master vanishes in mythology, **the** discipleship slides into pretence.

Let us observe however the strict limits and just application of this rule. It demands a true living soul, as the fountain of our faith, a being known to have acted, spoken, suffered, died, at a given intersection of space and time; it refuses to explain away this being into an imagination or a hope, consolidating itself from a nebula faintly floating amid the night of Hebrew fates into the central Sun of human history. But it does not require that we should go beyond the individual personal existence of this being; it does not require that we should accept all the relations by which it pleased his nation and his age to surround him, and conceive him to be so present in the line of events as they had imagined. Resorting to him for himself alone, we have at least but a secondary concern with the *system*, of which he was at the time regarded as a part. Having the *attestation* of his Advent as a Fact, we are past the point of having any interest in its *prediction* as a *hope;* the foresight of a thousand eyes could make him no greater; and their blindness would leave him divine as ever. And now that we see what he *has* achieved, and a calm, wide retrospect can assign his place in the course of Providence, we may well leave behind the dreams of his people, auguring what he must needs accomplish. The admission of Christ's reality, then, for which I contend, is simply a reception of him in his insulated, individual nature, apart from all the antecedents of his birth, the literature of his nation, the conceptions of his time; an acknowledgment of him, as of a spirit in heaven, exempt from the relations of lineage and clime, complete in its own identity, and sublime in its own free will. I ask for no assent to the Hebrew notions of the *capacity* in which he was to come, or even to the apostolic interpretation of the character in which he actually came; for no concurrence in the theory of the Messiah, as the theme of Prophets, and the consummation of the Law; for no special limitation of the world's early Providence to Israel, no local oracle on Zion, no favouritism to Abraham. The Christian appears to me in no way committed to the statements of the Hebrew scriptures in any of their parts; and though these venerable books must always possess the highest interest to the historian, the philosopher, and the poet that interest is entirely divested of all religious authority. Were we entirely ignorant of everything within the limits of Palestine before the hour of Christ's Baptism, destitute of all trace of a preparation of events, the world would indeed lie under a deplorable loss, and the sources of our faith be imperfectly seen ; but Christianity would still exist ; purer, though perhaps less powerful, for being made its own interpreter.

In one respect indeed the persuasive force of our religion would be greater under this imaginary change. The *personal causation* exercised by the mind of Christ would be less confusedly seen ; he would appear, starting up with godlike energy upon the field of the world, and with divinest tillage turning the waste into a Paradise. It would be impossible for us to be distracted from himself by the imaginary causes that brought him there ; impossible to think of him as an instrument framed by events rather than an absolute spiritual power, as an *effect* of given historical conditions, rather than the spontaneous creator of all that commends him to our reverence. Still more impossible would it be to resolve his whole being (except in name) into a fable, invented by Hebrew poets, and conformed to the models of ancient legend. In thus ascribing everything to the individuality of Christ, we should no doubt have fallen into partial error ; but into error far less extravagant than the opposite one, which makes Jesus himself a fiction of the age, necessitated by the state of the national mind. To the solution

P

of the problem of Christianity two things, it may be
admitted, are alone necessary; viz., a given condition
of Hebrew belief and anticipation ; and an actual
person to gather these Messianic ideals around him.
But he only can be held a disciple of the religion who
quite subordinates the first agency to the second; who
gives much to the prophet and little to his age;
who sees in him the primary and productive cause,
the spontaneous and mysterious originator, of the
heavenly truth that commands the reason, and the
unspeakable sanctity that awes the heart.

(2.) From this admission of the historical reality of
Jesus as the Author of the religion, we must advance
a second step, and ere we can call ourselves his
followers, must recognize him as the fairest form of
human sanctity and wisdom.   This also follows from
the very idea of revelation, and is indeed but an
application of the general principle which it involves.
If every man's religion is *his highest*, then they to
whom Christ is *not* the highest take their inspiration
not from him, but from that other nature, wherever
found, that transcends him in their thought.   If
genuine revelation consist in that surprise and
illumination of the soul by which a great mind opens
to view an undiscerned region of perfection, and an
intuitive sense of higher truths and obligations, then
he who has ceased to perform this office to our thought
and conscience, he who, once perhaps supremely sacred

to us, is himself o'ertopped in our estimates secret or avowed, has descended with us to a place human, not divine, and is to be deemed our prophet no more. And clearly, if Christ is to retain to our hearts this supreme rank among the things that have refreshed and elevated this world, we must be persuaded that enough is actually known respecting him to preserve to him so glorious a place.

Let it be observed, however, that in conformity with this rule Christ must stand at the summit of *realized and historical,* not of *conceptual and unlimited,* things. Of *the beings of pure thought* the most perfect is of necessity *our God;* of the beings *of actual life,* the most perfect is our *symbol of God.* Hence the bounding conditions under which alone reality can present itself to us may be freely admitted as restraining the merely imaginary transcendency of Christ, and making it a perfection not mathematical but moral, not of dimension but of quality. Our rule requires from him *no intellectual infallibility;* no exemption from all influences of an early home, of human ties, of national thought, of the oriental atmosphere of life. He was actually *in* these relations; with human eyes he looked round upon them; with a human mind he meditated on them; with human affections he loved them; with a human conscience he served them; and how then could he remain unaffected by them,—action without re-action? It is not even conceivable in mere imagination, much less possible in fact, that the conditions of our form of existence should be assumed without its liabilities; and there is nothing to deter a Christian from allowing some impress of time and place upon the Master's mind, some traces of the progressiveness of a human soul. It is not for even the highest child of God to choose the elements amid which he shall live; but to put a divine Freewill in their administration, and by the power of a heavenly spirit to transform their meanness into glory and compel their formal error to yield up essential truth. For myself, I can hear with tranquil heart and veneration absolutely unimpaired the announcement from the lips of Christ of expectations that were not to be fulfilled, of reasonings suited only to the times, of modes of conception long obsolete; and it seems a miserable pedantry, a wretched confusion of the form with the spirit of life, a foolish entanglement of Wisdom which is eternal with Knowledge which is mutable, to be embarrassed by the clime of foreign thought through which alone we can reach the Christ. The understanding of finite natures in their utmost greatness has innumerable meridians, from all of which the superficial look of the universe is different; but all are traced upon the same heaven of everlasting Reason, and stretch across the inextinguishable lights of a beauty that is infinite.

At the same time, though the devoutest discipleship

does not forbid us to notice a fallible, or in other words, an historical side of Christ's life, it certainly requires that we *somewhere* discern an infallible perception in him; that we feel conscious of *trusting* him; and confess him as the author to us of the truths we most deeply believe, and the duties we most reverently own. Nor is it enough that he appear to us merely as the publisher or even as the first discoverer, of these purifying agencies; they must come from him as *revelations*. They must have risen up within his soul as spontaneous, self-evidencing, authoritative realities, and have passed by like intuition to our faith, as heroism is felt to be noble, or space to be immense. Did he simply think them out by steps of articulate reasoning, and present them as the result of a critical balance of evidence, he might win our scientific assent, and be to us the head of a philosophic school; but would not be to us a spring of *religion*, unless the spiritual light he gives, instead of being gathered and diffused from the impersonal Reason which is the same in all, flows fresh from his personality, and speaks to us his moral nearness to God. There is the greatest difference between logical assent to the arguments of another and reverential owning of his diviner insight; the one is the precarious concurrence of equals; the other the golden link of trust by which the less hangs upon the greater in the family of souls. It is indeed the difference between natural and revealed religion. For natural Religion is that in which man finds God; Revealed Religion is that in which God fiuds man. Whatever sacred truth the mind wins by its own deliberate quest, and with full consciousness of the steps of thought by which it is approached, is referred to the former. Whatever divine apprehension enters unsought, enabling the conscience to see, "using itself as light," and subduing yet glorifying the soul with ineffable authority, whatever in short is immediate, intuitive, and above the personal level, will always be referred to the latter. Given to the prophet, not found by him, transcending his store of thought, commanding the sacrifice of his will, such discernment fulfils all the conditions of "Revelation" to him; and on its equally speaking for itself to other minds, places them in true relations of religious discipleship. All grace and truth arising thus not by any purposed use of means or exercise of faculty, but in fresh origination, come from beyond the lines of nature, and are, in the only precise sense, supernatural. They belong to that realm of free spirit, divine and human, of personal relation and communion, in which alone there is an unpledged margin of creative power; and Law, elsewhere advancing by the links of physical necessity, moves in the alternative lines of moral affection.

Whoever then recognizes in Jesus Christ such a new beginning of divine light for the conscience of mankind, and is at one with the characteristics of his personal religion and life, is no less a Christian (to use the illustration of an orthodox divine) than a disciple of Aristotle is an Aristotelian, and of Plato a Platonist. Only where these characteristics are deliberately disowned, where, for example, the Pagan ideal of self-assertion is preferred to the Christian ideal of self-sacrifice, or the personal relations of the Living God to the living soul are denied, does the name cease to have its proper meaning; and an alienation of feeling withdraws the mind from the school of Christ, just as it would be lost to the school of Plato by believing that " *All we know is phenomena.*" But, short of this, to relinquish or to withhold the name appears to me a surrender to the confused thought and narrow prejudices of the divines. They will disown you, unless, along with the characteristic features of Christ's own religion, you take also the *uncharacter-istic*, the mere current ideas which were in the very air and speech of his country and his time and which belonged to him no more than to every one of his contemporaries; which were not what he *added to the* world, but what he **did** not take away from it; the belief in Satan, in the demons, in the Messianic dream. As well might they forbid me to call myself a Platonist, unless, in spite of modern chemistry, I clung to the four material elements, and of modern astronomy, to the sphere of the identical and spindle

of necessity. Why should they bind you to *all* even
of the personal conceptions specially attributed to
Christ, and forbid you to say that the Advent which
he announced was not as near as he supposed ? As
well might they say, I am no Platonist unless I believe
the doctrine of pre-existent ideas and accept the polity
of the philosopher's Republic. Still more intolerable
is it when they exclude you from the discipleship to
Christ, unless you take, not only his own religion, but
all that others subsequently related, from mixed sources
beyond your estimate, respecting his acts and history ;
so that if you cannot reconcile the conflicting traditions of the Nativity or the Resurrection, you quit the
Christian pale. As well might they again deny me
the name of Platonist, unless I believe the philosopher's miraculous Sonship to Apollo (claimed for
him by his nephew and successor), or the story of
the bees of Hymettus settling on the child's lips while
he slept. Least of all are they justified in demanding
from you, as a condition of the Christian name, that
you shall accept the theories about the person of Christ,
which any later age, be it apostolic or post-apostolic,
may have constructed, in order to reconcile conflicting
tendencies and adjust the religion to the ideas and
exigencies of the time. As well might they once
more declare me no Platonist, if I turned away in
distaste from the New Academy, or disapproved the
mystic dogmas of Plotinus and Hypatia. All these

accessories being discharged, as mere accretions around the central life, to be taken or to be left without disturbing its repose, Christianity remains as the inner characteristic religion of Jesus, by which he reveals the living and ever living filial relation of the soul to God, and its ultimate self-harmony by absolute self-sacrifice. He only, then, who follows Christ by the leadings of pure intuition, displays the primitive spirit of religious discipleship.

(3.) This leads me a step further to a third requisite in Christian belief. Hitherto we have described a state of mind which might exist towards a being simply great and wise and singularly good; a state of mind differing little from that awakened by the familiar influence of genius and virtue; and it may well be asked, how do you distinguish between the faith in Christ and the admiration of Socrates, between the worshipper in communion with his Saviour in the Church, and the classic in the study of Plato in his closet? Is there a mere question of degree between the excellence of human instruction and the authority of divine command? and are genuine inspiration and the natural mental insight of lofty souls only two stages of the same thing? and if so, is Jesus merely to take his place among a class of lights of the world, separated from him by disparity simply, not by dissimilitude? In order to answer these questions most pertinent and just, I observe that

Christian faith requires the recognition of *something supernatural in the life or soul of Christ;* something that passeth all our understanding; and accordingly those who think *they can account for everything in Christianity,* who see some of its elements in the character of the times, and all the rest in intelligible processes of thought and inference in Jesus; to whom nothing remains unexplained and unexplainable, but the whole mechanism which manufactured the religion lies entirely open; can, by no extent of agreement in its doctrines, be constituted proper disciples of Christ as the author of a heavenly faith. *A thing accounted for* leaves no room for the true religious sentiment; to illustrate which general principle I will cite in conclusion an impressive statement of a German philosopher, free from all the supposed prejudices of the divine;

" What, in opposition to Fate, constitutes the ruling principle of the universe into a true God, is termed Providence. Where there is no forecast, there is no intelligence; and where intelligence is, there also is there Providence. This alone is Mind; and to what is of Mind alone respond the feelings which manifest its existence in ourselves,—Wonder, Veneration, Love. We can indeed decide an object to be beautiful or perfect, without a previous knowledge that it is the work of foresight or not; but the power by which it was produced, *that* we cannot admire, if without thought and without a purpose it operated in obedience to the law of a mere physical necessity. Even the glorious majesty of the heavens, the object of a kneeling adoration to an infant world, subdues no more the mind of him who comprehends the one mechanical law by which the planetary systems move, maintain their motion, and even originally form themselves. He no longer marvels at the object, infinite as it always is, but at the human intellect alone, which, in a Copernicus, Kepler, Gassendi, Newton and Laplace, was able to transcend the object, by science to conclude the miracle, to reave the heaven of its divinity and to disenchant the universe. But even this, the only admiration of which our intelligent faculties are capable, would vanish, were a future Hartley, Darwin, or Bonnet to succeed in displaying to us a mechanical system of the mind, as comprehensive, intelligible, and satisfactory as the Newtonian mechanism of the heavens. Falling from their elevation, Art, and Science, and Virtue would no longer be to man the objects of a genuine and reflective adoration. The works and actions of the heroes of mankind; the life of a Socrates, and Epaminondas; the science of a Plato and Leibnitz; the poetical and plastic representations of a Homer, Sophocles and Phidias; these might still pleasurably move, might still rouse the mind into an enjoyment kindling into transport; even so as the sensible aspect of the heavens might still possibly affect and gratify the disciple of a Newton or Laplace ; but we must no longer ask about the principle of our emotion ; for reflection would infallibly chide our puerile infatuation, and dash our enthusiasm, by the suggestion that *Wonder is only the daughter of Ignorance.*" *

* Friedrich Heinrich Jacobi. Werke. Vol. II. Vorrede, pp. 51–55.

LIVERPOOL, 1842.
LONDON, 1868.

XVI.

Characteristics of the Christian Theory of God.

———◆———

JOHN viii. 19.

"If ye had known me, ye would have known my Father also."

THAT pure and noble natures, when cast on foul and sordid times, should be vividly conscious of the Divine elements within them, and discern in them the impress and authority of God, is too reasonable and natural to excite surprise. The rare endowments of individual men are in fact the great instruments by which the providence of humanity educates and improves our race. They constitute both the credentials and the command to go forth and shed a blessing on the world. Respecting the origin of these peculiar gifts of genius or of moral goodness which impart an occasional brilliancy to human nature, a curiosity has always been felt. The sober language of modern philosophy describes them as inherent in the original constitution of the possessor; the enthusiasm of devotion treats them as the preternatural inspiration of God poured upon the mature mind; the speculative spirit of the East has often regarded them as the reminiscences of a former and Diviner State, where the soul dwelt within the mansion of God's mind, and beheld as realities those forms of truth and beauty and excellence which now are but the fading images of a dream. It is not however the *date*, but the *Divinity*, of these feelings and endowments, which concerns us most; and if they be accepted with fitting reverence, it matters little whether their chronological commencement be traced to a life preceding this, to the organization which has acted from the moment of birth, or to celestial influences more recently shed upon the mind.

Christ (if at least he really spoke as the fourth gospel represents) was deeply persuaded that parts of his nature were divine. In his idea of God, so great and tender, in his foresight of his country's fate, so distinct and sad,—in his pity for those whom the world would despise or crush,—in his repose on the feeling of duty,—the source at once of his serenity and his power, —he beheld something foreign to the land and to the life on which he was cast; something too vivid for a world where all things are shadows, and especially the things most pure and holy; something which must have been brought to him from the sanctities of an earlier existence, where his spirit dwelt in converse with the eternal mind. And where, indeed, in an age and nation all whose characteristic passions were fierce and exclusive, could any apparent origin be found for a conscience so sublime, a devotion so free, a humanity so disinterested as Christ's? If his followers, mere spectators of these qualities, have imagined that they proved him to be God, is it surprising that he who felt them thought that they came from God, and implied a former union with him? As no passion (it is sometimes said) can be born within the heart, till the mind is familiar with its object, so that deep yearning after the infinite Source of holiness and truth, of which Jesus was profoundly conscious, seemed to imply that he had once seen that perfect being, and been a tenant within the Divine nature. The impressions of that former state were to be found in his unerring moral and religious perceptions; they were venerated by him as the signatures fixed there by God himself; "The Father dwelling in him" by these traces of the past, unerased as yet by the rough experience of this world. In some sort, then, he conceived, two natures, resulting severally from the influence of two successive lives, dwelt within him; one from this earth, which presented temptation; the other from heaven, which vanquished it; the one, furnishing the suggestions of affection; the other, the counsels of meekness; the one, pleading the calculations of selfish ease and security; the other, urging to the enterprises of disinterested love; the one, prostrating the soul in doubt and fear before the Providence that rent the sympathies of nature ; the other, raising the affections to him in absolute trust on his Paternity. Had he yielded to the former of these two orders of his feeling, he would have spoken only of himself; because he committed himself entirely to the latter, which were of the nature of divine memories, he did only the things which he had seen and heard of his Father : his life and mind was the transcript and image of God ; so that he who had seen him had seen the Father also.

Whatever be the *origin* of Christ's identification of himself with the Father, whether in the system of ideas at which I have hinted, or in some consciousness either more or less awful, its *effect* has been immeasurable. It has accomplished the greatest and the most benignant of revolutions in the religion of the civilized world. It has made Jesus the representative of Providence ; has associated the peculiarities of his spirit with men's conception of God ; and added whatever is most venerable and beautiful to the image which they form of the object of adoration. Link the idea of Deity with the character of the prophet of Nazareth, and it can never be inflamed with brutality, or refined into a phantom, or frozen into an intellectual deduction again. While there is a trace of pity in the life of that meek Teacher, the Infinite will be a God of mercy ; so long as it is written that Jesus vindicated the oppressed and refreshed the penitent with pure sympathy, and drew forth the doubter from the deep, and touched the bier that the mother might have her own again, there will be a gentle Providence in heaven. Till it is forgotten how in the stern service of duty Christ wandered without a home, shaming the sancti-monions with his dignity, blighting the hypocrite with his rebuke, saving the deluded by his warning, and steadfastly setting his face to die that the work of life might be finished, there will reign above a Lord of the secret conscience, who holds justice and goodness in eternal respect. The great peculiarity of the Christian theory of God, derived from the contemplation of Christ as his representative, will be found in its *moral*, its *affectionate*, and its *spiritual* character ; these three words appear to me to describe the prominent qualities of the devotion of Christendom. And a brief reference to the two or three different forms which alone the idea of Deity can assume in the mind, will show how happily Christ has restrained the vagaries and supplied the deficiencies of the human imagination in its search after the Infinite.

The most remarkable religions of the ancient world were divided between two systems, which take their origin in fundamental ideas essentially different. The first conceived of God as a man ; as a mere gigantesque form of humanity; boldly ascribed to him all the processes of thought and emotion, the impulses and passions which agitate our nature. Everyone who has ever felt shocked by the representation of the Hebrew Jehovah in the earlier writings of the Old Testament; who has shuddered at the language of jealousy attributed to him by his Israelitish worshippers, understands the character and feels the dangers of this form of religion. It is abundantly vivid, but fearfully coarse in the impression it produces; by raising human nature, just as it is, into an object of worship, it tends to preserve the existing proportion between the animal, intellectual, and moral faculties; it associates the thought of Deity very little with the life of external nature, and very intimately with the affairs of society and life. Passions of preternatural vehemence, and volitions of resistless force, constitute in short the prominent notions of the Divine nature in this system. It deifies a bad and savage morality.

Directly opposed to this are the religions which reduce the Divine nature to a mere vital or mechanical force, pervading and moving the several parts of the universe, as the principle of life sustains the animal functions, or the tension of steam propagates power through the adjustment of a machine. The distinct personality, the intense consciousness, the voluntary activity, which the previous scheme assigned to God, here sink entirely away; the Deity and the universe merge into each other; neither is external or anterior to the other; the idea of *mind*, and still more the idea of *character*, has vanished from the faith; and nothing remains but a soulless personification of the physical energies, through which the order or disorder of the universe is maintained. Such religion is in fact nothing more than personification applied to the existing state of natural science; and had Newton lived among the Egyptians of old, he would have effected as great a change in their piety as in their astronomy. It is impossible to name a puerility too silly or a rite too gross for the genius of a material and pantheistic religion. It is not indeed to be denied that (in modern times) the fundamental principle of this scheme has been maintained by men of the noblest and devoutest nature. Perhaps, too, some faint approach to it may be discerned in the somewhat mystic piety into which all deep and cultivated minds are apt to retreat in their escape from the grossness of popular forms. But however innocent it may be, while existing thus only in the way of *reaction* against more formidable evils, it could never substantively occupy the minds of the great mass of men, without reproducing the effects which I have described from the religions of the ancient world.

Between these two ideas, of God as a magnified man, and as a mere dynamic energy, all antiquity may be said to have vibrated. The one embodied in religion a coarse morality, the other no morality at all; the one presented a being who might be hated as well as loved; the other, a being who could awaken neither aversion nor affection, but while exciting, like any deified force, slavish fear and superstitious hope, must remain as completely external to every moral emotion as electricity or heat. Long might the controversy of these antagonist principles have continued,—the vivid passions of the heart always tending to humanize Deity, and speculative science to fritter away every attribute of a thinking and voluntary nature,—had not Jesus issued from Nazareth, and been accepted as the religious link between man and God. As he was human, a verdict was thus distinctly given in favour of the Hebrew mode of conception; and our own nature, rather than the forces of the material world, became the illustrative type of the Divine Ruler of the universe. No one who ascends to the Creator through the analogies of Christ's mind can avoid ascribing to Deity distinct personality, intense consciousness, and all of humanity that is truly godlike. There is an end for ever to all the dreams of physical religion, and no subtleties can persuade us to worship again a mere Prime Mover of atoms. Yet the analogy between man and God is so restrained by the singularities of Christ's mind, that all its dangers are avoided. With him, unthinking impulse and blind emotion never won a solitary triumph; the love of duty ruled without a rival,— not coldly, not reluctantly and through fear,—but as a deep passion and pure instinct of the secret heart. The ineffable sanctity and spirituality of his mind, never seen before in a life so practical, present us with a selection of all the humanities which the imagination can invest with infinitude, and securely venerate in the being whom we adore. What gross or false morality, what harsh austerity, what relentless cruelty, what imbecile caprice, can for a moment adhere to the image of One who is in the similitude of Jesus? Perhaps the exemption of Christ from all domestic ties had reference to his great office of impersonating the eternal Spirit. In that other part of his mission, by which he became the model of our duty, it might have been well that he should sustain these near relations which group societies in families, and foster the divinest charities, and witness both the saddest weakness and the most amazing strength of the human heart. But the Divine goodness is impartial and universal; it does not depend on the position of its object; it is alienated by no distance; and stipulates for no requital. And there is a sublimity in that solitary position of Christ; wherein he stands, like Providence, dispensing his varied and exhaustless sympathies without reciprocation; sustained, not by the return, but by the simple indulgence, of affection; looking round on every class and lot, and directing on each the fit emotion and the appropriate effort; friendship to the loving disciple, stinging conviction to the artful foe; appreciation of goodness in the Samaritan, and indifference to the splendid pretension in the priest ; tears and rescue for sickness and the grave ; and the look of refreshing love upon the guilty, which best rebukes the guilt.

There is yet a third mode of regarding God, with which the Christian theory of his nature may be compared ; I mean that which presents itself in the philosophical reasonings of natural religion ; and of which the leading idea is that he is the great Designer, bearing the same relation to the universe that the architect sustains to his building, or an inventor to a machine. On no account would I throw any disrespect on the religious lessons of nature, and the devout acknowledgments of philosophers ; still less would I put them in any competition or contrast with the gospel ; for I regard them as comprised within the religion of Christ, and taken into its adoption. But there is a defect attaching to all these systematic views of God, which few who have attended to them can fail to have felt, and which goes far to prevent their acquiring general power. When the being of the Creator is shown by reference to design in the structure of nature, intelligence is the first property which is established as belonging to him ; this is the attribute which is repeatedly presented to the attention, as one con-trivance after another is expounded to us ; it takes the clear lead of everything else ; and moral qualities and feelings are introduced as mere derivatives thence, or admitted so far as seems to be consistent with its positive ascendancy. The general impression produced certainly is of an infinitely intellectual Being; and great hesitation and caution naturally arise in attributing to him any of the warmer attributes which move and win our hearts. The magnificence of his Omnipresence and the comprehensiveness of his understanding absorb every other impression, and seem to raise him above every cause which touches and kindles our affections. If all things are equal to him, we are apt to ask, how can he love? If all purposes are immutable with him, how can he have mercy? If the future is as clear to him as the present, and the happy issue of every grief is before him now, how can he have pity on our tears? It is useless to urge that there are arguments which just as strongly show that he cannot be without these affections; that he would not preponderantly bless, did he not desire to bless, which implies the aversion to suffering, and forces us to ascribe to him opposite emotions. The mind, familiarised with the idea of God exclusively in this abstract and logical school of thought, contracts an incurable scrupulosity and cowardice in assigning *affections* to him; and being at fault for some *measure* by which to determine the intensity of the moral attributes which may be safely referred to his nature, rarely contemplates him as invested with them at all. It is obvious that the progress of discovery in the various realms of nature, by augmenting the apparent

immensity of his being, and deepening the impression
of his boundless intellect, while it leaves his former
attributes where they were before, must tend not to
remedy but to aggravate this evil. It only helps
further to diffuse, instead of concentrating the idea of
the Father divine. Blessed then be the name of the
prophet of Nazareth, that in him we have a living
standard, a true and pure image, by which our
imaginations may wisely adjust their conceptions, and
our hearts regulate their love of the Providence that
rules our life; that he has taught us that trust in the
affectionateness of God which is the genuine Christian
faith; and that while science effects fresh conquests,
and spreads the thought of that great Being through
vaster cycles of Eternity and wider tracts of the celestial
space, he keeps our Father dwelling close within our
conscience and our homes, and presents him to the
tenderness of our heart, as well as to the admiration of
our awe-struck minds!

I have said that the Christian conception of God is
characterized by its *spirituality;* and this is true in a
genuine and positive sense in which it can be affirmed
of no other faith. Christ has rendered familiar to the
universal mind of Christendom a thought of Deity
intenser than Israel's visions and sublimer than Plato's
dreams. Many religions, I am aware, had said before
that "God is a Spirit"; and the most solemn picture
of his universal agency is yet to be found in the

psalmist's meditation on the question "Whither shall I go from his presence?" But when you look closely into the meaning of this doctrine on any but Christ's lips, you will find that it denotes no more than *negative spirituality,*—the absence of body,—or even less than this, the physical diffusion of divine power over an immeasurable extent. The sacred poet himself cannot escape from material conceptions of Omniscience. He represents to us the *largeness* merely, not the *spirituality* of God. To think barely of an *incorporeal* Being leaves us still at an infinite distance from Christ's representation of the Father. It is not that he exists wherever Space is spread abroad, and is conscious of the whole contents of Time; it is not that he pierces every cavern, and sees through every solid mass of creation with his Omniscient eye; it is not that he can command every force, and produce every imaginable movement in the universe, as easily as we can open our lips to speak, by the simple fiat of his Will; it is not that in fact he thus rules, without material frame, both the heavens and the earth, and that his thought alone issues the blast, and shoots the light, and drives the worlds; it is not this that makes him a Spirit in the Christian sense; for with all this he might be still an *External God,* always separated from us by some film of matter, so that when reading his expressions we are yet not in contact with himself. It is as a *Mind,* directly accessible to all other minds; seen most in the sanctity and greatness of others' souls,—felt most in the secret faiths, the true remorse, the diviner aspirations of our own; as an internal Deity known to immediate consciousness, and exercising that mysterious influence of spirit over spirit, the higher over the lower nature in infinite gradation, which would remain though the outward universe were cancelled;—it was thus that he was discerned by Jesus, and so revealed to us. Christ found an eternal Father *that dwelt in him,* an inseparable holiness to his desires, a constant heaven to his tortured affections. As he spake of this his Inspirer, he opened a new and deep fountain in human consciousness; and left behind him, when he departed, a " Comforter," a " Spirit of truth," that teaches faithful hearts all sacred things, tells us each " every hour what we ought to say " and do, and made us one with himself and God. I pretend not to define the limits of divine agency in the human soul, and to show precisely where man ends and God begins. It is the glory of Christ that he has for ever blended the two personalities in close relation ; made it impossible for thought to untwine them, and compelled philosophy to leave without distinction that which God has made so, and take away its hard lines where he has put the melting colours that mingle earth and sky. Meanwhile, what an awe is impressed upon our nature, when regarded as the dwelling-place of God ! What simplicity is given to the spirit of worship, when in life and death, in church and home, we bear within us both Deity and Shrine! What authority to the secret persuasion of duty, when known as the instant oracle of the everlasting Spirit! What respect, what tenderness is due to a tempted brother, when we look at his troubled soul as the theatre, dark perhaps but vast and glorious, on which God himself strives with Sin for Victory!

Looking back on what has been said, and endeavouring to define to ourselves the change which our religion has introduced into the idea of God, we perceive that Christ found, and assumed as a groundwork of the Hebrew's faith in Jehovab, the One Creative Cause, the awful Governing Power of the world. To this rude Theism he added two elements, by which it has been exalted into Christian faith. Himself becoming, as an Inspired Man, the symbol of Deity, he gave to the object of his disciples' Worship the attributes of his own mind, and led them to discern above a Ruler *affectionate and holy;* One to whom man was ineffably dear, and who would go to him to assuage his woes, to seek his heart, to save his nature from all that may ruin and destroy; One who would spread a watchful and delivering Providence over the abodes of human kind. And being profoundly conscious of the stirrings of a divine nature within him, and putting forth thence a transforming power upon all faithful minds, before which the selfish barriers of human passion and fear gave way,—kindling, in short, a felt sanctity where no such flames had darted up before, he created a perception of the *Internal and Spiritual God,* that comes and takes his abode with childlike and hospitable hearts. Thus to the orignal conception of God the Creator, he contributes these of God the compassionate Redeemer, and of God the secret Sanctifier. And these are the representations which have been degraded and hardened by a mechanical theology into the doctrine of the Trinity ; it is consolatory to those who protest against it as an unworthy relic of tradition, thus to detect in it an ingredient of truth, hidden though it be, and overwhelmed by gross mythological additions. Soon may the churches of Christendom reverse the steps by which they have wandered from the primitive and spiritual truth, disengage the worthless elements of ecclesiastic fancy, and accept again the simplicity of Christ.

LIVERPOOL, 1837.
LONDON, 1868.

XVII.

The Reformation of guilt not Restoration.

——— ٠٠ ———

LUKE xv. 7.

"I say unto you, that likewise joy shall be in heaven over one sinner that repenteth, more than over ninety and nine just persons that need no repentance."

THE ministry of Christ betrays a mind profoundly impressed with a sense of the evil and the universality of sin. Beginning with the call to repentance, and expiring with the prayer for forgiveness, he seems never to have quitted the presence of human guilt, and everywhere to have fixed upon it the same full, clear, unconscious look, divinely earnest and divinely sad. It was the look too *of a superior*, before which it cowered, like a detected slave before a magnanimous lord ; or burst into tears, like an unhappy son before a parent that loves him too well for his deserts. You observe in him one who had evidently been accustomed to a purer atmosphere, and discerned on all things the haze of moral evil, damping the fresh colours in which heaven, at morning, had bathed the world. He looked

on the countenance of human life, like a young fair
child on the face of a stranger, hard with selfishness,
and wrinkled with unsanctified care; with dignified
shrinking from the caress, with thoughtful wonder at
the disappointment, and yet the wisest feeling of its
significance.   This haunting perception, like all
discoveries arising from infallible instinct more than
from deliberate ideas, is evidenced rather by an inde-
finable spirit pervading the thoughts and acts of Christ,
than by the absolute substance of his teachings.   It
gives a tinge to many a parable, whose direct design
was local and incidental; and when the historical outline is gone, the heavenly and ineffaceable colouring
remains.   And when we place these various expressions
of his mind side by side, we are struck with the
discriminative feeling directed to different forms of
human character; as if his soul had been occupied
with the whole vast problem of moral evil, involuntarily
noting its divisions and measuring its scope; and
inspired to give, if not its speculative answer, at least
that practical solution which must precede this, as
certainly as moral action and affection are pre-requi-
sites of moral wisdom.   In the tales of the lost sheep
and the prodigal he intimates the true sentiment
towards special penitence, recalling the sinner from
the lapses of passion.   In the tares that were not to
be plucked up, but to flourish on the field of the world
and deform it until the great harvest, he touches on a

more terrible perplexity ; and compels us to ask, whence can come, and whither tend, those viler growths,—those hopeless weeds,—of human nature, whose species no tillage or transplantation can change, and which seem fitted only to be severed and cast away. In the publican who beat his breast, and only cried, "Lord! be merciful to me a sinner," he announces his sympathy with that permanent penitence, that inextinguishable sense of moral want, which his religion has been the means of introducing ; and which, while it confesses the perpetuity of sin, announces the immortal perseverance of the aspirations which subdue it. Of these three cases, *of special penitence ; of blind, animal, unconscious guilt,* and *of the abiding sense of sin which constitutes Christian self-abasement,* I shall at present advert only to the first ; and with an especial view to prevent any lax misapplication of the merciful spirit in which Christ treats it in the parable of the lost sheep.

We cannot look at the words of my text without noticing the bold, clear way in which Jesus speaks of heaven in the language of earth, makes them one in spirit and affection, and attributes to the dwellers there the same emotions that refresh and humanize our life below. The sainted blest, it seems, are not above yielding a surprised and rapturous welcome to one who had been dead, but was alive again,—who had been lost, but was found ; and herein surely they are just like ourselves; for who does not understand the joy which comes with a restored blessing,—with the sudden resurrection of dead sympathies,—with the gush once more into light and hope of some current in the affections which had long been flowing in the dark secrecy of despair? The intellect of a friend gives us not, during years of its best power, so pure a refreshment as at the moment when it first comes back upon us from the delirium of fever, with true but tremulous light. Nor does any point in the life of tried and faithful virtue give us an emotion comparable to that wherewith we see some deluded member of home and heart melted into new and better desires,—the barren soul stricken to give forth a fresh and pure stream. Christ, truest interpreter of the human heart (and if of the human, doubtless of the angelic too) does but utter the natural sentiment, that the frailest blessings are the most beloved; what so frail as those whose frailty has been demonstrated by their loss?

Jesus describes the feelings with which external spectators regard the restored victim of sin. That he is a more interesting object to them at the moment of transition to a better life than the character habitually good, is unquestionably true; that he is a happier, a safer, a nobler being in himself, or during any considerable period of existence an object of profounder sympathy, is both false in itself and an unjust inference from the parables in which the merciful spirit of Christ poured itself forth. In order to escape this inference, it is usual to suppose that by " the just who need no repentance," represented here as less interesting than the penitent, he describes with irony the self-righteous, the proud and hypocritical. In this case our Lord's sentiment would be, that there is joy in heaven over one sinner that repenteth more than over ninety and nine self-flatterers, too Pharisaic to repent. But the temper of serene compassion in which this series of parables is conceived is inconsistent with so caustic an allusion. Nor is there any occasion to ascribe this bitter irony to Christ, in order to vindicate his sympathy with the guilty. In defending himself under the accusation of associating with sinners, he can afford to rest upon their urgent wants, their out-cast condition alone; he need not step aside, in the spirit of insult, to deny to his accusers the credit of superior righteousness. When they complain of his mingling in intercourse with publicans rather than with themselves, who had a right to the Messiah's countenance and favour, he simply takes them up on their own principles. Admitting them to possess the kind of moral correctness which they claim, there is the less reason to regard them with anxious interest, and apply to them the machinery of reformation. At the same time the following parable, in which his accusers are repre-

R

sented by the elder brother of the prodigal son, intimates Christ's opinion of their virtue; that, however precise in form, it was merciless in spirit,— a selfish claimant on reward, rather than the cheerful tender of an open heart.

The cold tempers of theologians, that cannot imagine sympathy given where there is not approval, have perverted our Lord's treatment of guilt, so pure and lofty as well as tender, into a positive preference,—a preference dangerous as well as false, of reformed, or as they are called, converted minds over those that have never lapsed from their progress in Christian excellence. That the painter's art, which seizes on all the attitudes and seasons of strongest passion, should make a favourite of the convert and the Magdalene is not surprising. That the compassion of benevolent hearts should behold in the softening obduracy of sin a true refreshment is no more than natural. But the sentiments of pity and of hope must not be confounded with the sentiments of moral approbation; nor the rational estimates of a true conscience give way before the poetical love of contrast, or the craving for devotional romance. No penitence can entitle the penitent to the rank in our admiration and esteem which should be given to the perseverance of the uniformly progressive mind. I say however the *progressive* mind. For this is a very different thing from mere virtue, the bare punctuality of correct habit; the dull slaves of unobjectionable habit, who do indeed no great and crying wrong, but who bless their homes with no spirit of duty and of love, gladden society with no true sympathy, nor dignify their own soul with any growing thoughts and divine affections, are the greatest perplexity in the Providence of God. They are the only beings of whose state in the future world it is impossible to frame a conception. All other forms of human nature, even the saddest and the strangest, suggest to us some probable images of their immortality. The victim of mighty passions seems to bear with him thither a mind piercing enough to discern the wretchedness of his infatuation, a susceptibility to sorrow deep enough to deplore it, an energy of will powerful enough to seize on better aims, and step by step to win the way to repose of conscience and the peace of God. But the formalist sleeping on without a soul, in whose leaden nature not a vibration can be excited, how are we to think of him in a scene to which his usual round of action cannot be transferred ? where goodness does not consist in the attitudes or the punctualities of prayer, nor in nicely measured temperance of body, nor in exactitude of business, nor in a religious veneration for health ; but where the very principle of goodness must assert its vitality, and put forth a fresh growth ; where the warm love of excellence, which is the love of God, must break into original expression, and shape out new forms of conduct, and kindle to loftier aspirings, and glow with the naked sincerity of

adoration.   In giving the preference therefore to unimpaired virtue over reformed sin, I speak only of the
true excellence of a progressive nature, which has all
its faculties awake, which pursues a morality, worships
in a religion, and aspires to a happiness, possessing the
active sympathy of the reason, the imagination, and
the heart.

It has been urged that one who has had bitter
experience of guilt must have a more intimate knowledge
and a more vivid sense of its misery than those who
have but witnessed it; that he who emerges from a dark
past into the illumination of virtue must enjoy the
most intense relish from its peace ; that satiety in guilty
pleasures is the surest extinguisher of desire, just as
the child ceases to long for an indulgence which is no
longer forbidden.   Now there is no doubt that the fallen
and recovered mind has present to its feelings a
contrast of moral experience, a hell and a heaven of
memory, which can present no inducement to relapse,
and must create a sense of deliverance, a consciousness
of happy change, of lighter spirits, of more healthful
visions, of better prospects, altogether favourable to
continuance in the renovated habits.   But in this very
feeling there lurks an almost certain danger,—an
influence that may unnerve the energies of the
recovered will.   This perception of misery left behind,
this feeling of repose from the strife of ill, these tears
of joy as for a captivity reversed, what are they but a

form of complacency, an utterance of self-gratulation, a contented comparison of the present with the past? They tend to concentrate the attention upon this delicious retrospect of vanquished evil, to gather together all the moral emotions upon the process of recovery, and by this preoccupation of mind to sink into oblivion the future which should inspire a yet nobler ambition. The enormity of the guilt from which the once lost being has escaped totally absorbs the impression of present deficiency; the infidelity of conscience which appals him is in time gone by; his sense of shame is historical; his penitence an act of the memory. The present moment is his contrast to all this; it is his point of rest, his recompense, his heaven; his thoughts travel forward thither, and linger on a spot which seems so fair, and bask beneath its heaven no longer foul with tempest. And in this there is an attitude of feeling the very reverse of the genuine spirit of a great and holy mind. Such an enjoyment of the rewards of virtue, however natural after so recent a rescue from guilt, is premature and treacherous. It inevitably relaxes the forward pressure of the springs of the will which in the soul of genuine moral goodness is irresistibly strong. In a mind which has the true principle of progress, aspiration is never for a moment suppressed in enjoyment, the prospect before it never lost in the attractions of the retrospect, the conceptions of excellence and beauty and blessedness never satiated

but in that illimitable future, whose scenery rises
before its eye bathed in the light of vision, and en-
folded in the peace of God. The present is full, not of
querulous discontent, but of conscious insufficiency;
and no relish for praise, no respect for others' opinion,
can cheat the clear perception of their sober estimate
of existing attainments, or tempt the heart to dally
awhile in the ignoble ease of its self-love. The
intellect palpably feels the barriers against which it
presses, and longs to burst into the fields beyond.
The love of kindred and of kind, though so warm as
to refresh observers by the very sight, seems to itself
but an edge of sunshine beginning to glow upon the
margin of its selfishness. The feeling of duty, the
sense of the noble and the pure, the subjection of the
impulses of nature to the serenity of faith, the influence
over passive emotion of the inspiring ideas of a shelter-
ing Providence and an all-perfect God,—though such
as to impart an obvious dignity of character, are
deplored as faint and feeble still. In this state of
feeling is the essence of all human virtue, the great
and only security for progress; all goodness which
has it not is partial and counterfeit. And that it is
the tendency of reformed guilt, by driving the feelings
to the past instead of to the future, to abate and
extinguish it, is I believe confirmed by experience.
The religious world is full of these firebrands plucked
from the burning, as they rejoice to describe them-

selves. And do they not usually seize instinctively on those forms of belief which most speedily satisfy their complacency, which give them a short struggle of remorse followed by a long confidence of salvation, which enables them under the disguise of piety to boast of their improved condition?

Moreover, however paradoxical the assertion may appear, I believe that the actual experience of the sufferings attendant on guilt, tend to abate rather than to increase their influence as a warning. We may issue from them with no lighter opinion of their magnitude and intensity, conscious even that they were terrible beyond anticipation; and yet they will never operate upon us after the commission of wrong as they did *before*. An explanation may be found in the constitution of our minds. The pains of sin become, to those who have been its victim, pains of memory; not pains of conception, the outward signs of which have been observed in others, and their interior nature and intensity estimated by inference in our own imagination, but positive pains of personal memory. And it is a law of the human mind that remembered suffering ceases to affect it by degrees, and at length is even contemplated with pleasure. When any active pain is fairly gone, how difficult it is to recall it with any vividness of idea, and with what elasticity does the mind pass into the relief which succeeds, and instal its feelings in full possession! The affliction

which seemed to crush our very nature at the time
we learn at last to contemplate with melancholy but
peaceful emotions, and to speak of with hushed but
not troubled tones ; memory delights to travel over the
history again, and dwell on its most poignant moments
with tears of refreshing sadness. The aged, in the
frequent narrative of their early days, fasten on their
toils and griefs and perils, not less than on their pleasures. And thus, by a beneficent provision, the vividness of anguish appears only to distribute itself over
the circumjacent enjoyments, and impart to them only
a brilliancy and intensity of recollection. Nor are the
moral pains exempted from this law; and when placed
at a distance from us in the past, they cease to excite
a shudder or even to draw forth a sigh. We think of
them without shame ; they pass from warnings almost
into decorations of our being; they appear, not in the
awful hand-writing of conscience, but the animating
lines of history; and from the terrors are converted
into the romance of life. Thus the sense of evil
in wrong, of its injury to our nature, is attenuated
into nothing; the solemnity of disapprobation sub-
sides, and we are not incapable of being excited
again to a state of sympathy with our degraded
self. No, it is a fatal thing to allow moral evil,
that spectre of our early conscience, to grow familiar
to us as a corporeal reality, and transfer its horrors
from our fears to our regrets. To the inexperienced

in wrong, guilt and its woe appear clothed with an awe, a mystery, an impalpable gloom, which give them unrivalled power over the will ; they are the fiery lash that quivers in the grasp of an invisible fury,—or the solitary eye of vengeance that glares on us out of the darkness. But when we have dared to draw near and touch them, and they have become realities of flesh and blood, they will never operate upon us with like power again ; they may make us wretched, far more wretched than we had thought ; they may create loathing and self-abhorrence, and an ineffable sense of deterioration ; but they extinguish power. They excite misery rather than fear, and drag us to the torture instead of drawing us to the flight. They have sunk from the preternatural to the natural, from the ideal to the actual. We shrink no longer as from the invisible foe that once threatened to grapple with our will.

There is no such safeguard to the mind as the religious preservation of the feelings of the young conscience ; its estimates, its opinions, may change and ought to change ; but let the colour of its emotions remain unfaded. He who, by lapsing into a period of vice, clouds and pollutes these colours, may never hope for a perfect restoration of the same mind. He places a fatal chasm between himself and these early moral affections which, once insulted, finally retire. The continuity of the first generous impressions of life, the

persuasive shelter of them from all shocks of circumstance and example, is of incalculable moment to the
originality, the vigour, the happiness of the mind at
its maturer age. The interior glow of conscience,
once hidden by the visible blush of shame, shines
forth with no such pure radiance again. These
feelings may indeed partially recover, but they are
changed; they recover without faith. They are shy
and distrustful. They never venture themselves forth
in self-abandonment again. They depend upon the
kindling estimates of the judgment, and shrink behind
in melancholy reserve. It may be perchance one of
the destined blessings of the immortal future, that it
may recall to their full power the unrivalled memories
of early and virtuous life, and shed that graceful bloom
over the maturer energy of perfected existence.

LIVERPOOL, 1835.
LONDON, 1871.

XVIII.

Christian Self-reverence.

—•◆•—

JOHN xii. 24, 25.

"Verily, verily, I say unto you; except a corn of wheat fall into the ground and die, it abideth alone; but if it die, it bringeth forth much fruit. He that loveth his life shall lose it; but he that hateth his life in this world, shall keep it unto life eternal."

HAD Christianity not been Divine, it would have been pronounced the most imprudent of moral reformations; and yet has it been the most durable and glorious. It was a great experiment upon society, an attempt to change its feelings, its institutions, its morality, its worship; to create new types of individual character, new views of the vicissitudes of life, new ties of social union. It deals not at all with those small emendations which discreet men admire, and much with the abstract truths which they despise. Its power discards all appeal to those selfish interests through which alone, according to those who pride themselves on their sagacity, mankind are to be governed; and relies entirely on those convictions of truth, and feelings of right and wrong, and perceptions of moral beauty and greatness, and impulses of religious hope, of the existence of which, except as theological fictions, it is fashionable to doubt. Its great author, with a wisdom profounder than discretion, bade defiance to all rules of ordinary human policy; that they ever once occurred to his imagination he regarded as his bitterest temptation; that he thrust them from him, as his noblest victory. Not in the court or the council, but on the solitary hills of Nazareth, did he meditate the world's mightiest revolution. Not with any well-compacted machinery of human influence, any elaborate conciliation of human prejudice, but with the simple power of deeply moved sympathy and deeply imbibed truth, did he go forth to regenerate mankind. He was in a land where minds were singularly impenetrable, and passion invincibly strong; yet they were human, and must melt before the power of a divine wisdom and a diviner love. He wandered through the homes of his country, bringing indeed coolness to the fevered frame, and colours to the blind eye, and sounds to the deaf ear; but imparting also the holier freshness of penitence to the fever of sin, the scenery of life eternal to the dark mind of grief, the forgotten accents of conscience to the heart insensible to their solemnity. He earned the fate which is usual with such entire self-devotion, aiming to effect great changes in the world; he awakened into action, first the malignant passions of the bad, then the far more powerful and more enduring veneration of the good. He had left a silent, a wondering, an indelible impression of himself on a few whom his spirit had touched ; and thence the mission has spread in a flood of saving veneration over descending generations and a thousand lands. Doubtless the worldly-wise of those days drew sage lessons from his fall, and thought they had found another instance of the rashness of sweeping moral reformations, of the vanity of trusting to men's better sympathies, of the folly of refusing all compromise with their prejudices and vices. It seems as if Providence resolved to frown upon such narrow and vulgar sagacity, and to vindicate to all ages a higher order of wisdom ; for the death of Christ was the birth of Christianity ; the tragedy of the gospel burst into a triumph ; and at the same moment Jesus committed his body to the agony of the cross, his spirit to the God who guards the grave, and his memory to the eternal love and reverence of mankind.

True it is that the persuasion of miracle accompanied and aided the early diffusion of Christianity ; and it may be thought that without this the designs of its great teacher would really have been liable to the charge of enthusiasm. No doubt the belief in these supernatural accompaniments of the gospel was essential to its spread. Nevertheless the miracles, even to those who unconditionally accept them, operate rather as an influence in reserve in case of need, than as the every-day agency of Christianity,—as a fortress to which the threatened mind may retreat, when the moral feelings, which are the best persuasive to the religion of Jesus, are enfeebled. Our minds are apt to dwell too exclusively upon what they esteem to be the logic of Christianity, founded on its preternatural events. Satisfied I am that the heart of antiquity was far more deeply impressed by the moral elements of the system, by its natural than its miraculous phenomena; its pure worship, its lofty conceptions of duty, its unlimited promises for man. The character of Christ was the power by which the religion of Christ triumphed. It fired Peter; it melted John; it kindled Paul. It was the inspiration of their mission, the illumination of their life, the reward of their futurity, the sympathy which bound them alike to brethren on earth and God in heaven. If they speak of his miracles, it is less of the force of their evidence than the beauty of their beneficence. I hold it to be to the credit of Christianity, that it seized so strongly on the heart of mankind, that ages elapsed before the affections were cooled enough to part with it into possession of their mind.

It was then the moral spirit of the gospel, more than the logic of its miracles, which carried it triumphant through the world. And the peculiar feature to which its success may be mainly ascribed is precisely the quality from which the worldly-wise would have predicted its failure,—its *perfect and uncompromising truthfulness* to human nature. Had the policy of vulgar prudence been followed in the regeneration of mankind, some gentle ameliorations of their moral condition would have been proposed; existing errors would have been cautiously approached, and prevailing sins ingeniously circumvented; weakness would have been played off against weakness; conventional tastes and feelings would have been consulted in the purification of worship; and the more superficial of human desires in the delineations of heaven. A system would have been framed in the spirit of distrust of human kind, founded upon familiarity with its infirmities and an ignorance of its nobler capacities; upon the knowledge of men rather than the science of man;—a masterpiece of circumspection, instead of an enterprise of love. Interests would have been consulted, but hearts untouched; a party would have been formed, and society left unregenerated; and after momentary popularity, the tide of corruption would have rolled on, and swept away a force so puny. God, who framed the human mind, better knew how to touch its springs of power. He knew that there are in us two human hearts, the one the residence of interest and self, the other enshrining the vitality of love; that within our coarse and common nature there is an interior recess, the retreat of a thousand pure and

viewless emotions, where lurk unconsciously susceptibilities to moral beauty, and indistinct longings after
moral excellence, and tendencies to penitence, and
affections ready to spring towards the immortal. He
knows that however men might cling to their vices
they never really loved them; that sin was never satisfied with its state, and asked for connivance from others
because unsupported by sympathy with itself. He
willed to break up this whole system and make the
soul speak out at length its irrepressible love of the
holiest forms of virtue, its affectionate greeting of the
most majestic hope. He determined to call forth, as
the antagonists to the world's ills, the true and sincere
perceptions of its conscience. He introduced to it
the perfect soul of Jesus, and before this deep appeal
opposing passions soon died away ; here was the needful sympathy with weakness without one moment's
compromise, an appreciation of physical suffering with
the serenest supremacy of moral power ; a morality
perfectly human in its fitness to our affections, and
perfectly divine in its power to transform them ; an
exhibition, in short, of truth and holiness, in which
were realized the best dreams of the best minds, and
to which human veneration fled with instinctive eagerness, to repose itself at last beneath the cross with
pure and perfect content.

God, then, in his regeneration of the world by
Christ, yields us at once a perfect model, and gives no

sanction to piecemeal plans of improvement ; he stops not to negotiate with our infirmities, but addresses himself directly to the very highest susceptibilities of our rational and immortal nature ; he does not fear our aiming at too much, and dreaming too loftily of our prospects in the future, but invites us to elevate our faculties at once to the dignity befitting his children, and accept from his hands the responsibilities of life for ever. Herein, my friends, Providence teaches us a great lesson, which the world and our own hearts much need, and which is in direct contradiction to the time-serving morality of society. The lesson is this : to be always true to our best convictions and highest feelings; to guard them reverently as our guide, our strength, and never suffer them to be put aside by hope, or fear, or convenience, or the seductions of example, or the dislike of singularity, or the madness of party, or an impatience for success. The applications of the lesson are various. In the formation of our opinions it must lead us to shift aside no evidence, to stifle no doubt, to dress up no suspected fallacy, to retreat from no glimpses of discovery, but to be sternly faithful to our perceptions of truth, and repose every troubled feeling upon God ; this is the lesson to our intellect. In the formation and correction of our character, it must lead us to aim courageously not at improvement but at perfection, remembering that our poor ideas of perfection would be but an improvement after all ; it must

S

teach us to keep pure and high the standard within us, to insist upon its god-like right to obedience, and never to acquiesce in a life discordant with it, even though to-day may number a sin less than yesterday; this is the lesson to our conscience. In our advocacy of social improvements, it must warn us not to be laughed out of our conscientious course by a derision of theory, a contempt for abstract truths, and the pretence that men are not ready for our views; it should prompt us to answer, that we will try, if it were only to be faithful to our own minds; that men are always ready for the discussion of truth, however unprepared to act upon it; and that the ultimate construction, on recognized principles of social justice, of a great and healing good, is preferable to any immediate and petty abatement, on no principle at all, of some existing evil; this is the lesson to our public beneficence. I confine myself now to a few remarks on the lesson to our *conscience.*

In recommending the aim at moral perfection instead of moral amendment, let me not be understood as expressing any faith in sudden paroxysms of resolve. Nothing can be hoped from mere spasms of conscience; they are the wretched disease of prostrate sin, not the healthy action of progressive virtue. They proceed from no permanent feeling, and therefore lead to no permanent good; they are the delirium of the soul under the sting of shame, not the quiet and penitential prayer of illuminated conviction. Nor must it be supposed that any intensity of desire can carry us aloft at once, above the toils, the glorious but incessant toils, of a responsible existence. No bound can bear us to the eternal hills ; no burning emotions, like the prophet's chariot of fire, can cleave for us the clouds of earth, and before our time lift us on the whirlwind to the spirits of the blest. Step by step must the ascent be won, often, like the journeys of Paul, through perils of the wilderness, in weariness and watching. Let it be clearly understood that steady progress is the law of our moral nature ; and let there be no delusion respecting the amount of patience, of self-denial, of sustained energy, required to make that progress sure. But having once learned this truth, so as to guard against disappointment, the less we dwell on it in our career of self-improvement, the better will that improvement proceed. By perpetually thinking how gradual our improvement must be, we shall only make a slow spirit slower ; come the delay, if come it must, but never let our will invoke it. That the difficulties are great, that the resistance of temptation and the obstructions of habit are weighty, are reasons not for abating, but for nerving to mightier effort, the moral energy which is to sweep them away. If our powers be tardy, let our desires at least be swift.

It is a common and fatal error to suppose that in the

s 2

work of moral improvement, as in our worldly schemes, we must aim at no more than we can at once accomplish; and that there is the same imprudence in looking with intense longing on a lofty and mature virtue as in fixing our ambition on a station of renown beyond our reach. It is forgotten that the obstacles to the attainment of fame or empire are chiefly from without, from the order of society, and the passions and feelings of other men, which no mere vigour of desire on our part can materially change, and which therefore should fix an inflexible limit to that desire; while the obstacles which oppose our rapid progress in character are from within, from the bonds of habit and the vacillations of emotion, and the collapse of resolution, in short from the intrusion of false and seductive views at unguarded avenues of thought; and it is only because the love and desire of excellence is not yet sufficiently intense and permanent, because the sense of responsibility is not yet sufficiently vivid, the image of perfected goodness not yet folded to the heart with a homage deep enough, that we are unprotected from these enemies of our progress. To limit our ideal by what we are likely to accomplish is a miserable fallacy, since it is the ideal itself which determines how much shall be accomplished; the success must not graduate the desire, for it is the desire which creates the success. Paradoxical as the statement may seem, it is an important truth, that the great condition of spiritual growth is the eternal, the unwearied aim at impossibilities. To be penitent by inches, to select a sober slowness in the retreat from wrong, to wish no more than to be a little less selfish, or irritable, or useless, to-morrow than to-day, is the mark of an ignoble conscience, more anxious for comfort than for purity, and well pleased to linger in the precincts of its sin. To start into impatient and vast determinations, to glow with a sudden passion for duty and heaven, and then, when they cannot be possessed by assault, to depart depressed and vanquished, is the mark of a soul of more restlessness than power, of a kindled imagination and an untouched heart, of a youthful and selfish ambition, which, if it may not rush to the holy land with the splendour of a Crusader, has not love enough to take the garb of the meek pilgrim, and toil over sea and land, and tender in silence and solitude its offering of veneration. To set up within our mind an ideal of perfected goodness, the very image of Christ, to aim at expressing its beauty in the life, and, in spite of failure, to renew the faithful effort day by day, to feel a fresh penitence at every fall, and rise again saddened but not defeated, to have experienced that your yearnings after intellectual and moral good are never fully gratified,—to know moreover that they never can be, and yet to feel them still as the soul's inextinguishable life,—this is the mark of the noblest natures, the glorious infatuation, if you will, by which the mortal puts on immortality. There is an obvious reason in the very constitution of our nature why we should direct our efforts at once towards the model of excellence which approves itself to our conceptions, why, instead of being satisfied with less than is wrong, we should look in the direction of all that is right. Our faults are not mechanical and external things; they appear indeed in the life, but are issued from the mind; the sure results of wrong judgments and tastes and feelings there. There then must the remedy be applied; not to the action, but to the emotion. And to expel an emotion from the soul by a mere sentence of banishment is a natural impossibility. There is no way but to replace it by another, to substitute for the impulse which we would exclude a purer one which we would cherish. The tastes and emotions of goodness are the proper antagonists of those of sin; generous sympathies are the correctives of selfishness, lofty views of life and its purposes are the cure for indolence, the tranquil memory of Providence, for irritability, the vision of peace in heaven for unreasonable gloom. No effort can avail for the destruction of faults like these, except that which aims at the construction of the opposing virtues. The avaricious must strike into generosity at once; the morose into beneficence, the inert into energy. The slumbering moral perception must be awakened; the forgotten but not irrecoverable judgments of our better conscience must be revived; the love which gleams on us from the study of Christ must be nurtured; the convictions of which we have glimpses in our thoughts of God must be summoned steadily before us and entreated never to depart; the mind must spread around it the atmosphere of its purest thoughts, and freshen continually its best affections, that by the mere preoccupation of duty, the delusions of wrong may have no entrance. This is to act with perfect truthfulness to ourselves; there is no insult here to our noblest convictions, by acknowledging them to be true, and yet thrusting them aside. My friends, there is no weakness so wretched as that of a mind in discordance with itself, and acquiescing in habits beneath its perception of right. There is no power like that which is imparted to a man by self-reverence; clear from the lingering sense of shame that clings to him who feels better than he lives, he is free to welcome the open gaze of earth or heaven, and gladden himself with the love of man or God.

Sometimes the bold attempt to be true to himself and realize his best imaginings will doubtless fail for want of firmness. This however only shows, not that there should be *less* of such attempt, but more of it. Even then when through the cares of the world and the deceitfulness of riches his nobler self has been over-borne, and the lapse of years has been permitted to gather on him the crust of a sad selfishness, the struggles of better days will not be lost. Vivid thought and strong emotion may be sunk into melancholy and long oblivion, but never utterly extinguished. In some moment, when the benumbing influence of the world is withdrawn, when anxiety or grief open the closed avenues of the heart, we may be surprised by the memory of pure feeling, gushing upon us again, like the long hidden stream upon the earth, and flooding us with penitence, and inviting us once more to the peace which we had early sought and lost. It may be indeed that no such hours of reviving conscience may be given us on earth. The torpor of sin may remain unbroken till the grave has finished our probation, and the world of immortality has burst upon our view. But will not that be a moment of remembrance; will not the vision of that scene, once the object of our aspiring, will not the irresistible perception of that God, once the object of our prayer, will not the society of that Jesus, once our imitation and our guide, will not the embrace of those friends, once the witness of our struggles, bring back upon us the feelings so apparently dead? They will come, like the emotions with which the exile from his childhood returns to the scenes of his infancy, bringing an ineffable tenderness to his heart, and refreshing though mournful tears to his eyes; they will lead us to see our spirits as they are; they will conduct us to the blessed presence of our Father, and dictate the prayer, Father, I have sinned in thy sight. Even then will he not enfold us in his love and call us back, and welcome his children once dead, and now alive again, once lost, but now found?

LIVERPOOL, 1835.
LONDON, 1870.

XIX

𝕿𝖍𝖊 𝕷𝖎𝖋𝖊 𝖜𝖎𝖙𝖍𝖔𝖚𝖙 𝕾𝖆𝖇𝖇𝖆𝖙𝖍.

——◦——

LUKE xxiii. 56; xxiv. 1, 2.

"They rested on the sabbath day, according to the commandment. But on the first day of the week, very early in the morning, they came unto the sepulchre, carrying the spices which they had provided, and certain other women with them. And they found the stone rolled away from the sepulchre; and entering in they found not the body of the Lord Jesus."

No inconsiderable portion of the religion of mankind springs from the deep pity with which human nature, secretly waking to the truth, is forced to regard itself. The nobler faculties by which they feel themselves to be distinguished,—Reason, Conscience, Affection,— they necessarily and permanently attribute also to the Supreme Mind. They have no other type according to which they can frame their conceptions; this is the highest thing present to their thought; and this therefore they assume, silently and unconsciously, as the ground of all their worship. But besides this truly godlike characteristic, they fall into usages arising from their experience of weakness, sorrow, and sin. In the

agony of remorse they seek relief in fancied propitia-
tion. In the approach of death they administer some
rite, to charm away the terrors of the mid passage,
and secure the happy arrival of the departing spirit.
Under the pressure of fatigue and the need of an intermittent life, they adopt a periodic sabbath, to wind up
the weary springs of effort, and freshen the days
again. Half conscious that these things are con-
cessions to infirmity, man feels it needful to justify
them. And as he generally gives the grandest account
of his poorest doings, and makes up for the humiliation of his facts by the solemnity of his reasons, he
at once ascribes these things to God, insists upon
them as immediate mandates of his Will; and, the
better to conceal from himself their basis in human
weakness, endeavours to suspend them from the everlasting Power. And so it comes to pass that, while
the *unspoken* part of every religion, consisting of the
worship of God through what is truly divine in
ourselves, constitutes its purest essence, its most
questionable part, embodying fond and clinging habits
of the lower nature, speaks with the loudest boast of
authority, and most disdains the imputation of a
human origin. It is with the several faculties of
mind as with different individual men ; that the most
ordinary elements in our world are most anxious
to be thought of ethereal clay. There is something
affecting in this attempt of human nature to give

respectability to the necessities it cannot escape ; to hold up the head which shame and grief, if freely owned, might hang too low ; and cover with the decent robe of sanctity the infirmities else unsightly to behold. Sure we may be, that God, if he does not ordain these institutes of our childhood, at least will pity them ; and forgive the reverent theft if we steal unawares some colours of his heaven to adorn the sad ways our feet must tread on earth.

Thus, plain as it is that the " sabbath was made for *man*," adapted exclusively to a nature requiring, physically and mentally, variety and periodicity, the Hebrews were not content till they had applied it to *God*. Wondering about the source of an immemorial practice, they overlooked the infinite interval between the Divine mind and the human, and imagined that the Creator, after the fatigue of a six days' work upon the heavens and earth, *rested* on the seventh. It is not at all that men get tired, and cannot go on without a pause; it has nothing to do with any pretended flagging of their will, and exhaustion of their thought; it does not belong to them or their history at all; it took its rise in the biography of God; and they merely commemorate an incident in *His* Being, instead of yielding to a necessity of *their own*. Having once established themselves in this high way of thinking, they mistake their own custom for a rule of nature, and interpret by it events beyond this mortal sphere. They conceive that the laws of life and death and of all worlds respect it; and they push their sabbatarian fancies through the universe, seen and unseen. As God was thought to rest from creation on the seventh day, in order to *make* the sabbath, so was Christ supposed to rest in the tomb that he might *keep* the sabbath; though of this no evidence is offered beyond the fact that the disciples never went to look till the first day of the week, but stood aloof till then from the opportunities which furnished the discovery. Faithful themselves to the prescribed inertness of the day, they did not dream that angels could be free to pass from world to world and break the mortal sleep; or that the Life-giver himself could interfere with Death, and burst its seal, till the hour for work came round again. And so, the grave, having clutched its treasure just as the sabbath came, must keep undisturbed possession till it was gone. How the fact really was, which they thus believed, it is impossible to pronounce. The resurrection moment no one professes to have witnessed. It is in every way probable that Christ was not an exception to the universal human law, but an example of it, and that without interval the mortal melted into the immortal state. If he was permitted to manifest himself, and if the third day was the date of his manifestation, it might well be assumed as the time of his restoration; and from their own engagements the disciples would

fall into the conception that the seventh day had forbidden the functions of life, alike to themselves in the
city, and to the Master in the cave.

Be this as it may, from that very hour all things
are changed. Jesus at all events left the sabbath and
the grave behind him together. If that day really
held him back from his first heaven, it stopped holier
moments than it ever gave. How strange indeed the
Hebrew's whole conception of this institution was!
The most consecrated of times to him was a period
of *Divine inaction*, and *undisturbed human death!*
nothing so sacred to him as the day when God did
nothing, and life was stopped, and immortality could
not begin! the time which is only not fatal, in that
case, to all that is beautiful and good, and to the very
theatre that holds them, because it passes soon away.
Christianity makes us conscious that there is nothing
sacred, but only sad, in this: that it is fatigue alone
which demands an interrupted life; that natures and
spheres above our own are exempt from enforced
repose, and know nothing of the dizzied thought, the
sickened heart, the drooping will which compel us to
an interval of rest; that our noblest privilege is to
approach an existence so sublime, and to feel conscious
of capacities aspiring towards it; and that, at death,
we escape the sabbath world, and enter on a career
where, as the eternal Father worketh hitherto, we also
shall work without ceasing the will of our Inspirer.

This lesson is suggested by the record itself, after every allowance for its manifold imperfections and discrepancies. Assuming the very day and hours assigned, in which the Hebrew Christian discerned a homage to his sabbath, we may, with better right, gather from them far other thoughts. The opening of immortality to the Leader of our faith may intimate to us some features of our own, which are secretly legible in the laws of our own minds.

The Master's immortality is described as opening with the *morning*. Here, as in the poetry and prayers of every age, the new life appears as a *new dawn*. And who that has ever felt the early breeze upon his cheek, and flung into it his prayer of everlasting hope, can deny the harmony between the symbol and the reality? Not cooler would be the healing dew upon the late bleeding feet of Christ, or softer the air on that brow no longer stretched in agony, than the first touch of the calm life may well be to the wounds which the pilgrim bears away, and to the sense of mortal struggle from which he has just emerged. That heavenly life will come, to many a silent sufferer, burdened by a tortured frame, or wasted by a secret grief, or crushed by hidden cruelties, with the relief of dawning light to strained and watching eyes; the dim consciousness stealing through the emancipated nature like the widening streaks upon the East; and deepening and swelling, till the enveloping cloud of death

is kindled into glory.   To the troubled spirit of
delirium or of fear, so terribly speaking through the
eye of wildness and the voice of self-reproach, it will
come like the clear transparent hour, when phantoms,
flaming on the gloom, are gone, and shapes of dread,
seen in the uncertain light, retreat; when the fixed
outlines of God's landscape succeed to the restless
boundaries and haunting figures of the world of
dreams; and the gulf of darkness around the feet
is floored over by real and tender grass.   To the
tired and travelled mind, that has worn all common
experience threadbare, and trodden down its ways into
a dusty track, it will come like the magic colouring
that flies before the Sun, and decks the earth for his
approach ; making old scenes fresh again ; finding out
many a hollow and hidden place of beauty never
guessed before ; and dressing all things in the wonder
of a new creation.   To the deserted and lonely heart,
exiled from sympathy, and pacing the beat of duty as
a watchman of the night, it will come like the hum of
human voices cheerily waking up once more ; or the
matin chorus of birds from wood and field ; or the
laugh of little children that remind us of the kingdom
of God.   Not that we need claim all that is delightful
for the morning, and make it alone stand with us for
what is unimaginably fair.   Assuredly every time is
excellent as it succeeds.   Night also has its glory, but
with a difference.   It looks down with the beauty of a

divine pity on us, not of congeniality with us. We lie low, as a distant spectacle, to its thousand eyes, watching indeed with sacred vigils over us, yet lifted awfully above us. Drawing its curtain of silence round, it seems to soothe and nurse a world of various suffering, and glide with its whispering winds about us, to hush the sobs and compose the cares, of a sorrowing humanity; and to leave it to fresh hours and a more enveloping light to suggest to us the time when the tears of our infancy shall be wiped away. On the whole, who can doubt, that an insight, as from the effect of a new radiance, will dawn upon the soul on its immortal wakening. Without any change of law or faculties of the mind, the mere absence of disturbing causes of error, the clearness from false suggestion, the truthfulness of a position among nobler and more loving natures, are sufficient to secure a faithful interpretation of its own consciousness, a deeper perception than at the highest moments before, of the contents, the capacities, the obligations of its own nature; and an apprehension of new moral wisdom, loftier heights of divine perfection, opened by the revelation of this inner world. This at least we know, amid the vast unknown; that the conventional ways of this world do not reach thither; that its scornful reproaches, and its treacherous applause, entirely die away; that its false estimates and beguiling tastes can prevail no more; but only the simplicity of truth and the realities of God. *There* we cannot longer deceive ourselves; we cannot escape ourselves. No sophistry can live in that air an hour; no giddy dance whirl us away into mad forgetfulness. It is a turn out from the artificial glare and fever of the night festivity into the sweet atmosphere, and white light, and under the pale pure sky of opening day.

Again, the Master's immortality is described as commencing with the *Spring*. In the world's great year it holds the same place which it occupies in the circle of the day; partly suggesting thus by a new hint the same glad lessons; partly adding others of not less significance. In both cases it appears at the starting point of the mystic cycle of life, withdrawing our thoughts to the furthest distance from any goal; it exhibits an ascending climax of being; and plants our nature at the open gate of hope, with no exit within the sight of thought; and so represents to us, as far as a seasonal existence like the present can, the growing development and undeclining improvement of that higher sphere. It is as if God permitted the winter storms to be over first, lest in calling our spirits forward he should suggest any bleak images, chill us with the winds of mystery, and send us shrinking as from some pitiless alarms. We might not unnaturally have looked with too much awe into the vast unknown expanse before us; have recoiled from its touch, as from an icy plunge; have sat listening to the succession

of its moments, as to the running plash of the drip
into a hollow well, rather than to the sweet whisper of
the small rain upon the meadow. So we are not called
out to our celebration of the better life till the year's
sombre days are past; till flowers unasked are ready
to strew our way; till the fresh breath of all young
hearts fans into genial fires the embers of the old;
and on the growing earth a withered thought becomes
impossible. If ever, as tradition tells, the risen Christ
walked the fields and stood upon the hills of Galilee,
he doubtless saw in the natural scenes of this receding
world a fitting threshold to the spiritual glories of the
other. The great Life-thrill, undulating through the
substance of the mountain and the plain, touches the
deepest roots of beauty, pushes forth the folded bud,
and hangs out the promise of foliage as the glad signal
which proclaims, Lo! the Creator lives! The hidden
seed betrays itself where we had least suspected
it, and covers the dark mould with the blush of the
blossom and the promise of the fruit. And in how
many minds, in how many unreached parts of all our
minds, may not a happier season and a clime less
harsh, detect capabilities unsuspected now; penetrating
with a genial warmth to germs of thought and love that
lurk unseen as yet below the rough covering of the
outer life. Who has not seen, nay, in some degree
felt, the power of human genius to kindle by its
presence the minds before which it stands; to fill them

with its own glow, and make them partners of its greatness; to conquer them, not by sinking them in conscious weakness, but by lifting them into a like strength? And who can long abide with a spirit of noble and loving goodness, and watch its dear, heroic ways, and see it trembling with the sorrows of friends, yet wiping their tears away, bent beneath the cross of life, yet turning to say "Weep not for me," agitated by the sight of so much guilt and woe, yet resolutely working against them, and serenely trusting to the end, without feeling the upward pressure of better desires through the poverty of his nature, suspecting himself to be made for higher ends than he had dreamt, and gradually exchanging the morbid craving after happiness and ease, for the heathful love for whatever things are true, and pure, and good? And if this be so even here, if the great and excellent, by the light of their countenance, warm our best faculties into consciousness, and first find for us what we are; the world which is thronged with a higher race, of larger reason, of gentler affection, and conscience without guile, cannot but act as the vernal sunshine upon our nature, unfolding all its possibilities of beauty and of fruit. Not that we are to suppose ourselves misplaced, meanwhile, in this austerer state, or to complain of the drifting tempests though they must overwhelm us with sterility and death. Even the severities of the present, that seem to threaten a perpetual blight, may not be without reference to the more genial future; and the very snows that beat upon the exposed summits of our life, and bury them in barrenness, may be in preparation for the milder seasons of God, when they will flow down in fertility on the sequestered recesses of our nature, and make it rich and glorious as an Alpine vale. In any view, the discipline of the future cannot but be one of growth and progress, like the light and verdure of the advancing year.

Finally, the Master's immortality is described as commencing on a *working-day;* as introducing the entire system of working days;—a most unsuitable thing, if the future life were to be presented as a passive, dreamy state;—a most suitable, if the highest, freshest activity we can conceive gives the proper type of its experience. Nor is it possible for anyone who has the slightest acquaintance with the laws of the human mind, to doubt that those who enter that state, open into a career of glorious energy; else would all identity, still more all glory, or faculty of glory, be lost. Intellect that does not learn and think, genius that does not create, love that does not devise and work, devotion that does not aspire to ever purer perfection, present nothing but inconceivable contradictions. Nor does the external accompaniment with which we must fill the scene less plainly teach its intense activity than the faculties which are to be planted in the midst. The astronomer obtains a new station, without cost and trouble, whence to survey the grandeur of the universe, hitherto familiar only from his geocentric position. The historian stands in the living presence of the witnesses, whose silent page and broken fragments of speech he has questioned and half interpreted. What philosophies must there not be in a world which assembles and swells from age to age by new promotions the august council of the wise; where Socrates is safe from accusation, and Plato no longer dreams! What infinite depths of represented beauty, what schools of sacred Art, when Raphael and Purcell have so long been there! And amid those various ranks and ages of minds, what ample room for the most capacious enterprises of social beneficence, ambitious to take a productive part in the moral government of the universe! To learn from the elder sons of God something of the treasures of their memory; to temper and sanctify in young spirits on their novitiate the transports of their hope; to shield the penitent with a tender and heavenly love;—all the blessed offices, whether of pupilage on the arrival, or of guidance after the long stay, must be deemed among the familiar occupations of a state filled with past generations of the great and good. The fitness or unfitness for these higher engagements, though first pronounced by the award of God, is often visible enough to the eye of men below. As life after life is called away, the hardest spectator cannot gaze on all alike. Faith and fancy spring up and follow, with gladder or more reluctant wing, in one case fearing to go, in another grieving to stay. Soul after soul passes into the heavenly light; one becomes a blot upon it, and marks on it a black deforming outline; another, like a cloud, blends uneasily with it, dimming the glory, yet gathering it up and spreading it into colours rich and sad;—a third is absorbed into it, and melts as into a congenial element. Every noble attribute of this world helps us in our faith of another. The active, manly will, that has shown itself able to resign the faithful labour of duty for the patient quietude of suffering, affords us a glimpse of faculties ready for an immortal work. Yet, though we think of that scene as a *progressive* world, it is not, after all, vast power of genius or energy of resolve which we most readily place there. Life there wins its advances without strife and pain; no defiant obstacles provoke the struggling Will; the cross of agony, stripped of its victim, is left behind, and spreads its naked arms against the sky on our Calvary below. Our emancipated being rises into repose. And so there is no form of character which we more naturally follow thither, as to its native home, than the quiet mind, so balanced by pure and equable affections as never to sway from its own centre; which passes through the extremes of circumstance with a serene and touching constancy. Amid the vicissitudes of individual history, and the stormy changes of human affairs, the affectionate and permanent heart, the pure and living centre of private life, is the great conservative power of our world; ever reproducing, from age to age, groups bound together by holiest ties; saving from forgetfulness the sacredness of love and duty; upholding our genial hope for a nature still so fair; and even keeping alive our faith in the fidelity of God. Refreshing us while they stay, such spirits bless us also when called to go; leaving their calm image to sanctify the work below, and adorn the hope on high. They escape our humiliating conditions of toil and rest; and reach a state befitting their own pure constancy. Yes; it is only the labour we have for the bread that perisheth which spends and exhausts our strength : the hunger and thirst after goodness, beauty, truth, has nothing in it to weary and make us faint. Sleep and sabbaths die together; and they that reach that sainted peace shall neither rest nor droop again !

LIVERPOOL, 1846.
LONDON, 1867.

XX.

The Ascension.

———•••———

LUKE xxiv. 51.

"And it came to pass, while he blessed them, he was parted from them, and carried up into heaven."

As the collect of the day reminds us, Christians celebrate this morning the heavenly nativity of their founder. Though it deprived the disciples of their divinest glory, and declared the world unworthy to be the permanent residence of the Prince of Peace, though it call them to take annual farewell of him at whose feet they rejoice to sit, they yet greet it with joy, and place themselves for once in sympathy rather with the sphere which receives than with that which loses him. If the song of angels proclaimed, with generous gladness, his entrance into our world, so may the highest hymns follow his transition into theirs; and his mortal and immortal birth call forth an exchange of congratulations between heaven and earth. Nor is it merely in virtue of the sympathies which unite the whole

family of minds, in whatever part of the universe they
dwell, that Christians remember the Ascension rather
with the exultation of a triumph than with the grief
of a bereavement; they feel the act to be something
more than a mere personal retirement of Jesus from
the scene of his labours and sufferings; they claim
him as their representative, and see in his lot the
promised greatness of humanity;—in the glorified
Man of Sorrows the peaceful victory, awarded by God
himself, to unconquerable and martyred goodness;—
in his calm immortal retrospect, the regality of such
pure faith and truth;—in his tranquil vanishing amid
the spaces beyond our globe, an assurance that souls
like his are at home and free in the infinitude of God.

It is well said that, when he was parted from his
disciples, "a cloud received him out of their sight."
Alas! it is so with all who leave us to mourn that they
live with us no more.   Vain were it to speak with confidence, and wicked to speak without awe, of the life
which the prophet of Nazareth has lived for the last
eighteen hundred years.   He has at least passed
beyond the entreaties of the wretched and the claim
of sorrowful beneficence; on the ocean of eternity
there are not, as on the lake of Galilee, storms to
assuage and terrors to rebuke; amid the uncreated
light no blind cry aloud for mercy on their darkness;
in the pure abodes of mind no maniac implores his
pity with a shriek, nor any dead supplicate him with

dumb looks. Nevertheless, vast as the change must be into which one is introduced who goes behind that veil, only the narrowest imagination can permit itself to be staggered and thrown into serious doubt by the duration which our faith ascribes to the unseen existence. No wise man, capable of comprehending the contents and appreciating the capacities of such a mind as Christ's could have any difficulty, even now, in planning the occupations of two thousand years; or esteem a period like this disproportioned to the nature which God has given us to unfold, or the universe he has given us to inhabit. A far greater wonder is in truth before us every day; for do not souls actually come out of nothing into being, and where there was a blank new apparitions of humanity come into view? And to any perception not blinded by custom, this truly infinite transition, this leap out of the gulf of nonentity upon the shore of creation, must appear more mysterious than any mere extension of time, or migration in place, of existence already here. The wildest superstition has never invented anything half so miraculous as this one fact, that we, who once were not, now are.

The cloud which hides from us the state into which Jesus passed, hangs yet lower upon his history; touches even his sepulchre, and screens from mortal sight the whole process of his transition from earth to heaven. The picture which Christian tradition has delineated upon our thoughts, which the most beautiful productions of art have embodied and multiplied, of a visible and bodily ascension, can claim very little sanction from the sacred writings, and none at all from the gospels,—whence, I suppose, it is usually conceived to be principally drawn. Of all the New Testament authors, the only two historians who are said to have been eye-witnesses of the fact, viz., the writers of the gospels of Matthew and John, say not a word about it. The other two evangelists mention it in the fewest words, in which they present us, not apparently with the description of a stupendous sensible occurrence, but with an inference from their own minds. Luke's gospel limits itself to the words of my text, which affirm simply the separation of Jesus from his disciples, his vanishing away in benediction, and subsequent withdrawal to heaven; without stating that his transition was an object of sight. If we suppose nothing scenical at all to have happened, and no knowledge to have been given to the disciples respecting the fate of the Master parted from them, except by subsequent assurance, the language of my text would be no less naturally employed. The gospel of Mark, in a portion of the last chapter which is probably not genuine, has these words; " So then, after the Lord had spoken unto them, he was taken up into heaven, and sat at the right hand of God "; whence we can no more infer that the ascension was visible than that the sitting down at the right hand of God was so. It is not a little remarkable that in the newly discovered ancient manuscript brought by Tischendorf from the monastery of Sinai, the gospels both of Mark and of Luke do not contain the verses referring to the ascension, but stop short of that event. The sole authority for the prevailing form of this belief is found in the introduction of the book of Acts;—a work reputed to be the production of Luke, but in relation to the ascension quite at variance with the gospel bearing his name; since this event, which is here assigned to some hour of light on the fortieth day after the resurrection, is referred by the evangelist to the night of the resurrection itself. Considering the later composition and uncertain authorship of the Acts of the apostles, and its obvious inconsistency in this point with the gospel narrative, I cannot consider its testimony, however valuable in matters unembarrassed by difficulties, sufficient by itself to establish the astounding fact of a corporeal ascension from a public and conspicuous spot, in opposition to the total silence of every other sacred writer, whether reputed witness of the event, or known missionary of a true and early gospel. It appears to me evident that the ascension, like the resurrection, was originally taught in a more spiritual form than that in which it is now commonly held. There are good reasons for believing that these portions of the history of the resurrection which lay stress on the tangible evidence of Christ's corporeal identity, and describe his eating and drinking, formed no part of the primitive record, but were introduced for a controversial object.   And I would add that the silence of the evangelists, especially of the apostle Matthew and John, respecting the ascension strongly confirms this supposition.   For if these authors had really been writing narratives, not merely of some occasional spiritual apparition of Christ to his disciples, but of his bodily restoration to the incredulous hands of Thomas, to the table of their daily meal, to their fishing boat, and fire on the beach, if they had been conducting him through all these incidents of mortal rather than immortal life, how could they possibly cut short their history abruptly there, and leave him in the midst of particulars so purely earthly? how could they trust it to the reader's thought alone to finish the tale, and conduct him from such a scene to heaven?   Must they not have felt that, with the matter so left, they had not enabled the reader to dispose of the body of Christ?   that the conception of his retirement to another sphere was clogged with material ideas which it behoved them to remove by completing the story of his migration?   It is hard to conceive of a more painfully mutilated picture, or one less likely to have been drawn by an apostle, than that of a corporeal resurrection without any ascension; and as the two events were necessarily connected together, it seems probable that where the sequel is absent, the antecedent was not originally present. But it becomes comparatively easy to account for the silence respecting any ascension if we suppose the writers to have enjoyed and recorded merely such spiritual intercourse with Jesus as implied not simply his recovery of life, but a condition and form of existence clearly belonging to another sphere. In such case, the resurrection and ascension merge into one event, and consist only in the natural but ascertained assumption of immortality. This, under the sanction of the literary writings of the New Testament, I conceive to have been the original form of the recorded fact; the corporeal particulars relating to the resurrection being the later suppositions of Jewish theologians in controversy with the spiritualizing Docetæ; and these particulars necessitating the further addition of a corporeal ascension. Of the assured or intensely believed transition of Jesus to a heavenly life, the sudden re-birth of the religion which had been buried in his sepulchre, the total and sustained revolution of character in his followers, the conversion and whole life of Paul afford impressive and sufficient proof; with which, could I even doubt the immortality of Christ after having been the disciple of his spirit, and need external witness, I might well be content. To suppose that anything is gained to the evidence either of his immortality or of ours by the additional idea of a visible ascension, seems to me a marvellous mistake. So far is this from being the case, that the belief in the heavenly life must already have become strong, before it could even bear the weight of so oppressive a conception. No religious truth indeed could be established by any amount or kind of physical evidence ; the moment it becomes the subject of such, it passes from the infinite to the finite, and ceases to be religious. Under the influence of a natural delusion, the solemn convictions of faith are for ever struggling to find for themselves some external proof, and to descend into the rank of our perceptions of visible phenomena. Did they do so, they would simply abdicate their own divinity, lose that ideal character which alone renders them devout and holy, and become liable, like an incarnate God, lost amid the incidents of humanity, to all the sorrows and doubts and wranglings of interminable strife. But they cannot thus transmute themselves from moral to material ; and all the physical evidences of religion will be found, I believe, to be not the primitive foundation of any man's belief, or essential in any way to its support; but after-thoughts of the under-standing, vainly striving to realize in definite shape that which the conscience and the heart (or as I would rather say, the intuitive reason) compels us to receive as true.

Thus the fancy has not yet died out, that the idea of

a visible and corporeal ascension of Christ is at the very root of our belief in his immortal existence, and affords the only satisfactory proof we have of a future life to him or to ourselves. Yet it is surely obvious that, if our minds were not already furnished with the whole conception of that life, if we had not beforehand an inevitable faith in the godlike blessedness of such a soul as Christ's, the mere sight of his body carried into the clouds could do nothing whatever to supply these great conceptions. Were the same thing to happen to one who was less than man, it could not be affirmed to prove anything ; were it to happen to some evil man whose life had been a scourge to the earth, we should probably suppose that he was gone not to everlasting peace, but to unimaginable judgment ; and if this be so, we must evidently have a natural and intuitive faith in the Divine justice ; and instead of deriving our knowledge of the moral sentiments of God from the external fact, we are incapable of making anything of the fact, except as this knowledge may enable us to interpret it. To behold one of our race departing from this earth no more reveals to us the character of the hidden world to which he goes, than the spectacle of the emigrant's receding ship discovers the climate, the inhabitants, the extent, of the region which he seeks ; nay, not even does it demonstrate that there is such a world at all, except to those in whose map of faith it is already distinctly

U

sketched ; just as the departure of Columbus from the port would call up only images of despair and destruction in the minds of doubtful observers who saw nothing but the deep waste before him, and would suggest the picture of the blue water, and verdant slopes and boundless wealth of a New World to those alone who shared his own presentiments. Yet more evident is it, that a visible emigration from our planet can give no knowledge respecting the *duration* of the existence to which the traveller is removed ; the spectacle in no way provides against the possibility of extinguished life ; and the glorious idea of immortality is supplied, as the undoubted sequel, not by any evidence in the physical phenomenon, but from that treasury of infinite beliefs which is secreted in the depths of our purest nature. Look at it as we will, it is not the observed fact which proves the faith, but faith previously awakened that gives the religious interpretation to the fact. No ! the heaven to which Jesus retired, when his blessed work was finished, unsearchable by any human eye, was already open for his reception by the loving hearts of those whose spirits he had won ; who justly heard the will of God in the verdict of their own moral nature assuring them that such a holy one could never see corruption ; who knew he could not begin and end with being the Man of Sorrows ; and who, even if they had never before looked beyond this life, would have penetrated into eternity by the light of new love which had flashed within them under the action of his mind, and have spread abroad the everlasting heaven beyond this sphere, were it only as a tent for him to dwell in.

It may be supposed by some that the miraculousness of a visible ascension would give it an argumentative value in the proof of a future life, which, considered barely as a physical phenomenon, without regard to this peculiarity, it would not possess. But this will be found not to be the case, unless, as before, there be a preparation of previous faith, which is ready to take any hint, and use it as a plea for believing that which it instinctively holds to be true. To a mind unfurnished with the conception of anything divine, such a miracle would present merely the notion of some exceptional force. To a mind occupied with the idea of diabolic agency, it might present terrible apprehensions rather than tranquil hopes; nor is the time far distant in the past when analogous phenomena were regarded as among the possible effects of infernal agency. So that the moral impression of even the most clearly preternatural event cannot be deduced either from its physical character or its miraculousness; but is the spontaneous action of the observer's own mind, interpreting what he sees by what he believes. The sacredness of an occurrence is imparted to it by the devout soul before which it is displayed, and can create no heaven where there was none before.

In reverting from the notion of a visible ascension to the primitive Christian idea of an incorporeal passage from this world to another, not a single argumentative advantage is sacrificed. On the other hand, the human interest of Christ's removal to the unseen sphere is incalculably increased by divesting it of these bodily adjuncts. As it is usually regarded it is a solitary and insulated miracle, so unlike anything which can occur to others as to teach us nothing probable of the appointed fate of human kind; we cannot say, with any distinct meaning, that " *as* he rose, we shall rise also," for at every point within our observation the analogy distressingly fails. In the case indeed of our own departed friends we have a longer call upon our trust and faith than had the first disciples of the risen Jesus. The third day passes, and our dead do not revive; morning after morning dawns, and no angel descends to wake them from the sleep; the re-opened tombs show us no grave-clothes lying, no prisoners of mortality escaped; the footsteps of the departed are noticed no more in the scenes which they loved and left, and their voice never is heard to say " Peace be unto you; " in no breaking of bread are they permitted to be with us, but our eyes are for ever holden that we should not know them. And then how often and how mournfully may we look for their ascension in vain; no track to mark their upward flight, no whisper as of a receding soul's farewell; no illumined cloud to receive and transfigure them from our view; they abide within the wilderness of Night and Silence. And if our Lord's transition to a deathless existence be not a lonely wonder, but a species of the natural law of all our immortal spirits; if, in the scripture phrase, *as* he rose we shall rise also, then the analogy between his destiny and ours is essentially complete, though broken in some of its attendant circumstances. It may then be said, that we see in him what is the true lot of man; that which to duller eyes takes place behind the veil having been permitted, to the insight of apostles and holy men, once to pass before it, on its human instead of its heavenly side. They could not doubt, nor henceforth could any whom that spirit touched, that Christ was taken where dwelt the earlier members of our race; where now are gathered the spirits of the good from all later generations, down to the pilgrims that have laid aside their staff since last we were assembled here. And if so, though we cannot tell *where* is the region to which the emancipation of death delivers us, though we must consign ourselves like the blind to be led by a secret hand in a way that we know not, yet we perceive *when* the solemn passage must be made, and *who* will receive us at its close. *There* shall we find the glorious company of the wise and excellent, whose deeds we have revered, and whose thoughts have transmitted their inspiration to our souls; there, the contemporaries whom we have vainly longed to know, that we might tell them how our hearts had burned within us beneath the power of their fidelity and truth ; there the parents, brethren, sisters, torn from our passionate embrace ; there the forerunner Jesus, ruling still in the realm of spirits, as he did in the village synagogue, and does over the subdued minds of Christendom ; there the God and Father of all, to whom Christ hath already led our penetrated souls, and who to our purer thought will more nearly open the mysteries of his benign infinitude. But here we must pause, and let a silence fall upon a scene too holy for our speech.

LIVERPOOL, 1840.
LONDON, 1870.

XXI.

𝔍nfluence of the 𝔇octrine of a 𝔐illennium.

———◆◆———

2 PETER iii. 8.

"Be not ignorant of this one thing, that one day is with the Lord as a thousand years, and a thousand years as one day."

THE inextinguishable propensity of men to maintain a set of ideas altogether in advance of their practice, and in their disappointment at the actual to take refuge in visions of the possible, is one of the most significant of human facts. It has usually shaped itself into the obstinate belief, which, though it can only be true *once*, has existed *always*, that all "former times were better than these";—or else it has assumed the other half of the same conception,—that the "future times *will be* better than these." Faith in *perfection somewhere* has never been obliterated; in retrospect or in prospect it has dwelt secure, undisturbed by whole floods of misery and sin, overwhelming the present. It is the most vital of all realities, with which you can do nothing but drive it about from *now* into *then;* for when you are bent on dashing these fair visions, and point out such fiendish passions and biting woes and wide wasting corruptions as clearly prove that perfection is not a thing of experience, the human heart draws the strange inference, " the less there is of it here, the more there must be there." In the majority of systems, the belief in the past and the belief in the future perfection of human nature have been united; the present moment has been represented as the point of deepest degeneracy, the nadir of our sphere, the confluence of a descending and an ascending progression, the period in which depravity and wretchedness wring from the earth its most dreadful but its latest groans. The philosophy, as well as the poetry, of Greece and Rome had its dream of a golden age, when gods and men dwelt undistinguished upon a greener earth and beneath fairer skies, with no desires but those of innocence, no love but that of justice, no appetites that transgressed the simplicity of nature. The guilty passions which had interrupted this flow of peace, and drawn whatever was divine back to its native heaven, had acquired an ascendancy more and more terrible,—the merriment of license passing into the ferocity of war, and force, in its turn, decaying into avarice and fraud; till nothing was to be expected from an enraged and disappointed Providence than that in so dreary a winter of the world, some deluge should sweep away the polluted race, and even the brute tribes which they

seemed intent on copying, and prepare a cleansed earth
for a new creation of humanity. Had this been the
whole of the Pagan theory, there would have been
in it nothing characteristic,—nothing to distinguish it
strikingly from the Hebrew theology which teaches and
deplores the fall of man from the purity and immortality of Paradise, and represents even the physical
productiveness of nature as contracted in punishment
of moral ill. But the genius of the Heathen system,
its alliance, not with any high moral sentiment, but
with the cycles of the material universe,—appears in
this; that after its great catastrophe of destructive
flood, all things were again to return in the same
order; the same individual men to be born again, to
act again in the same scenes, and produce the same
series of events; and conduct the world once more
through the same melancholy successions of corruptions,
back into chaos and destruction. The whole theory of
society, expounded by the wisest Pagan philosophy of
the Stoical school, is comprised in this weary idea
of incessant revolution,—of rotation without progress,
—rotation as of an eccentric wheel, fast sinking and
slow rising;—an idea which could fire no will, warm
no sympathy,—not stimulant, but simply distressing,
incapable of any grandeur except that which it may
borrow from immense duration, and the solemn periodicity of Fate. Nobler in every way was the futurity
of the Hebrew, which passed into the *millennium* of

the Christian church. This belief, not even now
extinct, and in the early ages of Christianity quite
universal, deserves careful study even by those who do
not receive it as true ; as it singularly and beautifully
illustrates the peculiar genius of our religion ; and is
indeed so full of its best spirit as perhaps to have
conveyed more truth to the heart than error to the
understanding of its believers. According to this
doctrine the agent employed to consume the world's
accumulated iniquity was to be no undiscriminating
deluge, sweeping away the good and ill into one common
death ; but the commissioned Christ of God, who
should quickly descend to " burn up the chaff indeed
with unquenchable fire," but to " gather also his wheat
into the garner " ; who should bring swift destruction
on that only which hurts and corrupts in all the earth,
and gather all that is divine and fair into his presence
to adorn his reign of peace ; who should usher in a
thousand years, without the stain of blood, the sound
of weeping, or the spectacle of death ; free alike from
want and sin ; illumined by the universal intercourse
of holy wisdom and glad affections. And though even
millennial glories must have an end, they were not to
be put out by the mists returning from the abyss of
corruption, but to merge into the celestial state ; they
were to wind up the earth's history for ever; and
terminate in that tempest of judgment which would
transfer all that is human to other worlds. Thus the

Pagan *world prospect* was that of alternate renovation and relapse, in which the individual had no part except to tread again the same dull round, the happy embracing his joy afresh, and the miserable thrust into his woes; while the millenarian felt his foot on the first step of an Infinitude, offering the repetition of nothing, the progress of all things. His thousand years were as the silver twilight, interposed between the night of storm and the glories of an eternal day.

The comparison of analogous forms of belief in different systems is at all times instructive, and affords the clearest insight into their peculiar spirit and tendency. And in placing side by side the two superstitions which I have mentioned, a striking contrast presents itself to notice; that while the Pagan mythologist paid exclusive attention to that part of his scheme which had reference to the *past*, the Christian believer singled out from his faith its picture of the *future*. The golden age of the one was at the world's beginning; the millennium of the other was reserved for its end. Both acknowledged the miseries and guilt of their present era; both uttered the plaintive tones of human sorrow and confession; but from the one proceeds a dirge, from the other an aspiration. Both had their conceptions (in minds of the same order, not probably very dissimilar) of a perfect form of life; but with the one it was gone, faded into a tradition; with the

other it was at hand, glowing into a reality. In the
view of the one the world was sunk into decrepitude,
in the last stage of profligate senility ; in that of the
other it was on the very verge of rejuvenescence. The
one saw in its gleams of reviving good only the
declining beams of its god of light, frowning from the
angry West, with menace never to return; the other, the
Eastern streaks of promise that herald his approach,
and are indeed the very drapery of the Hours yoked
to his car of fire. The difference is distinctly
expressive of the true spirit of Christianity; which,
full as it is of penitence, is active and not passive ;
which presses ever forward with the passion for
improvements, instead of lingering behind in the
sadness of regret; which, instead of indulging us with
sentimental glances at departed good, sets an awful
future with sudden flash before the eye, and thunders
the word "Prepare"; giving to corruption a shock,
instead of a refreshment, and throwing society into the
energy of young life, instead of the sickly dreams of
moral death. The difference is that between the
organic atoms of a new world, and the ineffectual dust
of an old.

The history of the millennial belief is interesting in
another point of view. It shows the indestructible
faith which Christians always had in their religion, *as
a principle of justice ;* their affectionate trust in Christ,
and in that Providence of which he is the emblem, that

he will not suffer the wrongs and woes of earth to cry aloud to him in vain, but descend to heal them speedily. For if we separately examine the periods in which this expectation has been active, and the intervals in which it has slept, we shall find that prosperity extinguishes, adversity evokes it. So systematically true is this, that with no other guidance than this general rule anyone moderately familiar with history might infallibly conjecture the eras of each successive outbreak of this expectation. Long and silently may the oppression of some Christian class,—slave, serf, or heretic,—be seen to grow; but let it reach a gigantic form, and burst into violence, and up starts the millennial faith at its right hand, and full often slays the giant in the name of God. And if, after long laying to heart the spirit and the words of the divine Galilean, the universal impulse of the wretched is to cry, "Come, Lord Jesus, come quickly," what does it show but faith in him as the symbol of heaven's equity and mercy, an acceptance of his spirit as the expression of eternal rectitude and the ideal of perfect rule.

The belief in Christ's immediate advent was prevalent during the first two centuries of our era, almost till the gospel had exchanged its apostolic for an imperial dignity, and the crown of gems professed to reverence the crown of thorns. This was the interval which comprised its first struggle and its greatest power; when its moral energies grappled in

their young intensity with the consolidated forces of
philosophical speculation and mythological tradition,
and left them in the dust to die. Throughout the
greater part of this time, of peace always treacherous
and danger never far, the return of Jesus to sweep
away all other power, and reign, erecting a throne
where he had found a sepulchre, was the subject of
nightly prayer and daily anticipation. The long delay,
while it had made many apostates, had deepened
wonder, and awakened preternatural vigilance, in those
who were faithful still.   The number of departed
Christians waiting in heaven to form the procession of
their descending Lord, of friends to be given back to
the embrace, and holy martyrs to the veneration, of
the living, had reached an amount that no man could
reckon ; and the time must be at hand.   Every
symptom of the world's approaching ruin, every
portent of desolation, physical or moral, was noticed
and registered by some observant heart. Christian
prisoners of simple mind, who have never heard of the
marvels of foreign lands, are borne from their homes
in Asia to Rome, the centre of their abhorrence ; as
they approach its domestic territory, they pass within
sight of Ætna and Vesuvius, and whisper to each other
" I come to send fire on the earth ; and what will I,
if it be already kindled ? "   The puff of sudden smoke
declares the furnaces of judgment ready ; lo ! it
streams up, the flame signal of the Lord !   Some

disciples from the banks of the Rhone in the far West, are visiting the churches of Æthiopia on some embassy of faith and mercy; and as they cross the Libyan desert on camels' back and in manner otherwise so strange, what is that dim dry cloud, waving and travelling over the awful flat, silencing the jargon of the guides, and with whiffs of heat and darkness putting out the ruddy sun? It is the dread Sirocco, with its whirlpool of sand cloud-high, spinning like bubbles on a thousand eddies, but advancing like the rapid down its fall; as if the desert itself had been set upright, to find axis and orbit like a world! Here too, the pilgrims think, he comes; discern the giant image of the cross; and as they sink faint beneath the blood-red heaven, remember confusedly some gospel word about not going forth into the desert to meet him, and sun and moon extinguished at his approach. Martyrdom serves from time to time to quicken and almost to infuriate the expectation. The aged and venerable Polycarp stands unmoved in the flames, refusing to be bound, at Smyrna; he is commanded to warn his faithful band of disciples near of the vengeance that awaits their impiety from the wrath of Emperor and Jew; but he turns instead to the Pagan populace on the other side, and announces to them a swift destruction from a power more awful and divine. From that moment the Christians more intently watched; and when, a few years after, Smyrna was wrecked by an earthquake in the night, they welcomed its subterranean thunder as the growl of predicted doom, and walking through the rocking city, made their chant of hope heard amid the universal shriek.   And once at noonday, when the whole Mediterranean spread its blue waters beneath their serenest sky, a singular and sudden blackness arose in the furthest West; stealing up towards the East, it trailed behind it an ominous darkness over sea and land, while before it the Ægean glanced and sparkled still.   On a rack so visibly charged with no common storm, the Christians in Italy first looked wondering ; then, as its edge pushed on, those of Greece ; then those of Asia Minor, who saw it open, and burst on Palestine with a gleam and crash that struck all hearts.   Did they not remember then, that as the lightning cometh out of the East and shineth even into the West, so shall the coming of the Son of Man be, and remind each other that in the clouds of heaven he was to come ?   And were not the churches for many days like a chain of posts from Jerusalem to Rome, whose watchmen expected to hear and to transmit a cry of great deliverance ?   Nor was this eager faith stimulant of curiosity merely and enthusiastic piety ; but also of unexampled courage, disinterestedness and mercy.   Hunger and loathsome pestilence desolated Antioch ; the dying and dead lay in the public streets.   The Pagan governor, urged by the inhabitants to relieve by authoritative arrangement the sufferings of the starved and perishing populace, replied that the gods hated the poor. The Christians, poor themselves, and viewing in these calamities the predicted signs of ruin to the heathen world and triumph to their own, plunged into the centre of this misery, inhaled the breath of fever and of plague, and carried not only bread to the hungry and clothes to the naked, but with these the waters of life to thirsting souls, and the garment of joy to the spirit of heaviness. And in like manner, when at a later time the Goths, returning from one of their sanguinary incursions on the South, took with them some presbyters of Italian churches, so high was the courage and so divine the temper of these Christians, whose misfortunes filled them with more trustful faith, that the hearers' hearts were softened to admire, and their minds awoke to hear ; and the gospel, through the virtues and sufferings of these disciples, began to spread its civilization along the plains of the Danube.

In every subsequent age the same causes have re-excited, and the same symptoms have followed this singular belief. Discouraged by the flourishing and pampered hierarchy, it has taken refuge with the persecuted. When Constantine connected Christianity with the civil power, and endowed its bishops with wealth and dignities, the advent of the millennium passed from notice, and were scarcely heard of again till one sect at the reformation adopted them into its

x

faith.   The Anabaptists of Germany, an unlettered and resolute class, scorned alike by Luther and the Papacy, believed and proclaimed the coming of Christ to reign. And who were these bold prophets ? They too, like the early disciples, had been treated as the offscouring of the earth ; they were the trampled serfs of feudalism, whose toil had for ages been spent for others, and whose blood spilt in battles not their own ; their gain taxed without mercy, their produce seized, their homes insulted, their remonstrance spurned.   Their tears and their gospel had nurtured this hope, fanatic if you will, but nevertheless effectual ; for if Christ in person came not to their rescue, his spirit did in their own hearts and in their leaders.   They learned (in however wild a way) the great lessons of manhood which are inseparable from the idea of duty, the hope of life, and the faith of an impartial God.   From these first victims of Protestant tyranny, follow down the successive links of persecution, and at every point you find this doctrine start up anew ; the Huguenots in France, the Puritans in England, and the dreaded but devout Quietists among the disciples of Romanism, have all in their fiery hour found consolation in the vision of early deliverance and millennial peace.   Is it not then the form in which the Christian world has, in the successive crises of its agony, uttered aloud its unswerving faith in the justice of the gospel and the fidelity of God ?

One other remarkable operation of this tenet deserves to be briefly noticed, and can have escaped no careful reader of history. It was the expectation of a Christocracy, or personal rule of Christ over his disciples, that gave rise to the idea of *Christendom;* of a kingdom or polity of the faithful, uniting the believers of every land in ties of heavenly citizenship, compared with whose dignity and durability all civil and local bonds were mean and transitory. This deep-seated idea converted the Christian Church into a vast republic, penetrating through the substance of every nation, unaffected by changes of dynasties, and peacefully surviving the shock of successive wars. Its members sent to each other messages of peace and help across wide continents; its greetings were in no spoken tongue, but in the general language of the human and the pious heart; its ministers, using the language of Rome, consecrated by the pens of the western fathers, found a reception and a mission and a home wherever there was a church. The Ecclesiastical organization and the religious union, which arose out of this idea of Christendom, were essential to the very existence of all modern civilization. They clasped all Europe together in ages whose violence had ruptured every other bond, and thus saved it from universal wreck. When barbarism and warfare had annihilated all other cohesive power, these furnished a central attractive force compacting all disordered things till better days, and preventing confusion from dropping into utter chaos. The republic of Christ is thus the parent state of all modern nations, and has given rise to all that is binding in our existing civilization.

These effects has the millenarian doctrine undoubtedly produced. Nor need we, I repeat, think that it is a mere superstition that has wrought such marvels. For this tenet is but the incarnation, as it were, the grosser and more palpable embodiment, of a diviner faith in the spirit of Christ and the power of his religion;—a faith which history not refutes but justifies:—which it will justify yet more and more, till the gospel, having had final and freest course, shall have gathered in its latest glories.

While we drop its form, let us save its inner truth and retain its spirit. Discovering at last that the kingdom of God cometh not of observation, but lives within us, let it not sleep there in its idea, but go forth thence to struggle with the sorrows and the unrighteousness of men ; sustaining in us an undying impatience of every remediable ill, and a solemn vow that, be the years many or few, each one shall make its encroachment felt on the mass of suffering and wrong which hinders the approach of a more than millennial peace.

LIVERPOOL, 1838.
LONDON, 1868.

XXII.

Palliatives to the sense of Mortality.

———•••———

ZECH. i. 4

"Your fathers, where are they? and the prophets, do they live for ever?"

AMOS v. 8.

"He turneth the shadow of death into morning."

No one of reflective mind can avoid feeling oppressed at times by the mystery of death. Neither the vigour of life in the healthy, nor the brilliancy of faith in the devout, can always prevent that dark shadow from stealing in upon the thoughts to chill and sadden them. The spectacle of fearful disease, the picture of sinking age, the lapse of a domestic life, break our too solid security, and set our minds afloat as on a stream of resistless necessity, of whose rapid course we obtain a momentary and shuddering consciousness. The very custom and endearment of this world, which habitually deaden such consciousness, do but make it more startling and awful, when the sudden memory of departed years brings it home to us. And if then, in our darkness, we think it terrible to die; if we passionately throw forth our hands to seize and detain the blessings that drop from us into the abyss; if we feel awhile that the earth is too solemn with this region of Night around it, and cry aloud "How dreadful is this place!" if we privately wish that it were possible to dispense with death in the universe of God;—we yield, as I believe, not to any blasphemy of an unsubdued nature, but to the universal remonstrance of the human heart against the grave; to a feeling which we may gladly and innocently breathe to him that seeth in secret, though perchance it might be a new thing for him to listen to professions and prayers so true. Who will not acknowledge that it ingenuously states the universal remonstrance of the human heart against the grave? *To do without Death,* never to witness that heavy struggle, nor feel its prophetic shade stealing over life; to have in every sickness a knowledge of restoration, and no dread anxiety added to its pains; to launch out in freedom on those human affections which now, the more they love, must fear the more to lose; to feel the years run on, with no sad reason for numbering their succession, and celebrate our anniversaries without tears of memory, or abbreviation of hope; to be immortal here, and without the wrench of parting with one wanderer to see the world grow ripe in wisdom, and noble in goodness, and happy in the conscious presence of its God ; is a lot which no human imagination can conceive without desiring. There is a sense in which it is innocent to love the world and the things of the world, and in which the most affectionate and grateful mind will love them most. And were it the will of the Ruler of events to stop the laws of waste and death, and keep in action the causes of perpetual amelioration, I know no sphere more beautiful, no ties more holy, no occupations more delightful, no duties more sublime, than would exist for the race thus immortalized on earth.

It is however differently ordered ; and that is enough to show that this impression against death, though natural, though irresistible, though capable of being soothed only and not removed by religious considerations, is yet erroneous. Whenever we pass the veil, and can study our whole existence, the impression will doubtless vanish. We shall perceive and feel, what we cannot perceive now, its *actual* unreasonableness, its origin in ignorance and partial views. At present we must be satisfied with the humbler task of showing, not how it is, but how it probably may be unreasonable ; of pointing to the quarters beyond our knowledge, in which reasons may exist for the appointment of death ; and thus of awakening that feeling, not of assurance but of modest and affectionate trust, with which the heart, conscious of ignorance, is disposed to rest upon a Providence that doeth all things well.

According to the Christian theory of our existence, there are, and from the creation of our race always have been, two spheres for the reception of human beings, both of which must some time or other be each man's home. One is set apart for the commencement of existence, the nursery of minds, where the first trial of consciousness may be made, and the initiatory lessons of experience be learned. It would be office enough for one world, if it only bore us over that solemn step out of nothing into the great universe ; and when this mighty introduction is effected, and the first surprises of being have ceased, life is transferred to the other region, where it moves on an ampler theatre and exercises nobler powers. In the process of transition from one community to the other, we witness the departure only, and call it Death ; the arrival, alas ! is invisible and silent. The eye of science which sweeps the heaven, and numbers its worlds, and computes their distances, and measures their movement, can learn for us nothing of their life ; the midnight abyss is still and void ; no being moves across its track ; no thrill of life vibrates through its solitude ; all is the order of brilliant mechanism ; and we wander among its orbs in vain to single out the realm of the departed. Could we find it, what an hour for adoration would be the deeps of nights !

Now in seeking for possible reasons for the removal

of the human being from one world to the other, it is
obvious that there are three directions in which they may
exist. His departure must have an operation on the
community which he joins, on the community which he
leaves, and lastly on himself. With respect to the first
little need be said, because nothing can be known.
What offices of mercy, what enterprises of thought,
what mission for human energies, contemplative or practical, what new and various relations, may prevail among
the residents of the better land is a secret beyond our
reach; but knowing as we do that every age of mind and
every form of character are there, we must feel assured
that, among its infinite range of intellectual and moral
ranks, some place will always exist, some duty constantly
be found, nay, even some actual want often arise, for
fresh emigrants from this scene. Could we penetrate
the social organization of that state, it is surely conceivable that amid its busy throng of departed nations
we should find many a group that needed another
member, and could compensate the rupture of earthly
ties. There are indeed cases that it will go hard even
for the resources of heaven to explain. What place so
natural for the sister as the brother's side, whose nature
she refines and whose heart she replenishes with pure
and gentle thoughts? And what should the child do
there, poor infant, torn from a mother's bosom to be
thrown into that great world? We can only say that
he who watches the sparrow's fall will not forget to smile

on the infant's waking and hush the infant's fears; that he who devises the ties of kindred has an invention exuberant in blessing, and will find for the sister severed from her home some office fitted and native to a loving soul. Whilst we are in a position to see only the grievous side of these events, it is useful to remember that we perceive but half their operation; that there is a viewless scene which may be replete with the final causes of their occurrence. The mind is a stranger to the best emotions of our nature, that adjusts all its thoughts and affections to what it knows and can discern; that judges as positively, and feels as passionately as if that were all; that allows no self-distrust to steal from the vast unknown that is before, beneath, around the most penetrating mind. He has both the wisest and serenest spirit who tempers what he sees by what he does not see, who softens his conclusions from the actual by a remembrance of the possible, and feels as if his own experience and knowledge were but a speck of light floating in an abyss of mystery.

The wounds of individual affection habitually prevent our looking calmly and comprehensively at the operation of death on the community which is left. Constituted as the human mind is, it is a dispensation evidently essential to the progress of social improvement. The stability of age, the vigour of maturity and the enthusiasm of youth, mingled as they now are, moderate and correct each other, and

well conduct the world's affairs; but if the elder
generations never retired from the scene, age would
acquire too great a suffrage, and under the guidance
of its caution there would be a conservation of everything, with an improvement of nothing. Every
miserable prejudice would struggle on indefinitely;
error and superstition obtain the freehold of men's
mind; and all that is evil in barbarous times,
ignorance, and tyranny, and wild passions, bid a
safe and long defiance to the spirit of reformation. A
succession of minds must evidently tenant the globe,
if human civilization is to advance. It is precisely at
the intervals between generation and generation that
mistakes and prejudices drop out; discoveries and
experience are preserved, while folly is gradually
thinned off; and when the children of successive
ages begin from the point which their fathers left,
a rational hope is opened of mental and moral and
social improvement almost without limit. No class
of sentiments can now have a chance of perpetuity,
except such as will bear the reiterated scrutiny of
reason; no pleadings from the tenderness of age
can preserve a falsehood from its just fate; the
eternal mind of the human race · returns to it with
freshened power from century to century. The fierce
animosities of nations or of sects which deprave the
character of one period are imperfectly transfused into
the next, and may scarcely impart a tinge to the

succeeding. So that however slow may appear, in the view of our impatient expectations, to be the advance of the civilized community towards the peaceful spirit of wisdom and of virtue, it would undoubtedly be much slower if death were banished from the world ; and this stern messenger of God, though the constant invader of our private happiness, brings in his train the certain triumph of general liberty, righteousness and truth.

From these obvious remarks let us however pass to some considerations which appear to afford some insight into the probable operation of death on the individual himself; and to assign to it, in strict conformity with the laws of our mental constitution, a beneficent function.

It is evidently the plan of Providence that the human mind (I mean each individual mind) should be progressive ; and assuming the truth of our Christian estimate of its worth, it has indefinite capabilities ; new ideas may be added, and new modifications of feeling be imparted to its affections, without end ; it begins in short from nothing, and opens towards infinitude. Now to a being thus progressive the law of habit is indispensable ; ideas and feelings, once imparted, must have a tendency to remain, and to hold to the mind with a tenacity proportioned to their frequency and recurrence. It is this in fact which constitutes the power of mental acquisition. If every impression were effaced as soon as made, no stores of wisdom, or indeed of folly, could be accumulated; for the mind would be perpetually reduced to emptiness. And if ideas did not obtain a strong hold upon us by repetition, if every freshest impression had the same chance with us as the oldest, our condition would be no better; we could conquer no department of knowledge, and by no iteration of labour could we secure its treasures as our possession; the permanent and eternal forms of truth would be indistinguishable from the transient associations of error; and the great lessons of wisdom which are engraven in everlasting lines on the immutable face of creation would be no better than characters traced upon the sand. Nor would our capacity for moral attainment be any greater than for knowledge. No dispensation could become fixed, no permanent *tendency* be formed towards any course of action or emotion; the controversies of temptation would be for ever re-opened; and the past decisions of conscience successfully defied by each new impulse.

To our very existence then, as intelligent and responsible characters, the *law of habit*, which is in fact no other than the *law of acquisition*, is essential; and hence it is inevitable that old ideas, whether true or false, notions and feelings delivered to us from the past, acquire over us a power almost or altogether irresistible.

Next let us observe another quality, which is inseparable, even in thought, from the conception of a progressive being ; viz., an admixture of right and wrong impressions in his understanding, and good and evil feelings in his heart. In other words, a mind cannot be susceptible of improvement, without being both fallible and peccable. In what indeed does improvement consist but the gradual elimination of error, and the suppression of tendencies to guilt; in the substitution, that is, of true in the place of false intellectual and moral judgments. The conditions of our existence here absolutely forbid a perfectly impartial and symmetrical development of the human faculties. Each man begins his education in a position different from every other, and must see life under a different perspective ; each in his own centre is embraced by a circumference of influence with which the orbit of no other being can perfectly coincide. There is scarce a family without its distinctive peculiarities of understanding or of character, its exclusive tastes and exclusive infirmities; so that a type of genius, or a heritage of prejudice may descend by a law of natural entail. There is not a nation that has not ancestral opinions and local vices, and exaggerated excellences ; so that sentiments of morality and religion obtain a geographical distribution, and creeds may be coloured on the map. There is not a profession or set of employments exempted from the action of this law; and not a few of the speculative and practical varieties of human character may be traced to the constant suggestion of some particular order of ideas, or the persevering impression of a singular class of motives. Thus it is a necessity of our human condition, that we shall contract, amid our very earliest impressions, some wrong estimates and pernicious associations of thought. Moreover on these the congealing force of habit must seize, no less than on our justest notions and purest feelings; and when indurated by the frost of years, it is past hope that they should ever be broken and dispersed. The needful light and warmth are gone, when the sun of mortal life has sunk so low. Yet the mind's progress is threatened with permanent arrest unless these prejudices can be removed. Mere continuation in existence will never remove them. Here then we find that the very law which provides for our spiritual improvement threatens to impede that improvement at length, and to introduce disturbing forces of error, deflecting us from the luminous line of our career. Some corrective must be introduced, or the hope of orderly advancement is gone. The proper cure will be discovered by consulting our mode of treating mental delusions in their extreme case.

That extreme case we call the *loss of sanity.* I know of no definable distinction between a prejudice and a mania; they differ only in degree. Both consist in a wrong conjunction of ideas ; in the presence of some obstinate delusion, which prevents the accession of true impressions to the understanding. Increase the intensity of the prejudice ; suppose it constantly haunting the reason, and poisoning the feelings, and what does it become but madness. And so with vice ; it consists in the undue preponderance of some one passion or emotion, hurrying its victim to excesses that make ruin of his peace. Add a little more fire to the passion, or vehement tendency to the emotion, and the will lies prostrate, and delirium triumphs. It is terrible to think on what a tremulous edge the peace of reason for ever vibrates, and into what a deep calamity the over-balance of an idea may plunge us! Nay, as we are, it befits us not to be high minded. For it would seem, after all, that mental derangement is but relative. We measure insanity by its deviation from the average standard of human thought and belief; and may not the whole human standard itself depart equally from absolute truth and the perceptions of the Divine Mind ? Prejudices, verging on mania, are of every possible magnitude of circumference. Individuals have their singularities ; families, their intolerances ; nations, their antipathies ; tribes, their superstitions ; and may not a *world* itself have its misapprehensions and perversions of thought? Our whole race is, after all, but a family in relation to the great community of minds in the universe over which God rules alone ; and must be liable to have its sectional partialities and infirmities. And what treatment do we find most uniformly and naturally efficacious with the disordered spirits that are commended to our mercy ? We change the scene ; we take them to distant countries, where their eye may rest on new sights, and the ear be opened to new sounds, and the familiar causes, suggestive of perturbed thoughts, are far away. To the same process too we resort in order to banish the prejudices of education, and the vices of custom ; visits to other regions, where new modes of thinking are found, and new objects of interest created. And why may not this be the true purpose of our mortality ? We have all our infirmities and hallucinations ; all labour under some sad delusion of mind or heart. We, poor patients of Providence, are conducted to scenes remote, for cure, like the traveller of troubled reason to the warm South. As domestic bigotry is cured by mingling with other homes ; as the prejudices of profession are softened by the access of new studies ; as the pre-possessions of nations are removed by intercourse with other nations, so may our human narrowness be lost by mixing with other worlds.

If then each mortal, through that weary struggle, is to emerge into a clearer mind,—if he thus shakes himself loose from the fiends of beguiling passion and melancholy fear, Welcome Death, and a hundred

Y

successive deaths that can bring us deliverance like that! The law of mortality is then but the passport of emancipation that widens our human home; turning the villager into the citizen; the citizen into the man; the man into the denizen of the universe. To the ordinations of that law, wheresoever they may fall, it is for us to bow our heads, if with sorrow, with no sorrow that disturbs our trust.

LIVERPOOL, 1836.
LONDON, 1870.

As often as they drank the cup were the first disciples to remember Christ. A recollection so dear and sacred was not to be restrained within formal appointments and stated times ; but to be invited to their hearts at every season resembling that parting meal, or bringing back its affectionate and mysterious impressions. Jesus, on the verge of death, and wishing not to be forgotten by a world he had loved so well, that evening bequeathed his image to his followers; the divine lineaments of which would light up and glow within their minds, not only in solemn commemorative hours, but at every crisis that recalled either the scenery or the feelings of that night. And when would this *not* be ? In what moment of peculiar joy, or peril, or temptation, would not *some* portion of that picture, —so various, so beautiful, so sad,—recur to those who had witnessed it ;—witnessed it at first with dull sorrow that dropped in sleep, and then understood it with a vivid gladness that never slept again. The faces about that evening table, too dimly lighted to show all their wonder and their tears; the perplexed and anxious whispers here and there; the tender tones of the only voice inspired to speak; the untrembling hand that, with words of saddest intimation, passed the cup; the gracious form, kneeling to wash the disciples' feet; the look that traced Judas to the door, and the instant burst of relief that followed that trouble of spirit, exclaiming "Now is the Son of Man glorified"; —the moonlight walk, the silent streets, the pause on Kedron's bridge to listen to the stream;—the lulling wind that bore the Saviour's cry, and brought the disciples sleep; with all the solemn but dreamy memories that followed;—were too variegated with emotion, and too closely connected with every subsequent hour of effort not to gleam in fragments on them, in every grievous struggle or diviner excitement of their career.

Nor is it to the love of Apostles only that the memorable night of which we speak bears relation. There were features in it which associate it with passages of experience common to us all, and recommend its great lesson of Remembrance of Jesus to our wisdom and affections. Nor is there even a day in our existence, any more than in that of the first disciples, when to turn to his image, and invoke his spirit, may not prostrate a temptation, or invigorate an effort, of our conscience. Whether we partake of his cup of sorrow, or seize the draught of profound joy, it is well, as often as we drink it, to remember him.

It was at the *festal board* that Jesus made his appeal to the affectionate memory of his followers. And to revert to his spirit at such cheerful times will never be unwelcome except to those ignoble hearts that cannot, like him, blend the religious affections with the social. His own genial temper, that brought down Pharisaic reproach, because it refused not, on fit occasions, to make merry and be glad, can damp no innocent sympathies; can check no freedom but that which requires escape from moral restraint; and chill no enjoyment but that which insists upon oblivion of the great conditions of human existence. Not on the paschal meal alone did his benediction fall; but from the seclusion of that upper room in the city of Jerusalem it has spread wherever homes and hearts have been open to receive it. He,—true consecrator of our friendship and creator of the domesticities of life,—has blessed all our bread, and mingled his peace with the wine of our enjoyment; and shall we not remember him when we meet together,—if not his person always, yet his spirit, that we may know how to be happy without selfishness, and to abound without excess? What, better than his image, can rebuke the proud, luxurious thought, and fling across the too gaudy colours of outward pleasure those immortal memories, and low whispers of the conscience, which

sober, but never sadden, the spirit of the truly wise?
Will not his spirit silence the too eager solicitations
of sense, and fill us rather with quiet gratitude to God,
and ready mercy for the poor that lie not without the
most grievous sores at the gate of our abundance?
And whoever, passing the cup, remembers him, will
surely love the kindly and generous thought, wherein
is no shade of malignity, and the pure and temperate
speech that preserves itself cool and true amid the
false heats of a material life.

It was a *daily meal* at which Jesus desired his
followers to remember him. And of whom could we
then more fitly think, than of him that taught us the
prayer for daily bread, and made us feel that thus to
live is not the whole of life? Surely such a reference
would well reprove our artificial wants, and make us
ashamed of that elaborate anxiety about the meat that
perisheth, in which not a trace remains of his divine
trust; not one misgiving is felt in pulling down the
barns to build greater; not a transient look is spontaneously turned to Him that decks the lily, and hears
the raven cry. Oh! my friends, how few there are that
know how to seek what they may eat and what they
may drink, yet not, on that account, forgetting that
blessed bread of heaven without which, amid the fairest
show, the soul is wasting unto death! how few, that
caring for the following day, overlook not the mighty
morrow in this world,—the morning of eternity! Yet

did God never mean that the necessity of the outward life should crust over the deep springs of our
inner nature, and forbid the waters of true life to flow.
He has ordained no connection between the rugged
hand of labour, and the rough heart of selfishness;
between the spirit provident for earth, and the conscience thriftless for the skies. Indeed it is rarely, as
we pretend, the hard necessities, but rather the soft
blandishments of our lot, that indurate our affections,
and render us unfaithful to the high calling of God.
For one that is crushed by the cruelty of circumstance,
how many are there, even of the purest of us, that are
seduced by its indulgences! What obstruction from
without could not the divine spirit overcome in
Nazareth! The prophet who put his hand to the lowest
toil, and dwelt beneath the shelter of a cottage roof,
till he went forth, and had not where to lay his head,
—not only found for himself, but became to the world,
the bread of life. Let all who call themselves his
followers, and not least those who fare sumptuously
every day, see how divine a light sprung up in the
deep vale of his existence, and spreading from earth
to heaven, has since been leading many souls to God.

The hour when the injunction was given to
remember Christ was marked by *the gathering of
calamity and crime.* Treachery was in the room;
conspiracy was in the city; guilt was lighting its midnight torch; and already the hammer and the saw

were busy on the fatal cross. Before the moon, now high, had set, the tribunal of injustice was held, the hum of popular passion was heard, and the judicial murder was decreed. And before another day had passed, that form now thrilling with the last excitement of duty and affection, was stretched in silence within the sealed sepulchre. And in every season of consternation and grief, to remember him will be our safeguard and our tranquillity. His steady gaze upon the darkest fate, his calm submission to the temporary triumph of wrong, his meek patience till the vindicating Providence came round, his prompt efforts to console and bless, unexhausted to the last, can never rise before our thoughts without rebuking our weak terrors, and chiding our unfaithful thoughts. His trust, his love, his peace, are open in every emergency, to those that seek them. The Father to whom he cried is with us still, and no soul can look to him in vain. The same Providence shelters our life, and the same promises cheer our future. But then, to share in trial the courage of Jesus, we must remember him, not in name only, but with the very heart. Else, though we gather around the table of his kingdom, and seem to partake of the bread of life which he offers, we shall be like the disciples in that first night of communion ; who outwardly drank of the cup which he drank of ; but when the crisis in the garden came, they yet remembered him no more, and fled.

Jesus gave his apostles the command to remember him on the eve of a great mission ;—a mission whose responsibility he left them to meet alone. And well might the thought of him fill them and us with the most solemn conception of life as a high trust, and the world as a glorious theatre on which to spend and be spent in the service of duty and of God. His image, my friends, awakens us to a true faith in the comforter and inspirer of the strenuous conscience ; and sends us forth into any career, however difficult and noble, without fear and without reluctance. The genuine disciple of Christ, who is penetrated by his views of Providence, of life, of man, of heaven, becomes too familiar with the feeling of living on a great scale and for the sublimest purposes, to yield to surprise, or forfeit the calmness of a divine wisdom. The whispers of God enter the sanctuary of conscience, and bring access of unexpected strength; and when Christ and the Father have thus come and made their abode with us, by the inspiration of their power the severest yoke becomes easy, and the heaviest burden light.

LIVERPOOL, 1839.
LONDON, 1872.

WELL has this commemoration been called the "*Christian Communion.*" Not only is it a meeting of kindred minds to renew their common vows, and touch again, as with one hand, the symbols of their brotherhood; but it binds together in a unity unconscious and sublime a vast reach of centuries and whole families of nations. If we stood alone in Time, and belonged only to our own generation, these memorials could not be here. They are foreign to our present age, and come to us charged with an ancient meaning, and keeping open an everlasting hope;—strange and bold emblems, which our timid imagination would never have apprehended, had they not conducted to us the influence of a more fervent time, and become consecrated at once by an historic dignity and a pathetic splendour.

The faith which brings us hither is distinctly *retrospective*. We here commemorate the past; we avow our dependence upon it; we see on its dark brow the bright cloud that overshadows us with divine glory, and shuts us in with spirits of more heavenly race; and owning the need we have to pitch our tent with them, we renounce our self-sufficiency, and say, "It is good for us to be here." By the bread that is before us we confess that ancient hunger of the spirit which feeds on holy thought, and makes us pensioners still on the infinite wealth of the great Master-soul. In the cup, as we raise it to our lips, we solemnly pledge the mighty communion of dead who, in their moments of earnest life, have bent over it with like prayers. Every pretence at mere solitary wisdom we here resign; for our lonely selves we feel there would be no God, no glorious duty, no unfading hope; and we crave entrance only as poor sharers of that universal worship, which has brought the highest Reason and Conscience of every age, in proportion as evil spirits have been cast out, to sit "clothed and in their right mind" at the feet of Christ. Touching these emblems, we stretch our arm at once over eighteen centuries, and clasp an altar crowded already with millions of shadowy hands. We silently range ourselves with the eucharistic multitude that surrounds the slope of Calvary, and try to mingle our voices in the sweet and never-dying hymn they send across the plain of history. A spectral cloud of witnesses surrounds us as we sit here, and, with a murmur of immortals, sets us the note of endless aspiration which we too are summoned to prolong. We are in society here with the martyr,

clasping in the flames the truth we so lightly hold;
with the noble youth of fifty generations, taking their
first vow of consecration, and bending low on the
threshold of life's realities;—of the restored penitent,
daring to look up at the cross again, and reading
forgiveness in the drooping countenance of the dead
Christ;—of the dying, anxious, in the last breaking
of bread at life's evening meal, to rest, as the loved
disciple, in the bosom of Jesus, and amid this world's
mixed assemblage of the faithful and faithless, to
whisper, "Lord, is it I?"—of all devoted and apostolic
men, gladdening by their fellowship, and filling with
their spirit, even the outcast and the slave;—nay,
of the divine Master himself, who first drank of this
cup that we drink of, and washed himself the feet that
were called to follow him.   Amid this various throng
we boldly proclaim that we belong to a Prophet long
dead,—yet whose guidance is our divinest blessing
still.   Broken is the body, and shed is the blood, but,
as these same emblems show, immortal is the spirit,
of him who secretly presides at this festival of our
conscience and our faith.   And meeting here we sit
down at the banquet of ages, and exchange looks with
the circle of the saintly dead.

Yet this rite, commemorative as it is, has relation to
the *present* no less than to the *past*.   It does not *so*
direct us to the divine life in Galilee, and death on
Calvary, as to make us think that elsewhere there is

no God. The great Father who dwelt in Christ has not retired out of human reach, and become dumb to listening ears; the borders of his glory are never,—as some who are asleep persist to dream,—drawn up into heaven, but flutter still around for those who watch the flashing of their souls, and hearken to the rustling of their infinite desires. He is a *living* God, awake at this very hour no less than when the anguish of Gethsemane sobbed itself forth into the infinite bosom of his mercy. He is a *present* God, as close to us in our modern homes and at our immediate meal as on the grass of Olivet, or in the " upper room, furnished " in the city of Jerusalem. The sorrows he visits, the sins that shrink before his frown, the duties he measures out to faithful Wills, the affections he kindles with a heavenly fire, are no historical affairs that pass away and need him not again; but are the very constancies of our humanity, opening a perpetual commerce between his spirit and our own. Palestine was a piece of plain geography, till One came who transfigured it with the inner light of his own sanctity, and made it a Holy Land. And neither Christ in this world, nor angels in another, can stand upon diviner ground than we, as we pace across this bridge of awful life from nothingness to God. The Master whom we remember at this hour is no Redeemer unto us, but, on the contrary, our dangerous Tempter, if we regard him as absorbing the Divine Spirit from us, instead of

quickening it within us. It is the glory of true
Inspiration that it does not suppress and supersede,
but expand and vivify, the souls that recognize its
presence; it spreads and multiplies itself without exhaustion, and becomes more possible the more there
is. It is not like the mere cold light, caught only by
reflection, and leaving the face averted for a moment
in darkness still; but as the glowing radiance which
kindles that on which it shines, and sets it burning as
an orb self-luminous. It is the work of the inspired
Teacher to make us conscious of inspiration; to lift
us above ourselves into the higher sphere of meditation;
where the voice of mere desire, and the misgivings of
low doubt, and the atheistic dreams of a drowsy heart,
are hushed and shamed away by the startling clarion of
duty and the solemn touch of God. Into that height
of heavenly audience it is given to every soul to rise
through renunciation and lowly prayer; the renunciation, not of the nobler nature, but of sense and self
alone; Reason and Conscience keeping with Christ
the throne; passion and pleasure sitting submissive at
the feet.

LIVERPOOL, 1843.

THE dying sacrifice of Christ was, of all last hours, the most holy and divine. It is no wonder that again and again we turn to it, as the great model death, rebuking every mortal fear, and bidding us discern, in life's closing scene, not its deepest decline but its highest elevation. Private death is ever bringing its private sorrow and private warning; but when the soul of a Christ is called away, it makes at once bereavement and illumination to a world. It reveals to us the passing elements and real glory of our being here; its true place in the system of Providence; and how transcendent above the mere vital phenomena that perish may even *appear* the immortal spirit that endures. Expectants, all of us, of the same summons to depart, knowing each week that the steps before us are fewer now, we cannot but ask in our secret hearts, 'What is it that I approach to?' 'Why can I not shun it?' 'Where is this strange, impalpable necessity that will have me, and can neither be grappled with nor evaded?' 'Whither am I, a living man, answering to my name to-day, to sink away through the dark and infinite silence?' Our common experience yields us but a dumb and negative reply. The mean process of physical extinction, the disheartening ascendancy of animal phenomena in the crisis of departure, the sad stifling of reason and of love amid the dust of the crumbling and falling tabernacle, which are the symptoms usually presented, suggest nothing to elevate and console. And oh! it is a great thing to turn hence to the mighty spirits of our race, that, in parting from us, have seemed to lift themselves with conquering feet upon the mountains, and see the storms of life beneath them, and its everlasting canopy above; and more than all, to gaze towards that topmost point of human history, where Jesus stands, like a solitary figure observed at sunset on the highest Alp, his soul steeped in the hues of pure affection, and mingling with the glories of the upper world. The sublime tranquillity of the cross has given a perpetual sanctity to Christian death;—a tranquillity that penetrated and calmed whole floods of anguish, yet needed no high tension of resolve, but simply came from the unaltered presence of a surrendering trust and an exhaustless love.

We may well look up then, as we sit beneath the cross, with a wondering eye at the dying sacrifice of Christ. Yet that was almost a light thing to one who had completed his *living sacrifice*. The real wonder is not in the scene that astonishes and subdues us most, but in the whole history of which this is only the catastrophe. Every one's being is a consistent and inseparable whole, whose mortal end is but the natural sequel and significant expression of the rest,—the helpless outcoming of what *he is.* Live only the life of Christ,—be what he was,—and your death,—though it be on the softest pillow and amid the sweetest caresses, shall be holy as another crucifixion. Forget to seek him on the beach and amid the hills; desert him, when he has not where to lay his head; be anxious and troubled about many things, instead of choosing the good part; deny him in the palace, or betray him at the meal; and he will bend no look of parting light on one who has not drunk of the cup that he drank of, or been baptized with the baptism that he was baptized with. Hence the homage which we pay to his death is but another way of submitting ourselves to the authority of his life; and all our meditations on our own future are but an index pointing backward to some form of wisdom and duty in the present. Here, in this solemn hour, we cannot but think of the approaching " night in which no man can work "; but with far deeper anxiety and prayer must we remember the daylight hours that yet remain. For our departure, be it near or be it far, is a something that happens *to us;* while our time of tarrying is a trust that must be administered *by us.*

z

To the Christian it must always be a more fearful
thing to live than to die, seeing that he may live all
wrong, but cannot die amiss; that the one may be
guilty, the other only grievous; and one who with
faithful constancy has put forth the divine power
within him can always suffer with perfect trust the
divine power upon him, and say, " Lord, now lettest
thou thy servant depart in peace." No, it is not the
close, but the continuance of opportunity, that can
fill a disciple's heart with true solicitude; and the
prayer of his noblest spirit will be, not ' Lord, support
me when I go,' but ' Lord, help me while I stay.'
Never then, while an hour of responsibility remains,
let us cease to live in a sacred faithfulness, knowing
that we must walk to-day and to-morrow, and not till
the third day shall we be perfected.

But if the responsibilities of life are awful, its
freedom is glorious. While it lasts, it is given as
our own; when it ends, it returns to God; and no
other Will than His and ours can intermeddle with
the trust; what better conditions could any true and
loving heart desire? The hour of opportunity is not
lapsed as yet; it lies before us open and unpledged;
waiting to be filled with shameful negligence and mean
indulgence, or with the order of earnest duty and clear
affection. Year by year we come hither to seek from
the great Leader of Christian souls strength to choose
the better part; to learn of him that bore the cross for

us to take up, with courage divine as his, the yoke of
life which he has made easy and the burden he has
rendered light. We come to take that gentlest of
hands, that lifts the faith fast sinking in the deeps,
and submit ourselves to its divine guidance through
the scenes that are yet before us. And having taken
it, we must not let it go. It were a poor mockery
just to touch it and then depart, till we fear to lose it
altogether, unless we return to ask it yet again. We
cannot seize it at our pleasure, but must hold to it
with perfect trust. They only can be said to be faithful
disciples of the Lord Jesus who are retentive of his
spirit, and find it their true light of life ; whose tastes
and temper are in permanent harmony with that
wisdom from above that brings repentant spirits to
his feet. If we are truly possessed and penetrated
with his mind, we shall never, while an hour of
responsibility remains, cease to live in a sacred
fear and watchfulness for ourselves, knowing that we
must walk to-day and to-morrow, and not till the
third day can be perfected. While life continues, the
vigil of duty cannot be relaxed, and the effort to wake
up, and open our eye to the transient work beside us
and the everlasting stars above us, must be constantly
renewed. If we are true to him, we shall moreover
be full of helpful love for each other ; ready to toil
with thought and heart for the sorrows of them that
have none to help ; to lift the paralytic soul into the

healing stream at the moment of its flow; to open on the infant's heart the mild glance of heavenly wisdom, and extend over his head the benediction of a divine hand. Nor can we complete our fidelity to him, unless to his life of devoted action we join his spirit of quiet suffering, and give ourselves up in every lot with a trustful surrender unto God; not only resolute to bear, but disposed to love no other course than the way that he may lead us. To set us forward to this high end are we here this hour. Let us not quit this meeting-place of our mutual vows without some progress made. Here, as at the foot of the cross, let us lay down some infirmity or sin, from which we long to part, and which is fittest sacrifice for a grateful heart. Here, each season as we meet, let us take up some one of the high resolves which already, doubtless, have been too long soliciting our hearts. And thus shall we yield the true and faithful answer to the voice of invitation that always whispers to us here; "Come, take up the blessed cross, and follow me."

LIVERPOOL, 1844.
LONDON, 1872.

Communion Address.—IV.

To many ages has Jesus now appealed, desiring that
they would remember him ; and all have answered with
a ready heart, ‘Yea, Lord, we would remember thee.’
Yet that reply has been suggested by considerations
the most various ; and while the love that breathes
through it has been constant, the thought connected
with it has curiously changed.   The one thing about
which Christendom has been unanimous, and which
still kindles its inmost enthusiasm, is the majesty, the
beauty, the authority of its acknowledged Lord, and
the infinite debt it owes to so divine a sanctity ; and it
is not wonderful that a perfection comprehensive as his
should present itself to the mutable tempers of men
under different aspects, and draw to itself a reverence
ever altering in its grounds, and only permanent in its
intensity.   To none but the eleven gathered in that
upper room in Jerusalem was this usage that literal
act of memory, for which alone perhaps it was originally
designed.   Them, from the clear light of their later
ministry, it would throw back in fancy into the shadows

that hung around the approaches of the crucifixion. The grand and gentle look of Christ, as he knelt to wash their feet, while speaking upward in their faces; the melting tones of his voice, outwardly commanding their faith, but inwardly asking the solace of their love; his meaning glance at the traitor stealing from the room; the moonlit walk through the deserted streets; the dim terror of their hearts that made them start at the sudden tramp of their own feet upon the bridge; the cry of Gethsemane, faintly borne by the night wind upon their dreams; with all the feverish impressions that followed, from the burst of the band into the garden to the drooping figure on the cross, would reappear like a history come round again, and bring the promised sorrow converted into joy. Beyond the little circle present at that night these memories could not extend; and the early Christians, who missed these elements of personal attachment in the past, turned rather to the future, and assembled to " show forth the Lord's death till he come." When they touched these elements, it was with minds not affectionately lingering, but eagerly expecting; in the attitude of them that would watch and wait; who thought the time was well-nigh come when Christ, instead of handing the cup untasted, would drink with them of the fruit of the vine anew in his kingdom; and who felt themselves but prolonging the farewell meal till it touched and joined the banquet of reunion.

How curiously does our fallible thought blend itself with our infallible veneration, and the mistakes of our minds hang themselves for support to the truth of our love! But whatever these first disciples might dream about their Lord, in this there was no mistake ; they who had known him felt it was a grief to part, and those who had not were sure 'twould be a joy to meet.

With the continued absence of Jesus, new generations resorted to other thoughts. So dear a remembrance it was impossible to forego ; and as if it could not justify itself, some ingenious plea for it must be found. When the Christ proved not to be the prelude of a theocracy, it was treated as the mystic overthrow of hopeless sin and misery; it had not been the harbinger of the millennial morning light, but it had dispersed the cloud of wrath that hung like a night of thunder over the world. The church called men to this table, not with sentiments of memory, not with those of expectation, but with feelings of fear, to seize the sole shelter from unutterable horrors; or at least with gratitude, to bless the name of one who had delivered them from God. They were taught to look on Calvary, not as it sleeps in the sweet light of human history, but surrounded with a preternatural glare of struggling terrors and conquering mercies. They were led to suppose themselves distinctly contemplated in it, to feel the eye of the expiring

Jesus directed personally on them, and to listen to his cry
as the very crisis of their own fate.   And so when they
commemorate, as we do now, it is rather an event in
their history than in his ; less Messiah's sorrow than
their own joy ; and their voice is heard less in the
dirge of sympathy than in the song of triumph.
Nevertheless, let us join with them in such tones as
are in concord with our own ; for if the fancy be not,
as we think, right, the heart is not far wrong.   Jesus
was such a one as they suppose, only much better.
Had they really been in such a dreadful case, and
could he have seen them there, would he not
have cast an eye of mercy on them ; and, if that could
do them any good, have died to rescue, were it only *one?*
They do not mistake him then, except in supposing
that so dire a case could be needed to awaken that
self-sacrificing compassion continually moved by far
lighter woes.   So far as they read that mighty heart,
they do not read amiss; only with somewhat childish
fancy, matching the prowess of its pity against
imaginary monsters of alarm, instead of tracing its
tranquil and blessed work among the real grievances
and living sorrows of our humanity.

Thus far we join, in voice and soul, with all disciples
past and present.   If we could remember him in
person, it would be with the regrets of deep affection ;
if we were expecting him here, it would be with the
impatience of a glorious joy ; if we had been in the

view of his compassion, we should come hither with the gratitude of captives set free amid despair. But our real call hither comes from a higher source than any of these. It is not so much thankfulness for what he has done for us, as reverence for what he is in himself, that brings us to his feet, and keeps us there. And as indignation at wrong is degraded from justice into passion, when provoked by the reflection that the wrong is inflicted on others, so is the veneration for goodness lowered from the great faith of conscience to the common instinct of affection, when it requires a personal interest in the benefits it brings. We need not shut ourselves up in awful shadows to show how far the Galilean lustre shines. We need not pretend that he has "saved" us from any hopeless fate; we were always safe enough in the hands of God, nor could ever, in our utmost sin, desire removal from the healing shelter of his Will. Nor do we suppose that Jesus ever thought of us, or spread the generations yet to come before his compassionate view. It is natural indeed to fancy that what we see on looking back, he might behold in gazing forward; and, as in him were actually folded the germs of history, the mightiest growth of Providence, the blossoms of unfading hope, to imagine that he was conscious of it all, and beheld a visionary world clad in the graces of which he hid the seed within its fold. But it is otherwise with the sons of God; the view of Time is different from the view of Space; its intervals are not visible alike from either end; but the perspective, so clear as we gaze up into the past, was hid from those who looked down towards our present. Soft and prophetic as the light now seems that falls on Calvary, no ray of it was there to sustain the faintness of that hour; total eclipse blotted out the very sight of God; and if in the chill shudder any trust remained that he was there, it was the simple faith of a pure and heavenly soul that no film of evil can quench the everlasting orb. It is not till we strip that scene of the theatrical relations in which false theory and gaudy romance have placed it; not till we put ourselves back into that human point of view, which, like him that occupied it, may be despised and rejected of men at first, but ever proves the grandest after all, that we can apprehend its true simplicity. The peculiar glory of that sacrifice,—as of all sacrifice,—is this; that it was *not* for any clear end; that it lay quite out of the course of hope and promise, yet plainly in the line of the heavenly Will; that it was never planned, and yet was not avoided. To redeem a race by taking for awhile a mortal's sorrows were easy to any gentle heart; but to follow the beckonings of God into the gloom that seems to extinguish prophecy and to enwrap a world; to withhold no word of truth, and slight no thing that is holy, amid a thickening confusion and obscurity that look like the frown of heaven; to obey the Providence that appears to desert us all the while, and be obliged to cry " My God, my God, why hast thou forsaken me " ; this is the sublimest fidelity, supremely realized in him who is the author and perfecter of Faith.

LIVERPOOL, 1847.
LONDON, 1872.

Marriage Address.—I.

FRIENDS AND FELLOW-CHRISTIANS,

No more ancient or more natural sympathy is there than that which collects you here. You are come to watch a moment that is the germ of future years; and to think, with wondering heart, of the various lot and changeful discipline secretly folded within it. You are come to constitute a new home; to open another household dwelling for the Providence of our lives, and humbly to claim the children's blessing from their fathers' God. You are come to attend the young Christian woman passing from the lonely to the wedded life; and you esteem it good, in changing the human conditions of her lot, to enter with trust and prayer the presence of that Divine Protector, whose spirit gladdens our years at their commencement, nor ever quits them till they close. From all our hearts, —the young and unworn, the mellowed and mature, —there goes forth now a crowd of various sympathies, which draw close around this moment, to shield and bless it as they may. May the spirit of Jesus,—true creator of the sanctities of domestic life,—preside over our wishes of affection, and make them wise ; and the mercy of God, who hideth in his hands his children's days, crown them with his peace !

And you, my Christian brother and sister, on whom our united benediction falls, are standing on the verge of the most sacred of social relations ;—that wedded lot, which no one that knows how much may hang upon a human life can enter without awe ; nor any conscience wise in duty, without solemnity ;—yet no one, true to the cheerful faith and hope of Christ, without unutterable gladness. Of him you have already learned that the pure affections given to earth and home are not withdrawn from heaven and God ; and that the hearth where household sympathies vividly burn is the best altar for the fires of our diviner aspirations. You will walk within your house with that perfect heart of trust which, not content with securing mutual forbearance, will unconsciously prevent the very occasions of forbearance. You will together glow with grateful joy for the blessings of God's hand upon you ; together bend before him, when he " looketh from the cloud," and asks for tears ; together toil with lightened feet up the perpetual ascent of duty ; together find in your own peace a new pleading of pity for all who suffer, and be more ready even than before to succour them that have none to help them. Thus best does the Heavenly Father enable us to prepare for that last portion of our pilgrimage which we cannot pass together, but which one must be left to tread alone. Before the ample view of faith these solitary years shrink into a brief exile, not uncheered while it endures, and giving intenser transport to the embrace of the everlasting restoration. May this hope live within you both with such truth and power that, whatever be the allotments of a paternal Providence, the yoke of life may be easy and its appointed burden light.

1889.

Marriage Address.—II.

My Brother and Sister,

Meet and right it is that, in entering on the most sacred of human engagements, you have come into this public house of prayer, to place your new home in fellowship with the whole family in heaven and earth, and seek a benediction from the God of your fathers and the Providence of all our lives. For though there is no more private retreat than the abode of the wedded lot, there is not one more shielded and sheltered by a universal sympathy, which every good heart will meet with glad response. Nor is there any spot on earth that hides the secret of truer joys and deeper sorrows, and more naturally claims from our dim foresight the prayer for faithfulness and the surrender of trust. New dependence, new duties, intenser affections, bring with them a sudden affluence of experience which is apt to prove too much for light unbalanced spirits, and which needs, for its real blessedness, the restraining awe of conscience and the remembered presence of the eternal Holiness. The united life, no less than the solitary, is still within the compass and subject to the conditions of the Divine righteousness, and more than ever presses home the injunction and the aspiration to "be perfect as the Father in heaven is perfect."

And for those who have gained, as you have, the Christian insight into life, there is no conflict between the domestic and the heavenly pieties; the hearth where the household sympathies vividly burn is the best altar of our divinest aspirations. Poor and precarious indeed is the affection that plays with the mere sensitive surface of character, and looks no further than to please and be pleased, as if life were but a holiday; it soon entails a sickly fretfulness, and ends in a miserable partnership of self-seeking. But mutual love, chastened by mutual reverence, kept fresh by self-denials, and intent on the joint service of the highest ends, sets into permanent forms of dignity and sweetness that bespeak the inward peace of God.

With such perfect heart of trust in each other, and faith in your high calling to the life eternal, may you walk within your house through all your days; glowing with grateful joy for the blessings of God's hand upon you; bending together before Him when He looks from the cloud and asks your tears; together gathering, alike from joy and sorrow, a new pleading of Pity for all who suffer and have none to help. Such faithful fellowship will best prepare you for that last stage of the earthly pilgrimage which you cannot pass together, and which one must be left to tread alone. To the survivor whose mind has grown familiar with the large outlook of faith, those solitary years are but a brief exile, watched from above by a love so heavenly as to shed a soft light on the path to the everlasting restoration.

May the spirit of this hope live within you both with such kindling power that, whatever be the allotments of a paternal Providence, the yoke of life may be rendered easy, and its appointed burden light!

PRAYER.

O GOD most Holy, thou God of our Fathers! we remember how often thou didst gather their families in peace; and in all the sadness of their pilgrimage thy Providence was as the shadow of a great rock in a weary land. We now seek thy shelter and thy blessing, of whose faithfulness there is no end. Lo! the gates of another of our earthly homes are open unto thee; enter, O Lord, we beseech thee and dwell therein with all thy peace; adorn it with thy pure grace, to make it a place of accepted duty, and a shrine of strengthening prayer. Look down on the desires of the many hearts this day that are seeking for thy servants' house that only which is good; and make our benediction thine;

for though ours is not weak in love, thine alone is strong in power.

O Thou who readest thy children's future and concealed years, we trust their lot and lives to thee. Every joy thou bestowest, O make it by the gratefulness of their hearts a twofold gift. And in every trial which thou sendest, may a serene patience change the sorrow to a mercy that is divine. Then, having by love of whatever things are just and pure and true walked with thee here, may they and we be gathered in peace into that eternal home, where all the departed live with thee, and all that is lost shall be found again. AMEN.

1890.

CHRISTIAN FRIENDS,

In dedicating your infant by a Christian vow, you acknowledge that there is a sacredness in this young life; that it is not yours to deal with according to arbitrary pleasure and caprice, but only yours in trust, to be kept holy as the child of God, and passed into His likeness through the skill and discipline of life. In that fresh fair gift there is nothing spoiled as yet; and you would fain seize a blessing of heavenly grace, and wake in yourselves an eye of holy carefulness while still no shadow of evil falls.

To this end, you look round for help and protection less frail than the tenure of your individual lives and the pride of your personal resolves; you remember that as the child is enbosomed in the family, the family is environed by the flock of Christ, and all held together and led by the voice of the Good Shepherd; and you commend this little one to the shelter of his fold;— whether with strong life to go freely in and out for the full measure of days, or to be early carried, as the lamb in his arms, to everlasting pastures. Bringing your charge hither, you can be of restful heart ; never doubting that his Spirit in the Church below, or his benediction in the communion above, will embrace and cherish this emblem of his own kingdom.

Meanwhile, this trust for all the future will impart no languor, but rather a joyful fidelity, to the duties of the present. You will not be content with grafting the young branch into the true vine ; but will see that the sap of the living root flows in, that in due season the husbandman may not look in vain for the timely leaf and ripening fruit. Happily, there is needed for this end no labour but that of love,—no artifice but that of a pure simplicity ; for the soul most beloved of God and true to the image of Christ is but the deepest and most genuine form of our humanity,— the child's unconscious instincts of truth and reverence and pity guarded from corruption and growing into conscious obedience, and the open-eyed exercise of faith and hope and charity. There is not a different goodness for men below and for saints above ; but one Righteousness in the humblest home and the sublimest heaven ; so that the moral continuity of life is never broken ; and the simplest love of things pure and true, the willing service on the smallest scale, the daily self-denial, the sweetness and patience of domestic rule,—are the human beginnings of divinest ends, and make the lowliest already children of the Highest.

This it is that gives the sacredness to all our work and all our waiting; the daily duty, the daily cross, the trivial care, are for ever trying our spirits how they ring, and showing us in tune or in discord with the Holiest of all. In our homes, in the training of these little ones, the rarest faithfulness is the simplest too; it is but to stand out of God's light and give it way. If we never checked and disappointed the native wonder and uplifting of their hearts; if we never stifled the whispers of God stirring in our own souls and striving to speak out; if no self-will hindered the Holy Spirit seeking to make us the organs of a divine love and goodness;—then, all resistance thus withdrawn, the kingdom of heaven would find its realization in us and in our children by the power of spontaneous righteousness. The woe would then cease from the earth, against the hinderers of the little ones that believe in him.

And may the everlasting Father direct you in every effort of duty; sustain you in every care of life, and make all ready for the blessed season when the graces ripened by the gleams and tears of this earth shall be gathered and divinely stored.

1856.

Christening Address.—II.

CHRISTIAN FRIENDS,

To our human sense of dependence there must always be a certain sacredness about the *beginnings of things;* the little seed of mighty growths; the well-head of some widening stream of tendency. And if at the opening of a human life,—which is not only a *possibility of God's* but a *trust of ours,*—which calls us not only to watch and wait for *his* Providence but responsively to exercise our *own,*—we fold the gift to our heart with a tender awe, and ponder the future with silent wonder,—we do but yield to the double prompting of affection divine and human.

Unless there is some sin in being born, this child is given, a pure and unspoiled nature, into your hand; and would be taken into the arms of Christ, if he were here, and pronounced nearer to heaven than we. Not that there is any unmixed or angelic mind in the life of infancy,—any special grace,—or freedom from disturbing storms. But as yet no pledge has been given to evil, no advantage won by wrong; it is the open field, the unbroken force, the fresh heroic heart, the holy cause, before the conflict and the victory. All things are yet possible to God's spirit, where the artless susceptibility remains ; where conscience has learned no sadness and no cowardice ; and the inward pieties are damped and hid by no cloud of shame. The untainted humanity of childhood went to Christ as to its own,—the earthly opening to the heavenly fulfilment of God's Idea ; and his answering love seems to sanction the sigh of many a mother's heart, that infancy is gone so soon.

Yet, though in every human heart the strife of good and ill must come, and the child must pass the gate of the early Paradise into the thorny wilds, it is chiefly our own unfaithfulness, and the coldness of our higher trusts, that render this a fearful or unholy lot. The pure affections, the noble admirations, the clear truth, the gentle pieties, of the young soul, are ever ready to come forth and take their place of power above what is mean and selfish, if only they have the encouragement of sympathy and the fostering breath of a genial air around. If we always had a sweet and holy mind ourselves, if we went about every task with loving reverence, if it were evident that in commanding we did but obey and in guiding we only followed ; such a spirit would diffuse itself through the whole space around, as to hush the disorders of passion, and tempt forth spontaneously every promise and power of good.

The native force of the pure affections will be adequate to all demands, if only it have early practice upon the home problems, and learn courage at once from human sympathy and from communion with the eternal righteousness.

To parents touched with Christian humility and love, there is no more natural desire than that their children should be better than themselves. Yet how can dependent minds be lifted upwards but by the attraction of a higher spirit ? how pass beyond the level which is their measure day by day ? Must we indeed be content if they repeat our poor selves, and renew for the world the image which so disappoints our secret heart ? Blessed be God, there is no need thus to flatten the best inspiration of every worthy home. The child is formed, not merely by what the parents *have attained to be*, but also by what they *visibly aspire to be* ; not by the scale of their outward life alone, but by the measure of their inward worship,— by the tone of their love, the colour of their hope, the uplifted look of their whole being. This it is that reveals, more speakingly than any words, a higher than themselves, on whom they also depend, as the child on them ; that opens, though in shadowy visions, the steps of an ascending holiness which nowhere ends, from earth to heaven. In proportion as this secret reverence prompts the industry of the hand and the order of the house, mellows the tone of joy and calms the sorrows of experience, may the parents hope to be the organs of the Infinite Father; who will take their child whither they could not conduct him, and plant his feet where they have not learned to stand.

Thus may you dedicate this child to the service of God in the spirit of Christ; and may the heavenly Father, who has thus far been your comfort and your stay, still sustain you in every effort of duty and every care of life.

1861.

Funeral Address.—I.

———◆———

"IT is good for us to be here," said the disciples to Jesus on the mount of transfiguration, when, with prophets who had long been immortal, he spake of his own decease, which he should accomplish at Jerusalem. And good may it be for us, brethren, to be here, apart from the restlessness of our being, raised in thought above its ferment and its toil, and standing at one of those solemn points of our experience, where the living commune with the departed, and heaven and earth, the past, the present and the future meet and speak together of human duty and human destiny. It is good for us to be here, mortals in the presence of mortality; to learn again the ancient lesson, flung upon the ear by every funeral bell, and forgotten by the heart amid its crowd of cares, that all are treading a way by which there is no return,—a way from toil to repose, from the throb of pleasure or of pain to yon cold sleep, from friendship to a lonely grave, from the hopes and conflicts of probation to the place where the soul is sealed for judgment. If, brethren, we are a

wonder to ourselves that we have so much forgotten
these things; if we have often walked to the place
of tombs, and looked into the open grave, and been
compelled to take the measure of our days; if the
lost have often been the loved, and with the voice of
death affection too has mingled its tones of tenderness;
if childhood and age, the giddy and the wise, the holy
and the sinful, have all in turn fallen before us, and
read their separate lessons of pity, of awe, of grief,
and if still we have forgetfulness to deplore; if still
our chase after gain or pleasure is more eager than
becomes pilgrims travelling on a path like ours; if
still our spirits are unduly elated by success, tossed
by anxiety, and sunk in woes so brief as ours; if still
the quietude and sobriety of a mortal expectation has
not settled upon our hearts; then it is good for us
again to enter into this house while the mourners'
tears are flowing, and the mourners' prayers ascend.
While upon the mount Jesus was learning the story
of his decease, below him far rolled the murmurs of
human population; and while here, for a few moments,
we retire from the movement of life's procession, to
look on the fixedness of life's end, we may become
elevated spectators of the scene from which we have
retired; and to know how soon we shall drop from the
number of its actors, to realize the silence which must
soon still our every energy, may cool the fever of our
passion, lighten the brow of care, abate the intensity

of worldly pursuit, and render serener and more sedate the spirit both of grief and joy.

But is this all, my friends, that this hour can teach of life? Is its only lesson to be that all is transient, all fragile; that we must diminish our interest in life by reason of the shortness of its span, that we must not pursue earnestly because pursuit plunges into vacancy; that we must not labour strenuously because its rewards all drop from the hand in the paroxysm of death; that we must not be glad without measure because joy is preparing to be quenched; that we must not love with the soul's depth and fervour because there is close at hand a severing of ties, a woe of bereavement, a solitude of pilgrimage? Are we to spread the pall over life, and make it one long procession to the tomb? No, brethren, there are in death far more and better things than these; it has a promise by which it gilds life's scenes more than it beclouds them, inspires more than it depresses them, and restores a hundredfold the fervour of hope which its first impression may abate. When Jesus was told of his decease, it was by the vision and voice of immortals; and, brethren, an immortal too it is, who here, though dead, yet speaketh to us of our destiny. It is indeed but the shell of life which remains with us; but while we take our farewell of this poor dust, it shall be to us a reminiscence of the habitant that has fled, that has passed the dread secret, that has gone to the land where are the abodes of the happy pious, where the generations of the earth now live together, where the energies of the mind are nobler, and its affections deeper, and its conscience more quickened to duty, and its knowledge vaster, and its perspective wider, and its employments more beneficent, and its penitence more purifying, and its companion Jesus, and its illumination God. Thus, brethren, if we be at this moment in contact with death, we are also on the confines of immortality; if we be in sorrow, the sorrow imparts to our hopes a relish, a beauty, before unfelt; makes us love these hopes more; it urges us to take them into companionship and yield them our confidence; it tempts us to try their power, and drink their interior spirit, and stir ourselves up to the inspiration of their guidance. How many a stricken mourner has gone in utter and broken anguish to the grave to weep there; and the tears have softened the heart for prayer; and the prayer has kindled up the invisible into life; and the invisible is full of peace and motive and power; and its light is fairer for being shed upon the margin of darkness; and the affections are re-animated with its glow, and he that came to pay his tribute to mortality stands over the elements of dissolution, a conscious immortal; he that was haunted by phantoms of death becomes surrounded by images of life; he that in his sadness had taken his measure of human existence, and been full of trouble at its briefness, sees it spread out a boundless career, and lost amid the passes of a glorious distance.

From Jesus the heavenly messengers departed ; the bright cloud floated by ; he and his disciples descended from the mount ; they mingled again with the homes of their country and the toils of life ; but the blissful remembrance of their interview remained, the hope was thenceforth awake, and its spirit of serenity and power upon them. Thus be it ours, knowing the mighty destiny which is in reserve, to carry its spirit hence into the humbler vale of our being, to feel its inspiration of duty, to reflect its lustre in our affections, to wield its power in every struggle with evil, to inscribe its peace in our inmost hearts, for there are times when more than earthly peace is needed. In this spirit may we wait to join the blessed, that are ever without fault before the throne.

1833.

———••———

' But thanks be to God who hath given us the victory through our Lord Jesus Christ.'

So ends, as with a burst of triumph, the Apostle's glorious remonstrance with mortal grief and fear. And such is the chorus of Christian joy into which, when taken up by the voices of faith, the tolling bell of natural sorrow rises and is lost. But are we called to join in that high strain over our dear brother now departed, the daily associate of our circle, the promised heir of so many noble aims and intellectual gifts; and does the seal of final silence lie upon those lips which were open only for the true and right; and is the light of those patient looks quenched so soon ? Then indeed it needs some firmness of faith, some elevation above the darkness of the hour, to attune this moment to any words of " thanks" and "victory." Yet even here, amid the very tears and prayers of bereavement, they meet our sadness, though they sound of joy. The deeper affections of our nature, though we call them by different names, are never far asunder; it is but a superficial sorrow that can bear no light, and but an empty joy that shrinks from the pathetic shade of life. So let us yield ourselves to the Apostle's invitation, and take up his mood. Here, in presence of these poor remains, say utterly in soul 'This mortal shall put on immortality'; here, in sight of that last slumber, inwardly repeat, 'We shall not sleep'; here, with eye fixed on these memorials of the earthly, rest on the thought, 'We shall also bear the image of the heavenly';—only make an open way of trust and love for these blessed lights to fling themselves into the heart of all the shadows; and, as the finite clouds disperse and the infinite calm looks through, not even the lonely and the weary will refuse the song, 'Thanks be to God that giveth us the victory.'

The surprises of death are ever new. We have seen the summons come at every hour; in the fresh morning taking by the hand the little child; abridging for manhood the noon-day heats; calling the aged to his evening rest. Yet never do we hear the words, 'Behold, the bridegroom cometh,' but it strikes upon the ear as a midnight cry; and the dread wonder never wears away. Blessed be the tender mercies of our God that they also are ever new, and freely flow, with tide that never ebbs, into the windings and recesses of the inmost grief. Till we kneel and cry in our Gethsemane, we know not what angels there are to strengthen us ; or how the experience of human anguish may be the birth of a divine repose. Bitter as it is to say farewell to the companions of our way, who can deny that Death transfigures life with a tender glory, and establishes such communion between *there* and *here* as to give a sacredness to the one, and take the strangeness from the other ? Who would accept the irrevocable Past crowded with retiring shadows, without the opening Future, ever peopling with approaching forms of light ? As friend after friend is taken from our side we are the less detained by the world we cannot keep, and gain the clearer view of that to which we tend. The pathway of ascent to the everlasting hills is stripped of its desolation by the footprints of our forerunners, who stand already at the summit, where our life is hid with Christ in God.

Here, as we wave the last adieu, and let the spirit pass to God who gave it, we cannot but compare the going thither and the staying here. And solemnly as we may think of the approaching night in which no man can work, with far deeper anxiety and prayer must we remember the daylight hours that yet remain. Our departure, be it near or far, is a something that happens *to us ;* while our time of tarrying is a trust that must be administered *by us.* The one is in the safest hands,—the providential care of God,—and can in no wise fail of being best ; the other, in the feeblest and most doubtful,—our own poor Will,—and cannot for a moment sleep secure. To the Christian it must always be a more fearful thing to live than to die, seeing that he may live all wrong, but cannot die amiss; that the one may be guilty, the other only grievous. Ah no! it is not the close, it is the continuance of opportunity, that fills the disciple's heart with true solicitude; and the prayer of his noblest spirit will be, not " Lord, support me when I go," but rather " Lord, help me while I stay." The dead have no doubts to bear, no weaknesses to fear, no temptations to confront; for them there are no tears of shame, unless for ills which they indeed may be in a position *to see*, but which we are in the place *to do*. While we turn to their image with the eye of reverential sorrow, they from their securer station may gaze on us with looks of saintly hope, dashed however with no faint shadows of a holy fear. Touched by that glance, may we live in a sacred watchfulness; knowing that we must work to-day and to-morrow, and not till the third day shall we be perfected.

1858.

Funeral Address.—III.

PSALM LXXXVIII. (*with omissions*).

O Lord God of my salvation, I cry day and night before thee; let my prayer come before thee; incline thine ear unto my cry; for my soul is full of trouble, and my life draweth nigh unto the grave. I am as one that hath no strength; thou hast laid me in darkness and the deeps, and overwhelmed me with all thy waves. Thou hast put away my friends far from me; mine eye mourneth by reason of affliction.

O Lord, I stretch out my hands unto thee. Wilt thou show wonders to the dead? Shall thy loving kindness be declared in the grave, or thy faithfulness in destruction? Shall thy wonders be known in the dark, and thy righteousness in the land of forgetfulness?

So unto thee have I cried, and in the morning my prayer is before thee; why hidest thou thy face from me? Thy sorrows come about me daily like water; they compass me round. Lover and friend thou puttest far from me, and mine acquaintance into darkness.

Or PSALM XXXIX.

Or PSALM XC. (*with omissions*).

Lord, thou hast been our dwelling place in all generations. Before the mountains were brought forth, or ever thou hadst formed the earth and the world, even from everlasting to everlasting thou art God.

Thou turnest frail man to dust, and sayest, Return, ye children of men. For a thousand years in thy sight are as yesterday when it is past, and as a watch in the night. Thou carryest them away as with a flood ; they are as a sleep ; as grass which in the morning groweth. In the morning it flowereth and groweth up ; in the evening it is cut down and withered.

Thou settest our iniquities before thee ; our hidden sins in the light of thy countenance. All our days vanish away ; we spend our years as a tale that is told. The days of our years are three score years and ten ; and if, by reason of strength, they be four score years, yet is their pride labour and sorrow ; for it is soon cut off, and we fly away. So teach us to number our days, that we may apply our hearts unto wisdom.

Return, O Lord ; how long ? O satisfy us early with thy mercy, that we may rejoice and be glad all our days. Make us glad according to the days wherein thou hast afflicted us ; the years in which we have seen evil.

Let thy work appear unto thy servants, and thy glory unto their children. And let the beauty of the Lord our God be upon us; and establish thou the work of our hands upon us; yea, the work of our hands, establish thou it.

JOHN XIV. (*parts*).

Let not your heart be troubled; ye believe in God; believe also in me. In my Father's house are many mansions; if it were not so I would have told you. I go to prepare a place for you; and if I go to prepare a place for you, I will come again, and receive you unto myself; that where I am, there ye may be also.

If ye love me, keep my commandments; and I will pray the Father, and he shall give you another Comforter, that he may abide with you for ever; even the spirit of truth, whom the world cannot receive, because it seeth him not, neither knoweth him; but ye know him; for he dwelleth with you, and shall be in you. I will not leave you comfortless; I will come to you. Yet a little while, and the world seeth me no more; but ye see me; because I live ye shall live also.

These things have I spoken unto you, being yet present with you. But the Comforter,—the Holy Spirit, whom the Father will send in my name, he shall teach you all things, and bring all things to your remembrance, whatsoever I have said unto you.

Peace I leave with you, my peace I give unto you

not as the world giveth give I unto you.   Let not your
heart be troubled, neither let it be afraid.

These ancient tones speak to us still, and are as
sweet and sad as if flung from the voices of to-day;
for the chords of the human heart are stretched as they
have ever been ; and when they are struck by the hand
of death the same music trembles forth again.   The
act of the living in taking leave of their dead can never
cease to be sacred and pathetic, till man sh all lose the
thought and love that make him Man ; and as we
engage in it here, as we shut up, "like a tale that is
told," the life which can now speak its story only
through our lips, we stand at one of the sublimer
points of our experience.   Fall where it may, the
mortal stroke shows us how much may be wrapped in
each single life.   It is not only the collapse of manhood
in its full strength that, in the wreck it makes, reveals
how we all hang together.   No little child can be laid
upon the bier without rending the fibres of an
immeasurable love, and leaving them to bleed at every
pore.   No aged friend can be taken from our midst
without a thousand inroads on customs long and dear,
and a fading of some warm colours from the glory of
the Past.   And who can forget that as in life we are close-
knit together, so in death we are not long divided? that
already every name is on the roll-call of God, and, one

by one, we must soon answer Yea, Lord, here I am, and go? And though it is ever hid from us who shall be next, yet ere many days have run some one of us, it may be you, it may be I, will take that silent place, and not hear the solemn words or the funeral bell, or see the tears of faithful friends, but pass through the shadows into the great company of the departed.

To look lightly on that mysterious transition is to be incapable of thought. To haunt it with terrors is an illusion of distrust or an augury of sin. To meet it with triumph is the inflation of presumption. To approach it with perfect faith and serene hope, owning the darkness which calls for trust, expecting the light which love and reverence predict, is the true temper of the clear and pious soul. Once gain assurance, through peace of conscience and sweetness of affection, that you are in sympathy and communion with the divine Righteousness, and you will believe that union eternal; where God loves once, he loves for ever. Clouds there may be that hide that future from an eye so dim as ours; but this at least we know, that the pure conscience, the high aspiring, and the will of sacrifice are fit for any world, and cannot miss their home in the universe of God. In this simple modesty of faith, and with no troubled hearts, let us part with each righteous forerunner that leaves our sight. The long voyage is over; the storms are past; the eye is no longer strained upon the stars above or the shifting

lights below ; the anchor is dropped in the quiet
haven.   There let us leave him in perfect peace.
What better land may encircle those calm waters, what
fairer fields may clothe, what softer skies may over-
arch its everlasting hills, what city of the blest may
crown its heights, it is not ours to tell.   But there too
is the colony of God ; and where all things best are
possible, there is neither shape nor hue, neither good
nor beauty, that is too divine to be.   Whatever is
perfect, God will provide.

What then remains for us, thus committing the
body to the earth, and the spirit unto God who gave
it ?   To return to our place in the present, and infuse
into it a fresh sacredness from mortal memories and
immortal hopes.   The last breath of each completed
life is a new commission to the incomplete that are yet
upon the field ; bids them pick up the dropped arms
of Christian conflict ; and sends them into higher,
larger, and later service.   Be it ours to accept the sad,
yet glorious promotion ; to take up all our possibilities
of duty and shrink from no breadth of obligation that
is according to the measure of a man ; to use our
visions of the perfect world in mending one that is
imperfect ; to heal every wound, and abate every
grievous ill in the sphere committed to our care, till
it is ready to be offered as a province of the kingdom
of heaven.   In the love and service to which God
invites there is no fear but that of sin.   The ever-

lasting mercy folds us round. Be we simply faithful to the best we know, our sacrifice will be divinely owned; and it will be well with us in every life and every transition that may await us.

[*At the Grave.*]

Man that is born of a woman is of few days and full of trouble; he cometh up, and is cut down like a flower; he fleeth as it were a shadow, and continueth not.

In the midst of life we are in death; of whom may we seek succour but of thee, O Lord, who hast pity on our sorrows and art grieved in our sins?

O Lord God most holy, O holy and most merciful Father, waken us by the visitation of thy good Spirit, and save us from sinking into spiritual death.

Thou knowest, Lord, the secrets of our hearts; shut not thy merciful ear to our prayer; and spare us, O Lord most holy, till we are fit, through the repentance of our hearts and the discipline of thy mercy, to join our sainted forerunners, and be with them who are without fault before the throne.

To God pertain the issues of life and death; it is the Lord,—let him do what seemeth good in his own eyes; his Will be done on earth as it is in heaven.

Now we commit the body to the earth, and the spirit unto God who gave it.

I heard a voice from heaven, saying unto me, Write;

from henceforth blessed are the dead that die in the Lord; even so, saith the Spirit, for they rest from their labours, and their works do follow them.

Hear our prayer, O Lord, and let our cry come up unto thee. Often do thy clouds gather around us, and thou coverest us with thy storm. With much mercy look on the sadness of thy servants; and though thou makest our strength to decay, yet let thy hand of grace be with us, and thy promise comfort us. O eternal God, with whom do live the spirits of them that depart hence in the Lord, after thou hast led them through the troubles and temptations of this world, and lodged them in the bosom of thy everlasting peace; teach us, while here, to imitate their lives, so far as they have been well-pleasing unto thee, and to unite ourselves unto the same service of thee, by a pure faith, a holy hope, and a never-ceasing charity. And when our summons shall come, O let thy mercy support us, and thy spirit guide us. Lead us through the valley of our death safely, that we may pass it patiently and with a perfect resignation; unto the end rejoicing in thee, in the hope of thy mercy, in the refreshment of thy spirit, and the expectation of thy glory.

And now may the Lord bless us and keep us; may he be gracious unto us, and give us peace, both now and evermore. AMEN.

1869.

Funeral Prayer.

[In the house.]

O FATHER everlasting, in whose hands our times are, Thou art our refuge in every lonely and troubled hour ! Source of light eternal, we look to thee; and though thy cloud is round about us, and its shadow covers us, yet we know that thy mercy is undimmed, and with perfect trust we wait for the brightness of thy love, as they whose eyes watch for the morning. We own thee as the only Lord of life and death ; do with us as thou wilt; call us to our work, or to our rest; bid us take our burden, or lay it down; we murmur not, O Lord; only abide with us by night and day, and be our strength to do and bear thy perfect Will.

Thou hast sent among us thy sad messenger, O our God, and taken from us the dear companion of our way, with whom we took sweet counsel, and divided every duty and every joy. In the sorrow of our hearts we remember the long years gone by, and bless thee for the sacred ties that are severed for awhile, for the faithful love, the gentle patience, the single eye to whatever things are pure and good, which made his life fruitful in hidden blessings. Thou hast withdrawn them into thy mystic shadows; thy will be done. Only, take not *all* away; by the image in our souls leave us whatever has been sweet and true and sacred in the presence which here we shall know no more; that it may yet render us more ripe for the everlasting restoration.

O God, thou helper of all our need! Look upon this home with thy tender mercy. Sustain and comfort every mourning heart. In thy keeping are the living and the dead; and all are safe, till thou bring them to thine eternal light. Give us strength to return to the quiet duties of our place. With chastened desires, with better aspirations, with truer diligence, with less trust in ourselves and more rest on thee, may we dedicate ourselves anew to the service of thy will; that, in the faith and spirit of him who was made perfect through suffering, each may be ready to say, whenever the hour shall strike, 'Father, I have finished the work which thou gavest me to do.' AMEN.

1884.

ADDRESSES

DELIVERED AT

VALEDICTORY SERVICES

ON OCCASION OF

STUDENTS LEAVING

MANCHESTER NEW COLLEGE

TO ENTER THE MINISTRY.

Valedictory Address.—I.

WOULD that I could leave behind me any last thought that could help you a little way up the height on which I fain would see you stand. What can it be but some word of sympathy on the student's struggle to harmonize his intellectual and his spiritual life?

You mingle with associates in study who are preparing themselves for other fields of personal labour and human service,—medical, legal, scholastic; you measure yourselves with these in the class-room and the examination hall; and naturally use the same standards and form the same appreciations; and acquire the habit of working from the same motives. In boyhood, and so long as education is rather an *end* than a *means* this is innocent. *Culture* then is the admitted aim.

But when your heart has caught sight of an ulterior object, and *that* the furthering of the Christian life and the work of an evangelist, the studies, still as indispensable to you as to your associates, stand in quite a different relation to the end which prescribes them.

What the surgeon, the lawyer, the scientific teacher learns, constitutes the very substance of his profession, the rules of his skill; and only in virtue of its contents is he *what he is.* His occupation is *an Art;* and the perfection of the art lies in the perfection of the knowledge and of its application.

It is otherwise with you; and no more fatal blight could fall upon you than to conceive of your future engagement as an Art. If your mind were a magazine of all that scholars know, and the sciences report, and philosophy thinks, you might still be without the word of converting power, and have no access to the callous heart and the impure will.

Nay more; if you were the administrator of some divinely ordained rite, *i.e.* of some magical medicine for human ill, you might indeed carry healing *to a disease,* but not any *rescue from sin.* And if you conveyed some divinely dictated gospel, you might inform a misinformed understanding, but not on that account change the direction of the affections and the will. And in both cases you would be the mere dead medium for *transmitting a foreign gift;* nothing would depend on *what you are,* everything on *what you have.* Hence the sacramental doctrine that the *divine efficacy* is in no way intercepted by the unbelief or corruption of the priest, and that true doctrine will not lose its promise of salvation to the belief though received from a bad man.

You have no such external media on which to rely, and which make it a non-essential matter what you inwardly are. Religion, as we receive it from Christ, is an *immediate relation of spirit to spirit;* with movement now from God's spirit to ours; now from ours to God; and now from one human spirit to another. **And** there is *no passage of it,* from spirit to spirit, through heterogeneous conductors, *material* or *logical.*

Hence, both the **difficulty** and the simplicity, of the life to which you are giving yourselves;—*its difficulty,* because it is not *an office,* for which you can come to us and say, 'Show us the way; teach us to handle the tools; give us the skill'; because you must go upon your healing errand without any *Materia Medica* to work with and then watch for the desired cure;—*its simplicity,* because it is *a call,* asking for nothing but pure self-surrender and self-expression; carrying you indeed to others by unspeakable attraction, not however with any doctoring or indoctrinating contrivance, but with intuitive entrance into their nature, and sympathetic fellowship with them, only from a deeper interior of experience and a soul of larger resources.

The shrinking of unregenerate men from this sublime immediate relation has led to the exaggerated estimate of "*the means of grace*" which are supposed to be the peculiar charge of the ministers of religion, and to the disavowing of much *real* "*grace*" which comes without these "means." To many a soul there is revealed some gleam of the life of God with us in objects and events, in times and places, in common duties and relations, not hitherto consecrated by us; and whoever fixes its flash for us in thought and speech, or in a silent picture, or in music without words, or in the mere look and manner of some simple act, is in holier orders than any Bishop or Presbytery ever conferred. Be he poet, or artist, or guileless organ of love and conscience, he is possessed by the secret sanctity of things, and opens the divine meaning with which they are charged. To Christ, this Divine meaning in the world was absolutely universal; it broke forth from every scene and incident that struck upon his attention; the field-flower and the bird of the air; the sea-beach and the mountain top; the village home and the lonely desert; the blind by the wayside and the scribe that boasted of his vision; the widow self-forgetful of her poverty, and the youth sorrowful amid his wealth; the sinful woman in her tears, and the sanctimonious Pharisee with his frown; the priest's hypocrisy, the child's innocency, the Samaritan's mercy; the Hosannas of the people, the betrayal in Gethsemane, the tragedy of Calvary;—all fell into place before him, as the lights and shadows of a Divine drama, every feature of which, though it be in the very anguish of love, does but bring him nearer to the Father.

This conscious union with God, as it is the essence
of Christ's power, has to be reproduced in every one
who conveys that power to other souls, or sustains
it in them. It was *his* inspiration; and it must be
yours; not by reciting it about him, but by the
personal possession of its life. In our time also, be
assured, the true minister has *to be himself a fresh
fountain of Religion.* If he only tries what he can
get from the Father's well, he will find that he " has
nothing to draw with, and the well is deep "; he must
" be himself a well of living water, springing up unto
everlasting life."

You think perhaps that such Christ-like spirit is
rather given than gained, and is not at your own
command. Not, certainly, *unless* it be given; but *if*
it be given (as it assuredly is), and in so far as it is
given, it is yours to surrender to it, or to slight it and
let it pass. A pious soul will stand upon the listen,
will pause upon every suggestion of reverence; will leave
spaces from which hindrances are kept away; will
not allow the times for meditation and prayer to be
crowded out, or inserted between quite uncongenial
engagements; and will keep up a close communion with
the great and quickening spirits of the Past that have
widened the horizon of sacredness by their " vision
and faculty divine."

Is there then no religious function for all that you
learn during these College years? No *positive or*

creative function, I am willing to allow. But a *regulative* function, in the absence of which a simple effusion of your personal devout affections must run wild and incur the risk of finding no response, I no less eagerly affirm. The spiritual message has to shape itself into forms of thought, and will be intercepted on its passage from soul to soul, if embodied in intellectual conceptions that are not common to both; if one thinks to be true what the other knows to be false, the devout appeal will go forth, but will not go home. Hence, a certain harmony of modes of thought between the speaker and the hearer is an indispensable condition of spiritual influence; and since that harmony has no security but in partnership of *Truth*, we cannot spare any attainable knowledge, if we would protect the messenger of God from delivering his true message beneath a mask of folly. But the whole object is *to prevent* the human imperfection of the medium from spoiling the Divine power of the Spirit.

At first view, the enthusiastic student might see something depreciating in the place which is thus assigned to the intellectual engagements of his college years. If they are not, like those of the other professions, the implements and resources of the end he has in prospect; if their relation to that end is only that of a *restraint* upon going amiss; are they not reduced to mere negative values? and how are we to expect, from such an estimate, the zeal of the scholar, or the prolonged and intense mental efforts of the mathematician or philosopher? Shall I surprise you if I reply, The subjects which I seem to displace from their just honour, I really lift, by the very act of which you complain, into their true dignity? In denying them to be the means subservient to an ulterior Art, I affirm them to be an *end in themselves;* and to be treated as *good on their own account* is a nobler homage to them than to be pursued as useful for something else. If the motives which sustain the intellectual industry of the medical and the law student are not similarly present to *you,* all the more are you at liberty to rise above all interested ambitions, and surrender yourselves to the pure love of knowledge, the sacred thirst for truth, and beauty, and spiritual good, wherever found.

This I seriously take to be your distinctive privilege; you are free, as hardly any others are, from the temptations of competitive intellect and the vain egoism of culture; and invited, on the very gate of entrance upon your studies, to pursue them, not for what they *give,* but for what they *are,* and achieve in them, not what your task-work requires, but whatever a generous enthusiasm may prompt you to undertake, and a sustained diligence enable you to accomplish.

What more then can you wisely ask from heaven

than this ; a life, surrendered on the intellectual side, to the pure attraction of all light ; and, on the spiritual, to the service of all that is lovely, and right, and holy, and a living communion with the Perfect and ever-lasting Love ? Such is your call; remember it with joy and thanks ; and hold to it with simplicity and faithfulness.

Valedictory Address.—II.

———•••———

IT may seem to be no happy duty which devolves upon
me at this season, to stand up year by year, and simply
say that saddest of human words,—"Farewell." But
the regrets of life are in closest contact with its hopes;
and if it is appointed to the old to be for ever taking
leave of something they have loved in the past, it is
their privilege to prepare the elements of a better
future, and to enter into the joy of those who will
serve and gladden it. Though you set me here in a
retrospective attitude, and bid me face the shadows and
the echoes of bygone years, you will not chain me by
the head, like the prisoners in Plato's cave, that I may
not turn round to catch the abiding lights and living
tones of which they are the semblance.

For nearly seven years have we kept step together
on the track of life; and, ere we part, it is but natural
to pause and think whence and whither we have come.
May we not say it has been a continual ascent? Have
we not, like a group of travellers, reached by steady
toil the mountain ridge, whence our several paths

diverge, each down its lonely valley, excepting that of
our guides who must return the way they came ?
Looking forth from the height, we can clearly see the
little station which we left together. But as the eye
sweeps elsewhere round the horizon, who can notice
without awe the countless radii of possibility that join
it with his feet ? Is he to pass by those bright
villages, sheltered by stately woods and standing
sentinel over sunny fields ? or, through those mountain
gorges, black with the brooding thunder or boiling with
the eddying clouds ? or, over yon hardy moorlands,
tearful with slanting rain, yet touched with floods of
gold ? We cannot tell. We only know that all belongs
to the beauty and the glory of the world ; and the
experience of all is available for the sweetness or the
strength of human life.

The change of mental station which is effected by
the period now closed is unique in life. Nothing
analogous to the emergence of the Schoolboy into the
Scholar can ever happen to you again. You may learn
new languages ; may think new thoughts ; may explore
new veins of natural law or human literature ; but no
addition to the materials of knowledge or to the skill
in using them can compare with the very birth of
thought itself ; no fresh evidence on the great
problems of existence, with the first discovery of what
those problems are ; no growth even of religious
character, with that transforming contact of God's

living spirit with ours which thrills the conscience wakening to its responsibilities. I protest to you, I look with growing reverence upon a manhood worthily assumed by a mind of developed powers, and render to it a more willing homage than to grey hairs and length of days. To pass from the boy's loaded memory and tabulated knowledge to the subtle sense of literary beauty and the large scenery of historical imagination ; to exchange the stock heroes of the school theme for those real intimates who, in the poetry, the literature, the philosophy of a distant age have struck upon the cords of living sympathy ; to step forth from the cabinet universe of the early fancy into the open infinitudes of space and change ; to learn to be alone, and find, with the " companions of solitude," friendship which can never deceive nor perish ; to be transferred from the unquestioning trusts of earliest years to deep-rooted and firm-grasping conviction ; to quit the careless joy of childhood, and take upon the heart the burden of human guilt and sorrow, and vow to it the service of a life-long Pity ;—this is little else than to " be born again " ; and this has for ever spoiled you for the old instinctive life in which so many remain mere overgrown children to the end ; and dedicated you irrevocably to the higher necessity of consciously working with God.

So vast and various a change cannot be hurried in its accomplishment ; and the fulness of its contents

seems to stretch the years devoted to it.   Yet, long as
they appear while they run on, you find, now that you
look back upon them, that they do but bring you to the
vestibule of the august temple of religious thought;
whence only gleams can be caught of lofty aisles and
cloistered   walks   not   measured   yet,   of   ancient
monuments still unexplored, and stray tones be heard
of prayer and hymn in some sweet but unknown
tongue.   All that we could do has been to place you
face to face with possibilities of knowledge, and leave
you on the threshold of divine truth, with the spacious
perspective before you in which it lies.   Ere the view
is forgotten, while it is clear in your eye, and is still
humbling your individuality in the presence of what so
far transcends it, resolve to enter in and penetrate more
deeply than hitherto into the sanctuary which you have
approached.   The chief benefit of an ample culture is
perhaps to be found in the large ideal space which it
spreads around our life, drawing out your affections on
various lines   unknown to others,   mingling your
sympathy and admiration with the distant and the past,
and saving you from being distracted by the noise and
crushed by pressure of the hour.   You will religiously
guard this privilege of calmness and of breadth; will
not suffer yourselves to be snatched away by the rush
of the present, and deafened by its momentary cries;
but will qualify even your compassion for its ills, your
labour for its good, and your welcome to its truths, by a

secret sense of wider relations in which it lies. You will show how false is the common prejudice, that the scholar among men cannot be the prophet of the living God ; how it is the attribute and glory of both to be lifted out of the low plane of the immediate hour, and rise to a diviner point whence it is possible to look fore and aft, and fetch in thence visions of warning or of solace to touch the torpor or sweeten the sorrows of to-day ; and how the sympathies of thought, whether they wind downwards from the contemplated Past, or the imaginary Future do but swell the purifying stream as it flows through the Present, and mellow the fields to a richer fertility. It is the Omniscient whose name and nature is Love ; and it would be strange indeed if they who are kindled with some few rays of his intellectual light were not also nearer to him in tenderness, in patience, in constancy of beneficent activity. And so, in bidding you adieu, it is my quiet hope that, whatever may be your work, you will not find its force enfeebled or its spirit lowered, by the memory of your years with us.

1875.

Valedictory Address.—III.

THIS evening closes a long companionship, and extorts from us the *"Farewell"* which is always itself a sigh, and should not die away except in thought and prayer. Of the feelings which fill this hour, I do not forget that the hopes belong chiefly to you, and the regrets to us. We have sailed the seas together till we have brought you to a point of new departure; and now, while we retrace our way, like the pilot returning home, you push on into fresh latitudes, and spread your sails for more adventurous winds. As we rest upon our oars to wave "Adieu" and watch the receding ship, we well know over what joyous waves it bounds in its first liberty, how bright the widened horizon looks, and in what sweet haze of wonder lie the lands beyond of unexplored life and possible achievement. The mature it is often said, and still more the old, forget that they have been young, and are apt to check the fervours which they have outlived, and damp the spirits they no longer share. But short indeed must be the memory of their heart, if they can ever witness without sympathy the crisis of moral experience which we mark to-night; when the preparation for living is over, and the reality begins; when the soul moves out into unsheltered responsibility; when the Pity and indignation long stirred by the thought of human ills are free for the conflict with them; when the moral enthusiasm which has gathered strength with waiting years is flung at length into its sphere of opportunity. The hour which you have reached is one which can never be repeated. From the seat of quiet spectator you are flung among the actors of the great human drama; and the very next scene will put you to the test, whether its spirit has true hold of you, and you are equal to its high demands. It is a grave, yet an inspiring change; *grave*, because it will find out your weaknesses, and mark every missed opportunity with a shadow of unavailing regret; *inspiring*, because asking nothing from you but what you can surely give,—the free surrender of *yourselves*, the life of pure simplicity, the word of truth to your own best thought, the deed most natural to a considerate and tender heart. If you had any part to play, we could never have taught you to assume it. To be what you are, to say what you think, to teach what you know, to do what you most revere, and make no peace with what you inwardly abhor,—this is the sacrifice, neither impossible nor ignoble, which you descend into the world to offer to the Lord of conscience and the Searcher of hearts. Only in speaking the word which is most deeply your own, will you utter that which is not your own, but the Father's who sends you ; only in acting from the inmost shrine of your own spirit, will you do *His* work. Resigning our poor guidance, we commit you to that higher care of His which is never withheld from those who trustfully seek communion with Him.

1877.

Valedictory Address.—IV.

In the ritual of human life, it has often been observed,
the gladdest incident is, with one exception, also
the most pathetic; and it is amid all the brightness of the wedding that tears will force their way
from some of their deepest springs. It is no idle
fancy to say that, in our present gathering, many of the
same elements mingle and make the interest of this
hour; the separation from one set of precious ties and
knitting of others more enduring; the passage from
guarded and guided years to those of full exposure and
completed trust; the struggle of the heart between its
retrospective tenderness and its **transporting** hopes, and
its inward prayer that it **may** be true to both; and, in
the distribution of this mixed experience, the fall of
the shadows **chiefly** on those who stay, and of the
brilliant lights on those **who go.** It is equally natural
that we should be sorry to lose you, and that you
should be glad to leave **us**; and freely as we give you
your · joy will you patiently bear with our regrets.
Representing as I do the Alma Mater that has so long

cared for you, I may be pardoned something of a mother's weakness in parting with her sons.

As we here take counsel together for the last time and look back over our academic relation, we cannot but ask what chiefly it is that you will carry away with you as the fruit of all these years ? Nothing half so good, I delight to own, as that which you brought with you, which we did not give you, and which it is our purest satisfaction that we have not worn out or taken away, viz., your vow of self-devotion to the service of God and the conflict with human sin and sorrow. This inward call, this yearning of the heart to become the organ of Divine truth and pity to the world, is the supreme preparation for the work of an evangelist; the prerequisite at first, the crowning essential at last; as much above all that we could impart to you, as heavenly insight is above earthly skill. Under the guidance of such a sacred aspiration you came to us, and with it still unexhausted, nay intensified, I believe, you leave us. In a " school of prophets," like ours, it is not always easy to keep the human teaching and the divine in living harmony and balanced power; through various weakness the schooling too often stifles the prophetic spirit; or the prophetic spirit creates impatience at the schooling. And there are occasions when the Teacher, in an agony of disappointment, has to ask himself, " What have I done with this poor youth, that, as his intellect grows, his soul is withering? What canker have I planted, that the tender tints are gone, and the foliage of reverence drops, and there remain only dry and ashy fruits?" But here there is no place for such sad words. You, at least, have not been with us seeking mere culture and learning under the plea of religion. You have not fallen from your first intent, or ever let its fire die within you; and in bearing it with you, to consume the difficulties, and animate you under the sacrifices of your life, you take what you brought, and what far transcends the whole that we could give.

But though "the Sword of the Spirit" can be tempered only by heavenly power, it needs a trained hand to wield it for the rescue of the captive, and the piercing of the guilty heart; divine as it is, its strokes, if flung about by the wild impulse of an unpractised will, may only beat the air and waste the enthusiast's strength. And what we do aim at during the years you spend with us is to surround the central inspiration of your life with well-ordered faculties, and place at its disposal the utmost available resource for acting with power on the souls of men. Comparing in this view your entrance with your departure, see at once how the same affections, which persist all through, gain quite a new aspect when they rule over the larger and the fuller mind, and are ready to come forth with a tone and volume of which they gave no sign in their first simplicity. Where before you dimly felt, you now

D D

distinctly think; where before you arbitrarily thought, you now persuasively speak; where before you blindly believed, you are now preferentially convinced; the aspiration which before was a vague drift of nature is now the luminous purpose of your will. A more **discerning** insight into human life has deepened your compassion; a wider horizon has calmed and elevated your faith. Nature is vaster, history is longer than you had imagined; and if under the immensity of the one your personal life seems quenched and silenced, it kindles up again at the great chorus of human voices that is flung from the past, and whose many languages are but the parts of one harmony. It has ever been the glory of the Bible, among sacred books, that it has maintained in its disciples the consciousness of an historic life, and rendered it impossible for them to be born and die in the present; they belong to a spiritual kindred that runs through thousands of years; and they must know the story, and admire the deeds, and sing the song, and pray the prayers, of their saintly forefathers. Studies wider than the Bible, which place it in its true relations, and introduce us to other monuments of human thought, expressive of the same affections, and witnessing to the inward unity of mankind, extend and intensify this noble influence. And to meet, in a primeval Oriental maxim, with a touch of mystic piety that would be natural to-day, or in a Greek epitaph with a cry of grief that seems an echo of our own, is **one** of those pathetic experiences, in the neighbourhood of which nothing little and nothing ungenial can live. This ampler world, these new dimensions of sympathy, these purer and more copious springs of devotion, you will take with you hence; and however modest may be the outer scale of your life, they secure to it, if **you** are true to them, an inalienable peace and dignity.

This silent enlargement of your love of God and fellowship with men is incomparably the noblest fruit of your studious years; for it is an increase of energy and vitality to the primary and permanent source of all religious power, a more complete possession of every faculty and feeling by the spirit of holiness. Quite secondary to this, yet of great relative importance as its instruments of action on contemporary minds, are the intellectual aptitudes and gains of positive knowledge **with** which your College period has enriched you. Without these, although the inward unity of religion might be profoundly felt, its outward differences, with all the problems they present, would remain a helpless phenomenon, without interpreter; and as of these it is, as of all facts temporarily obtrusive, that men are most conscious, he who does not know their distinctive speech, their history, their relative strength and weakness, the secret of their hold upon the human heart, **may** prophesy for all time, but not **specifically** for his **own.** In order to **aid** the struggling thought, to lift the depressed affection, to rekindle the languid faith, to enlighten the undiscerning zeal, of your neighbours to-day and to-morrow, you must be able to read the map of their mind, and find the lines of steerage which will extricate them from their straits and shallows. When the older forms of devout belief fall into difficulties and cannot adjust themselves to the meaning and speech of the living generation, no one can mediate between the new conceptions of finite things and the undying worship of the Infinite holiness who is not intellectually at home with the former, as well as spiritually at rest in the latter. The true and the good must not be severed, as they are sure to be if they are delivered over to separate representatives ; and they can be maintained in harmony only by minds able to survey and revise their relations. Still, *the matter of knowledge*, though an indispensable part of your outfit, is *not* the matter of religion ;—is for you chiefly a *defence instrument*, enabling you to clear and hold the ground of your position, and pioneer the grand assault of the prophetic spirit upon the sins and grievances of the world. *When* that assault begins you must parley no more, but charge direct upon the conscience and affections of men ; and *until* it begins, you have not entered upon your function, but are yet displaying your credentials and lingering in preliminaries. So far then as we have furnished you with the needful materials of knowledge, we have been engaged in but a subordinate task; nor should we be faithful, if we did not warn you against trusting in it, and resorting to its fruits as something primary. Keep up, improve, enlarge, what you have learned; but in your daily work, forget it. It is yours to live in the sensitive and moral experiences of others; to face, with quiet eye and clear heart, the inner realities of human life, and touch them with a true sacredness; and, for this end, the simple feelings that first brought you to the feet of Christ, the love and reverence, the aspiration and trust, that made you long to speak and act for him, are your commission and your strength.

1878.

Valedictory Address.—V.

IF you were to ask me what part of my life I should
be most glad to live over again, I should eagerly name
my College years; and feel that, could I but repeat
them, with my present knowledge of their lines, my
whole existence would be lifted to a higher plane. If
I were to ask you, whether you would accept anew the
term which you complete to-day, your heart would
sink within you at the proposal, and you would resent
it as an attempt to baulk your life of its proper end.
Whence this strange perversity in our discontent, that
the very period which those who cannot have it would
joyously enter, others who are in it no less joyously
quit? In part, no doubt, it is, that the fair look of
things never comes quite up to the point at which we
stand, but, to be seen for what it is, must keep some
distance. The sunset light is not rosy to those who
are bathed in it, but only as reflected from the far off
rocks and snows which it picks out for evening glory.
And so from the present station of experience, the
beauty of life may naturally make its escape, for the

old into the past, for the young into the future. But over and above this optical variation from the different point of view, there is a real and justifying ground for both your feeling and my own,—which will be yours hereafter; and inconsistent as they seem, neither of them is without its essential truth.

It is surely not without reason that we who are in the thick of life's battle, weighted with its responsibilities, swaying with its pressures, breathless with its haste, should deplore our poor equipment and precarious strength, and long for the irrevocable years of preparation in which we missed so much that now we want. Once entangled in the fight without our proper weapons, it is too late for us to return and fetch them; if thrown upon the field with a false conception of its dispositions, we risk all by a change of front in the midst of action. When we have left behind these priceless years that build up the boy into the man, we soon become awestruck by their decisive character; and discover that the habits we have neglected to form, the knowledge we have failed to master, the thought we have omitted to clear, the aspiration we have suffered to flag, are to be the wasting canker or the piercing thorn of all our life. It is no wonder therefore if many a sufferer from such weakness of his own cries in his heart " Give me back those golden morning hours, that only time of easy and elastic freedom, when all noble possibilities were at their greatest, and all pure inspirations in their freshest strength! How reverently would I use their moments now, and turn their unclouded light on dark places in my view of things which now haunt me with a painful mystery!" You cannot deny that it is a time of peerless privilege, when no heavier burden of duty is laid on you than to let your own mind and soul expand and energize, and survey the field on which they are to live, and draw near to the spirits, divine and human, with whom they are to commune; when the joy of growing faculty meets its own check in the humbling infinitude of truth and intensity of beauty; when the eye of wonder is kept for ever open to new visions, and things seem large and affections deep enough for you to learn and love eternally; and through the literature, philosophy and prophetic voices of many ages you are introduced to the august and gracious company of the wise and saintly. It is a season that comes but once; and happy are they to whom its glory of opportunity is revealed while yet it stays!

And yet there is just cause for the student's joy that his last session is over, and the hour of his release has struck. It is not surprising if, after years of intellectual work, he sometimes finds his attention wander, and eager reveries agitate his lonely hours, and a restless enthusiasm invades and spoils his calm contemplative existence. For, after all, *Thought* is for the sake of *Life*; and cannot, in any healthy mind, be indefinitely fed upon itself, but nurses an irresistible thirst for its proper end. And it is no less natural for the learning and meditative mind to pine from dearth of action, than for the over-worked and hurried will to complain that there is no time to think. In the very midst therefore of the real sorrow of leave-taking, I yet defend your joy; and even congratulate you on your escape from one or two especial dangers attaching to the studious years of those who undertake the work of an evangelist.

One of these is incident to the very nature of our work together. We have to teach, you have to learn *Theology*; and this keeps us always at one remove from *Religion*. It is the *theory* of things divine, not the sanctities themselves, to which alone we can try to introduce you; and it is reached only by considering whether we are to think of them in this way or in that, by comparing and criticizing human conceptions about them, or interpreting the propositions assumed to say what is truest about them. All the objects of our study have been *notions* and *beliefs* shaped by predecessors, on which we sit in judgment as if superiors, and which, if approved, are but the media or intervening element through which we prefer to seek our way to God. We see him therefore, not in any immediate relation, but only as reflected in other minds; and to the vision we carry the mood appropriate, not to the living presence

of an infinitely Holy one, but to a probable hypothesis
awaiting our scrutiny.   In our Academic work, we are
conversant only with ideas; we live upon books; we
discuss opinions; we analyze the logic of creeds; we
ponder the sayings of the wise; and these are all human
products, though they may make mention of things
divine; they have for us a literary and historical
interest, but no more *sacred* character than a legal
judgment or an art critique.   You will not suspect me
of depreciating these studies of the records and varieties
of religious thought.   Without them we should indeed
stand helpless before the great problems on which all
that is sublime and sweet in life will always wait;
—problems which transcend the resources of the
solitary intellect, and which yield only when the choice
spirits of our race take counsel together.   But still,
there is something to be feared from the habit of
looking at spiritual things with the fastidious analytic
eye and growing familiar with them at second hand;
the inward reverence is chafed away by too much
speech; the heavenly perfume is carried off by the
" winds of doctrine," till the fresh altar flowers drop
their petals and lie dry and dead.   The mood of the
Scholar is, in short, quite different from that of the
Prophet; and if it is with a sense of deliverance that
you emerge from the long preponderance of the one, I
gladly refer it to the compressed force of the other,
brought at last to a moment when it may breathe freely

and lift up the voice as witness for God. It is a blessed change to have done with philosophy and divines who speculate about heavenly possibilities and find yourself in the train of Christ who lives in their reality; to pass from *evidences* to Him that is evidenced, and from the strain of intellectual constriction be handed over to the repose of a personal relation; to revert, with larger mind and deeper soul, to the child's *immediate* apprehension and simple trust, and " speak that which you do know, and testify that which you have seen." Be it only in the spirit of a divine self-surrender, men will receive the testimony as true.

Another danger is inherent in the student's life, in so far as it is a period of *Self-culture*; whose pursuits are selected and proportioned largely with a view to bring the faculties into a preconceived state of attainment and expertness. This aim is no doubt present in all education, and has a legitimate place in it throughout. But in the earlier stages it is pursued *for* the child by his teacher, and need not be his own animating motive; whereas in later years it steps forth into the front, and for the pure love of knowledge is apt to substitute the mere desire of accomplishment. Whether, in a large view of social ends, this incentive is overworked by our public systems of mental training, I will not here consider. But this I must say; that among those who dedicate themselves to the service of

Christ's religion, the kind of temper which is fostered in the sphere of intellectual competition, the ambition for distinction, the mutual admiration, the thirst for praise, the pride in finished skill, are very much out of place; and are in fact quite left behind by all the more saintly spirits, however marked their genius,—by a Leighton, a Pascal, a Newman. They know themselves to be another's and not their own; and if they set themselves to gain new knowledge or to learn an art, it is not to enrich or decorate themselves, but to get ready some fresh sacrifice for others. No self-contemplation, though it be directed on the regulation of mind and character, can ever do more than the negative work of moral police; warding off the assaults of ill, and keeping the enclosure of the soul swept and garnished, but kindling there no spiritual life, and filling it with no consecration. Refine it as you may, it will only take you, with labouring feet, to the summit of *the Law*; if you are ever to launch thence into the free air of the gospel, you must trust yourself upon the wing of self-forgetfulness and self-devotion. You must cease to choose, and let yourself be chosen; content to be the organ of that Highest Will that speaks in your compassionate enthusiasms, and mingles with the tenderness, the purity, the aspiration, of your prayers. Thus to be at disposal, as the ready vehicle of divine light and love, is true fidelity to him who lived and died to do not his own will, but the will of the Father in heaven. That you welcome the moment which drops every Stoical hindrance to this higher prophetic life, is no ingratitude to the past, but only the claim of your full discipleship.

1879.

Valedictory Address.—VI.

WHEN the hour strikes to close some human relation, its solemn tone so vibrates through the heart that we would rather listen to it till it dies away than break in upon it with our poor words. It is the significant privilege of our nature to look with a certain awe at that which can never come again ; to put some pathetic mark upon the dates of things ; to remember our anniversaries, to count our generations, and take our road-side rest by some milestone on the way. To such a place of pause we are brought to-night ; and ere we bid adieu to our endearing companionship of life and studies, and pass you through the gate whence the track must be your own, it is natural to compare its beginning and its end, and measure, with faithful conscience, what it has given, and what it has taken away.

Replace yourself at the moment when you took the first step on the path which here ends ; remember what you were ; and especially what was the decisive impulse which then diverted you from the market or the forum and joined you to the train of Christ. Was it not (for I will take it at its poorest) a simple enthusiasm for Divine things, a longing for a secret walk with God, and a wonder that men could be so insensible to the "holy ground" beneath their feet, and the heavenly light around their head? With the film removed from your inner eye, you looked with only weariness at the competition of gain and honour, and with irrepressible pity on the struggles of the baffled and failing. Life appeared to you too solemnly placed, and too grandly endowed, to be surrendered to selfish pursuits and material well-being; and you took up your vow of service to others in loyalty to him who came " not to be ministered unto but to minister." Such, I believe, was the spirit which possessed you at the outset, and called you to become an organ of the Divine love to suffering and unawakened men ; a spirit already eager to test itself by self-sacrificing effort, and partially exercised in the Sunday School Class and other forms of Christian work. With this God-given baptism you came to us, and " we have baptized none of you "; and it is so truly the prime essential, and looks so like the only one, that we may well turn with some misgiving to the other end of the story, to see what has been added to it, to justify the expenditure of all these years.

Glance then at the contents of your altered mind at the present moment, and see wherein the difference lies.

It is all summed up in a vast accession of knowledge, indefinitely widening your intellectual horizon, and opening to you unsuspected fields of thought and wonder. You have entered far enough into a few of the sciences to embrace in your conception the great hierarchy of natural laws. You have grown familiar enough with new languages to see how flexible the moulds, yet how constant the matter, of human thought and feeling. You have learned not only to count the centuries by rota, but to identify them by their scenery and recall the acts of their great drama; till you have found your life in the present at once infinitely reduced and infinitely enlarged, by its place and affinities in Time. By the simultaneous study of three great literatures, the Hebrew, the Greek, the Roman, your mind has been held in contact with the several affluents of our modern civilization, and acquired the scholar's discriminative sympathy with all. Under guidance the most exact you have surveyed on all sides the birth scene and age of the religion you mean to preach; so that the records fall into their place, the agents separate their parts, the blended stages become successive, the mythical accessories drop away, and what was before the object of a confused faith passes into the sublimest of portraits and the most touching of histories. You have followed the strange process of spoiling the essence of Christianity by amalgamating it with the prevailing humours of eighteen hundred years; of reversing the transfiguration of Christ, bringing down that glorious form from the illumined Mount, and losing it in the darkening vapours of human thought and life till its divine features are forgot; and a spiritual religion has become sacramental, a simple superlatively complex, a universal exclusive, and a solemnly personal fundamentally vicarious. And, **finally,** you have not been left wholly without insight into the attempts of philosophers to solve the ultimate problems of the universe; you can tell, on looking round, whether you are in the Academy or the Lyceum; you can read the thought that lurks behind the calm brow of the Stoic, the abstracted look of the Mystic, the smile of the Epicurean; and into your appreciation of modern systems more pressing in their claims you can carry many an interpreting light of analogy and contrast, to facilitate your final apprehension of what is possible to the Reason, right to the Conscience, and true in the Religion of our nature.

Such then is, on the one hand, the inspiration with which you came; and such, on the other hand, the knowledge which you take away. What is the relation between the two?

(1.) Do you find that there is *no* relation between them? that all this intellectual growth has gone on outside your spiritual impulse, and has no vital union with it? Do the roots lie quite apart from your original self-dedication and from your acquired learning ; so that you are servant of God on one day and secular scholar on every other ; and there is no common life between the largeness of your thought and intensity of your piety ? If so, this is not the result which we have *meant* to reach ; and were it too frequent, it would justify the popular doubt, what good there could be, for the service of a religion accessible to all, in a mass of learning which no Apostle ever needed, and no one in his spiritual hours could ever use. There *is* no sacred good in vast attainments, unless the soul to which they are added can send through them the flash of its thought of God, and fuse them down to the enrichment of its love and power.

(2.) Or do you find that the relation between your first divine call and your gathered knowledge is one of antagonism ? You expected perhaps, when you set yourself apart for divine service, that all your preparation would be aglow with the enthusiasm of your purpose, and that your progress would be elastic with the spring of an exhaustless strength. And on discovering that the path of your advance was as laborious, as monotonous, as much in the dust, as if it led to some earthly mart instead of to the Prophet's Mount ; that language and logic, science and history, exercise the same faculties, whether the learner is to be lawyer or divine ; that criticism of a sacred text is neither more nor less dry than of a classical; you were perhaps disappointed to be so plunged in mere intellectual life, and impatient of it as training you away from your end. In weary moods you have asked, it may be, 'What shall I do with all this burden of knowledge? Can I not teach men their duties without being at home with all the chemical equivalents, and the equations to curves of each degree? Shall I bring them nearer to Christ for being able to count and date all the Uncial manuscripts? or kindle the love of God the more for cramming my memory with the nonsense of quibbling councils and exploded philosophies?' These are natural questions; expressive of the first and superficial revolt of the inward pieties against not only the apparatus of systematic theology, but all preoccupation of the mind with finite things. And it is quite right for the conscientious student to stand on his guard lest his daily work should dry up the ground of his religious affections; and to be profoundly aware that, if left to itself and allowed to usurp the command of his nature, it will assuredly do so, and leave its spiritual branch with only the withered foliage of a season that is gone. But to treat this danger with mutinous impatience instead of with manly and reverent vigilance, to seek shelter from it in devout ignorance instead of conquering it by holy thought and discipline and prayer, would be to set up a civil war among the faculties of the soul, and to betray the one supreme trust committed to the scholar, of reflecting in himself the unity and harmony of the divine empire which he surveys.   To the spirit and power of religion, *his* pursuits are neither more hostile nor more favourable than any others.   God is not to be found in the *matter* but in the animating *soul* of life ; and there is no daily work which you may not find desecrated by querulous routine, or consecrated by the heart of loving service.   It is as easy to sin and fall away from God in labours of charity and services of worship as in the study of Assyrian Antiquities or the interpretation of a Pagan philosopher.   If herein I speak, as I am persuaded, your own permanent conviction, then,

(3.) The relation between your acquired store of knowledge and your first self-dedication, is one of intimate blending and harmony ; and the early intensity is only diffused through and over a greatly enlarged mind, meeting there nothing that it cannot penetrate and glorify.   A true call of God begins with his kindling in the soul of his young servant some little spark, or laying some small live coal that burns of itself from the mere air it finds ; you may add much to it and pile upon it what you will; it will all turn to fuel, though it be hard as stone ; and there will never be more than a momentary question whether the fuel or the fire will prevail ; the central heat will radiate through the mass and stir it with strong vibrations till it is all wrapped in one altar flame. This it is that makes the crowning glory of these college years,—that your studies, instead of overshadowing and dwarfing your Religion, are taken up into it, to give it their dimensions, to suffuse it with their intellectual light, and receive from it the fervour of its reverence and love. The whole theory and practise of our relation to each other rest on the conception that to the Christlike mind *nothing is secular ;* that a universal gospel embraces all human interests, of thought and character, of person and society, of art and letters, of the present and past; and that its minister and representative should accordingly have a certain elevation of mental position, commanding some sympathetic survey of the whole contents of life. How can he speak to *all* men if he is stranger to the characteristics of any? how find what sanctities are possible to them if he presents only a blind side towards what they think and feel? If our aims for you have been large, they are no larger than the Soul of man with which you have to deal, or the Spirit of Christ which creates that soul anew in the likeness of God.

1880.

Valedictory Address.—VII.

—••—

DEARLY-BELOVED pupils, in age my sons, in spirit and mission my brethren! Never does our relation appear to me in a light so clear and sacred as on the anniversary which gathers us here. The whole life, whose morning is on you, whose evening on me, seems to lie before my eye; and, as I gaze at it on your behalf, to distribute its inward history into three sections, which in the healthy and happy soul are softly blended by an undertint beneath their superficial hues, but in the sadness and confusion of our hearts are often set at variance and cancel each other's blessings. There are the years of early wonder and enthusiasm, when first the mind, as if cleared of its childish mists by a shower, looks into deepened skies above, and freshened colours on the earth below; and custom has not yet crushed the wild flowers on the grass, or construed them into weeds; and the tale of heroism brings the flush into the cheek, and the sight of wrong wakens the passion for redress; and every neglected duty presses the spirit into the desert, and never halts till it hears the sob of remorseful prayer. You at least will not deny that this season at the end of boyhood is one of natural piety, when finite things swim in the currents of an Infinite Will, and the human lot is awful or glorious because it is also Divine : for precisely *this* it is which has determined your path of service, and in your self-devotion to others made you children of the temple where God and Man may meet.

This self-dedication introduces the next period, and decides what its contents shall be. Not that the inspiration which brings you here needs any tutoring of ours, or can receive from us anything but reverent recognition and sympathy. The spirit of God perfects its own call and asks no aid from us ; and to the prayer, the conscience, even the questions of a child, I have often surrendered a heart that would be callous to less simple fervours, It is not mere folly that tempts so many pious souls to despise human learning. Were there nothing to be considered but the purity and freshness of *the inward spring,* I know not but we too might be content to exclaim, ' Father, we thank thee that by the mouth of babes thou perfectest praise.' But we have also to reckon with *the outward conditions* under which your word has to be spoken and your work to be done. Your times have fallen, not indeed at ' the end of the ages,' but in the rear of a vast procession of forerunners, with whose august voices you may dare to mingle yours only when you have duly listened to their strains, and caught something of the richness of their tone. The message which you have to deliver is wrapt in the scriptures of an earlier world, and needs to be disengaged from what is obsolete and local, and made to live and breathe in the atmosphere of to-day, and ring in the ears of the village or the city throng. The very universe which you will interpret as the appeal of the Infinite Mind to the finite, and which is the measure, not indeed of **Him,** but of what you can say of Him, is so transformed in these latter days as,—in spite of its " ancient hills," and its " everlasting stars,"—to be virtually a " new creation," wherein all history is but a beat of its pendulum, and the span to Milton's " Empyrean " but the step of a child. It is to study these things, to bring your mind into free accord with them, and place at your disposal the wealth and depth of conception which they supply, that your academic period is set apart. To know *as it is* the system of nature which is God's outward expression ; to save the pearl of great price in the divine story and word of Christ from its imperfect investiture ; to commune with the noblest spirits of the Past, and learn what they have thought on life and death, on good and ill, and every mystery divine and human, is a needful discipline and enrichment of your own faculty, if it is not to run dry, and an outfit that can ill be spared, if you are to reach what lies at the heart of the present age. That it is in which we **try** to help you; for, in spite of Pauline example, we would not **force** you to renounce all "excellency of speech or of wisdom"; or fear that the spirit of God will desert such gifts, if only they be humbly consecrated to **Him.** As far as in us lies, we set you in the way to gain the exact and scholarly Mind, the clear and various Reason, the large and chastened Imagination, the **firm** grasp of your own thought, the tender sympathy with truth and good in foreign forms, the grateful friendship for every soul whose genius stirs or whose wisdom enlightens you, though looking into your eyes only from the silent page.

Suppose this task achieved, and that our joint pains, —yours and ours,—have rendered you at last (so far as the years permit) the finished Scholar. To what does it amount, when measured by the supreme end to which your life is dedicated? Have we done for you the same thing which is done in the hospitals for the students of surgery, and for the untrained pleader in the Inns of Court? Are we to think of the calling which you have chosen (or which has chosen you) as simply a *skilled Art,* like Medicine and Law? To make experts in these pursuits, the instructor has to begin at the beginning, and to raise the whole structure of conceptions from the foundation to the crown; and the total characteristics of the physician or the advocate **are so** much added on to the common staple of our humanity. Is it so then with *your* function

too ? have we been at the beginning of your *Religion* ?
Have we ever sought to approach its springs, unless it
be in fellowship of love and prayer ?   Do we pretend
to change its source or its securities, and *prove* it as
our finding of God, instead of accepting it as *His
finding* of us ?   Through you, as its organs, it is to
pass from mind to mind ; can its fervour and its flash
be transmitted by rules of persuasion and ingenuity of
address ?   Is it not rather by the spiritual contact,—
torch with torch,—of natures similarly charged, set on
fire by the first soul on which the lightning falls ?
Take away this primary inspiration, this awakening
touch of the Infinite Spirit upon the finite, and do
you think that, left to your own resources, you could
convert so much as *yourself*, or draw from another the
tears and cry of conscience, ' I will arise and go to
my Father " ?   No ! the best that we can give you is
but secondary and instrumental,—fuel to feed a flame
that is kindled from on high.—It is not Learning, it
is not Thought, but Divine Pity, that plays the part of
Missionary among men ; and the Scholar, if he be no
more, wins no heart to goodness, subdues no will to
God.

What then is the question that most weighs upon
us, when we have brought you to the verge of your
third period,—the test and goal of all ?—Were we to
" magnify our offiee " and see nothing beyond it, we
should be content with the conventional standard of the

College class-room, and ask only what is the sum, and what the characteristic, of the accomplishments you will take away; and if all were bright and well, should feel a warrantable pride that a good name was added to our roll. But another feeling glides to the front, and eclipses this natural care for the success of our proper task. You come to us by a sacred leading of the Spirit, you have lived with us for the exercise and culture of the mind; you leave us for the work of the Spirit, and just in answer to that first call virtually say, 'Here, Lord, I am, ready for thy word and girt for all thy will.' As we stand then to-night on the dividing line between the scholarly and the spiritual years, our paramount anxiety must be that that gracious leading of the Spirit survives to take you on; that we deliver you back to the same holy guidance, with larger thought and deeper heart and surrender no less free; and that you may not have forgotten your early vows or fallen away from your first love. In all pure religion, in the inward experience perfected in Christ, there is a sweet patience and continuity by which it flows on, now on the surface and now in hidden caves below, through all intervals and vicissitudes. It never changes its tenure or its source, so as to become more a knowledge and less a trust. It is always, and equally, *both;* given in the very essence of human Conscience, and inevitably mingling with the life of thought and love. With Faith we begin; and with

Faith we must end ; and when Samuel the child grows into Samuel the prophet, he hears the same voice, he yïelds the same service ; and though he now knows the ways and thoughts of men, his heart is beyond, in a divine realm that embraces these, and shows what they *ought to be* and *shall be*. So may you all live on through your probation in the simple habits and deep trusts of your first piety. Were the effect of our teaching to be that you started back from your own enthusiasm, and became accomplished only as critics of the living beliefs of others, I could wish myself accursed for having blighted the flower and forbidden the fruit of your early devotion.

And now let me brace my heart to say the annual *Farewell*. To the constant sadness of that word there is added, this year, no little special sorrow by the remembrance that, of the trio who had entered with us on their first studies I have now only one to name. Of one we have all taken leave together around the open grave ; the tolling bell and the whispered blessing have spoken our Valediction for us ; and voices unheard by us have welcomed him to higher service than any for which we could prepare him. Another who will be with us no more is indeed present to invite our best wishes, and worthy to receive them, if he would let me speak. Nor is he careless of them, while knowing them to be his ; and if he takes a silent leave it is not because the Past is indifferent to him, but because the Future is unknown.

As I review in memory the many years which you have passed with us, I have no fear lest they should have spent the earnest purpose that brought you to us, and left you becalmed and helpless for the voyage that is before you. On the contrary, if I mistake not, the blessed breeze that is to bear you on was never fresher; so as even, it may be, to take away all regrets for a life less congenial to you than that which you are ready to enter. Be it so; and God speed you! Faithful and devoted action, the soul of love and the will of duty are the supreme end and crown of thought; and it is not necessary for *every* apostle to be the pride of Gamaliel, ere he is taken captive by the vision of Christ. If Christianity could *win* the world through so variegated an agency as that apostolic band, the ascetic James, the impulsive Peter, the doubting Thomas, the apocalyptic John, supporting or resisting the ideal enthusiasm of Paul, surely it may *keep* the world through all " diversity of gifts "; the weaknesses of each being dissolved and volatilized under the possessing fire of God and love of Christ. Farewell! and whatever good prophecies you fulfil, remember now and then those who have hoped and promised well on your behalf.

1882.

Valedictory Address.—VIII.

My first embarrassment to-night is to know by what appellation I am to accost you. Yesterday my pupils, to-morrow my brethren in a common work, you hover to-day between the two relations, and can be addressed by the name of neither; yet precisely for that reason,— because you have reached a moment of transition,— I know you to be possessed by the attributes and affections of both. And to me also it should relieve my Farewell of its sadness, that the Past which it closes has all its significance from the Future which is now at hand; so that it is only the spring-tide that is over, while the summer glow and the autumn fruits are yet to come.

What, I wonder, was the secret feeling that first drew your heart towards this ministry on the verge of which you stand? what the vision that brightened your entrance on the years you have spent with us? Let us say, that the glory of Divine things had dawned on you, and was yet fresh upon the young soul; that the inner meaning of worship, so long shut

up in the shell of custom, had broken upon you and
found out your springs of awe and infinite aspiring;
and that nothing sank so deep into you as the tones
of prayer, or melted you like the favourite hymn, or
seemed sublimer than to speak for God to men. To
live entirely in this high atmosphere, or on its verge,
was it not to gain a vast horizon, and be lifted into
perpetual calm? to look down upon the surging
passions of the world below, with no share but that
of pity for their cries? The early dream which draws
many a fervent youth into the temple, wearying of his
workshop and even truant from his home, is the
yearning to be about his Father's business, and
escape from the littleness of temporal cares into the
solemn sphere of things eternal. He deems it incon-
gruous for an immortal nature to spend itself in
buying and selling, in eating and sleeping, in multiplying perishable wants, when only one thing is
needful, that can never be taken away. When once
he has felt the sweetening dews of the heavenly
grace, he dreads lest his spirit should dry up beneath
the hot breath of human competition, and its tender
colours fly in the glare of public life. He will trust
himself to no such tainting scenes; having found the
fountain of peace, he will never quit it more. His lot
shall secure the consecration of his heart and will. To
serve the altar, with hand never far from its purifying
touch; to have the mind in permanent contact with

holy writ and saintly examples; to be the organ of others, not in their gains but in their prayers, and linked to them only by the common sorrows and supreme affections of humanity; to be pledged to work which most carries the Sabbath air all through the week; to have every heavy cross made light by an habitual love elastic to bear it; what is this, he thinks, but to live above the level of temptation, and conform at once to the relations which shall never die?

If it was in such mood of natural enthusiasm that you were drawn to the Christian ministry, it attracted you as something sanctifying and intrinsically divine; as an office securely railed off from all that was common or unclean, detaining you on holy ground, and, by pre-engagement with the highest communion, laying to sleep the lower desires and sordid interests which make slaves of other men. It needs no long experience to dissipate this illusory reliance on the outward lot for consecrating the inward life; and you already know that it is no less vain to expect the saintly mind from saintly opportunites, than to excuse our sins by anger at our temptations. You have discovered how possible it is to be intellectually engaged with the most vivifying truths, while spiritually untouched by them; to study a sacred text as coldly as a newspaper advertisement; to follow the steps of Christ even to Gethsemane, and be within hearing of his voice, yet fall asleep and be unable to watch with him one hour; to say you pray, without praying; to teach about the Spirit of God, yet not be in it; to pass through the Sunday hours with a week-day mind; to dwell on the new-birth with unregenerate heart; and expatiate on the solemn grounds of the Infinite Love and the eternal Life with untrembling thought, and soul empty of their wonder and their joy. You cannot draw any line among external things or intellectual acts that shall separate the secular from the sacred; there may be devotion in the workshop or at the boat-helm, and profaneness in the pulpit or at the grave.

The enthusiasm of imagination persuades us at first that to be familiar with the vast range of theologic thought,—to "understand all mysteries and all knowledge,"—must harmonize the mind with all that is divine in human relations, and silence the discords of the personal life. Is it really so? In your years with us you have gained an outlook over an immense world, of natural law, of human experience, history, literature and faith, and of the everlasting Will which unfolds itself in these. Is it a matter of course that this flood of outward light also steeps your soul in sanctity? On the contrary, it has shown you that, for the balance of the soul, there is needed another and an opposite order of expanding radiation from the world of spirit forth upon the universe which is opened to your view. You remember perhaps what Plato tells us about the way in which Vision comes to pass; from the secret chambers of the bodily eye, when we look through the window of its pupil, there issues forth an inborn light which meets the arriving beams of the external day; and only on the greeting and mingling of the two does any true perception flash upon us; if we withhold the mental light, "seeing we see not, neither do we understand"; if night withdraws the physical light, the closing lids imprison what is ours to sport with us in the phantasms of our dreams. No happier parable could there be of our spiritual experience. To read the meaning of the universe aright, we must bring to it something akin to what we take from it; if we carry into it nothing ideal, we shall find it all material; if we fling upon it no asking thought, we shall gain no responsive insight; if we go to it without reverence, we shall discern in it no sanctity. The merely recipient nature *learns* nothing, but only feels; it is the quickened spirit that is the condition of all our apprehensiveness; and in the world under its religious aspects, as a theatre of discipline and duty, all its significant characters, however deep and pathetic may be the things they really say, must remain undeciphered, like an inscription in a forgotten tongue, except to the supreme affections and energies of the soul. By what signs can love make itself known to the heart that has no sympathy? or a Moral administration, to a mind without conscience? or the beauty of holiness to the cynic and the egoist ?   The drowsy and the carnal temper has no organ for the divine elements of life, and can no more reach their altitudes than the paralytic can climb the Alps; and to one who is not yet converted from this sleep of nature, the tender lights and mystic shadows of human experience are as much hidden as the loveliness of dawn from the cattle on the hills.   To the spiritually dead, nothing really lives, but only moves with a meaningless automatism; let such " dead bury their dead, but go you and preach the kingdom "; sure only of this, that the work will not consecrate you, but *you* must consecrate the work.   For this, its crowning baptism of power, trust to no favouring circumstance, to no native intellect, to no acquired learning, to no conscious art ; these are but imple- ments, to be wielded by orders from the ultimate sanctuary of the spirit within.

Do you ask me whether, even *there*, you can escape from yourselves, or do more than obey *your own orders?* whether in the inmost recesses of the con- science, you are not still at home?   Were it so, it is most true I could not ask you to *inspire yourselves*, and, of your own will, play the double part of God and man.   But precisely here it is that we know ourselves *not left alone;* that we do not create our own highest vision of the right and holy; that it is given us, ready clothed from its august authority ; that the conscious- ness of it is human, the source of it divine ; that it is therefore the true meeting point of the Holy Spirit and our own, the living touch of Moral sympathy between the finite and the Infinite mind. In following the supreme conception that haunts us and giving ourselves up to what, in our heart of hearts, we venerate most, we enter into the experience of Christ, and know that our judgment is just, because we are doing *not our own will* but the *"will of the Father in heaven."* The inspiration is His; the surrender only is ours. And so, we break the bondage of Self and fly to the everlasting arms; desire, and fear, and doubt, and self-consciousness pass away, and in the freedom of love and simplicity of trust, we can become organs of a diviner life than ours, can warn and testify, console and plead, not in words of our own thinking or tones of our own voice, but as from an invisible lyre on which the Spirit of God is breathing while his prophets touch the strings.

In this faith lies the secret of your calling. Instead of its outward "business" implanting in you any inward holiness which terminates in union with God, its very life starts from the stirring of his Spirit moving on the deeps of yours and wakening it to its new birth; and then completing itself through your self-abandonment to him, conveys a true sacredness, a divine beauty, into every relation which it controls and every labour which it requires. The larger the capacity of thought, and the wider the horizon of knowledge which you have gained, the more intensely needed is that spiritual enthusiasm which shall carry its answering fire to every divine gleam that lies upon so vast a field. In yielding to it, you will reconcile the affluence of the student's practised faculties with the repose of the child's trust, freshness of unspoiled affections, and the simplicity of the Christian mind.

Go then with a heart of faith and courage! The field is clear; set a steadfast hand to the plough, and trace the furrows deep and clean; scatter good seed and spare it not; and may the Lord of the harvest make the ingathering glorious!

1883.

Valedictory Address.—IX.

THOUGH it is no longer my office to speak to you as my pupils, it is my privilege yet once more to speak to you as to my sons,—be it only to embrace you with a parting blessing on the borders of your promised land. Believe me, I do so with joy; I brush aside my tender regrets, and mingle my heart with yours, and say that this is a glorious, if also a solemn moment, full of a meaning which can never repeat itself in life. So far as that meaning looks forward to your future, I leave its interpretation to the friend who follows me; so far as it looks backward, on the years now closing, I will try to draw forth its chief contents.

If the many attempts to reduce history to Law have detected anything like a rule of order, it is this; that, in its growth, the human mind moves by intermittent pulses, now of propelling, then regurgitating, force; the former bringing the times of creative genius, exuberant in original production; the latter, relapsing into the repose of spent energy, but living on its rich inheritance, submitting it to critical analysis, and framing from it rules of taste, which thought and taste are never to transgress;—never, *i.e.*, till the next vernal glow pushes off the withered leaves to make room for a new creation and start the world afresh. And thus, large conceptions, deep insight, divine fervours of affection, alternate with the imitative pedantry and superficial gloss, and rhetorical raptures of a conventional literature. And the Story of Religion exhibits a similar alteration of the *Ages of Faith* and those of *Reflection;* the first, when the souls of men, conscious of the living God, are wielded by infinite convictions and mighty passions, and flung into heroic enterprises and strenuous abnegations and sublimest worship; the others, when the Spirit having fled from the organism of thought and habit which it justified, nothing is left but first a sleepy formalism, then a waking scepticism, startling the church and the world into Reformation. And so, as surely as the declining year undoes the work of summer, and strips her foliage away, and can only store and count her fruits, and turn all her beauty into *use,* is the poet succeeded by the critic, and the prophet by the scribe, and the visions of saints by the doubts of *savans.*

The life of Society is that of the individual "*writ large*"; and each of you may perhaps find in his own experience, something like an epitome of this law. The play of impulse goes before the studies of reflection; and all purposed Art is but Nature looking at her image in the glass. The free air of child-hood, its grace and glow and movement flashing as a swallow's, are but the rise and fall upon the surface of inward waves of instinctive feeling that flush the transparent features and command the supple limbs. Of all the dexterous things which the child will learn to do, not one will have the daring beauty of the sport or heroism which does itself uncon-sciously.

We are not long surrendered to this precarious rush of " chance desires "; every step in our education is a reduction to rule of what was spontaneous before; and one by one the wild provinces of accidental passion are annexed to the empire of the Will and adminis-tered by organized thought and disciplined method. But the encroachment of reflective Reason upon the native haunts of intuitive affection is gradual, and by no means equal all round; and the region which is last invaded and longest retains its simple faith and unquestioning devotion is the mountain boundary of Religion. There it is that heaven and earth visibly blend, and within its zone we feel the embrace of the everlasting arms; we are slow to let the logical engineer push his survey into it, and project his audacious roads; and would fain reserve it as the eternal retreat of unmeasured Nature, where the wild flowers and the glacier have their way, and the heats of life are escaped and even the clouds may be transcended.

At the age, therefore, when you resolved to dedicate yourselves to the Christian ministry, you were led, I have little doubt, by a simple unbroken enthusiasm of reverence and trust; by a piety and charity which made nothing seem so sublime as worship, nothing so blessed as to lift the souls of men to God. Whether we ascribe it to spiritual growth or to divine conversion, there is no time like that when the sanctity of life and the immensity of its relations first burst open upon the mind, and the living touch of the Divine sympathy thrills through the trembling heart, and the silent thought flows forth in waves of prayer which leave all tones behind, and realities of love and duty seem pure enough to shame all Sin away, and, though simple as the sling of the boy and the stone from the brook, of power to lay low the most giant wrongs. Was it foolish in our forefathers to stand in awe of this stage of the Soul's life, as the " Call of God " to his more intimate service? Are we any wiser, if we contradict and laugh at them? It is at least the spirit's " Age of Faith," through which he wins us to himself; the startling hour when, the latch being lifted and the wicket opened of our bounded nature, we find it to be the gate of his Infinitude.

He who has been thus "born again" sees all things in the light of the diviner world that has dawned upon him ; and full of pity for the multitudes that hurry and strive after phantasms in the very midst of the only realities. That the vision by which he is possessed has any dependence on his own moving nature, that it can ever waver, or fade, or be eclipsed, that the film which has cleared away from himself he should be unable to remove from others' eyes, it is impossible for him to suspect ; and so ready are bystanders to reverence the signs of higher inspiration, that often he is encouraged to fling himself at once upon the prophetic gale that bears him, and rush like a hurricane upon the unbelief and uncleanness of the world. Far be it from me to disparage any servants of God, who thus *hasten* to answer his first elementary appeal, and, in trusting his strength, forget that it has to pass through their weakness : from the sheepfold and the fishing boat, from the loom and the last, many a seer of Israel, many a missionary of Christ, has gone forth to bear the burden of the Lord or do the work of an evangelist. Nor do I doubt that if (in the temper of an older time) you had yielded at the outset to the exclusive enthusiasm of the spiritual life, and, careless of human thought and learning, had taken your vow to be thenceforth *only* " about your Father's business," the word of your ministry might have been with power, and your self-devotion have brought many wanderers home. God has proclaimed his love of simple affections and transparent truth in this, that to only one thing has he given higher persuasive energy than to the dithyrambic fervour of a sincere and worshipping soul.

Why then does this not content us? Because it would seal up our opening nature with an abrupt arrest; and thereby disqualify you for acting upon all who live and move beyond that limit. In its instinctive affections, in its intuitive apprehensions (and on these rests its religious faith), the mind is but at the beginning of its life; and it is in its mode of dealing with these, after they have been given, that the whole of its characteristic history, its intellectual range, its moral capability, its proper personality, consists. The self-conscious Reason wakes, and plays the critic to all the contents of the spontaneous experience. For the energy of personal religion it may be sufficient to breathe still the sweet air of childlike trust and tender conscience and believing prayer, untroubled by vexing doubts and anxious thought; but, for the religious teacher and guide, the counsellor of troubled souls, it is impossible to stand still upon his intuitive or inherent pieties, and merely reiterate their authoritative messages. These, he will often find, have ceased to wake the echoes of other hearts; and unless he can not only deliver them as a testimony but render account of them as truth, they will but die upon their way. That others may feel them, he must *know* them; must already have turned them inside out; found them ensconced in the ultimate strongholds of reality; distinguished them from counterfeits and illusions; defined their relations to each other and their permanent place in human nature; and disengaged into clear light their sublimest historical impersonation. Without this you may be a religious animal, like the Apocalyptic beasts that worship before the throne; but not an *adoring intelligence*, like the strong angel, flying in mid-heaven, with an eternal gospel to proclaim to the dwellers upon earth. Without this, your faith may be true, but is unverified; your enthusiasm may be impassioned, but it is blind, and will not help you to be leaders of the blind.

It is to effect this conversion of instinctive trust into intellectual vision, that you have spent with us the years which close to-night; to throw the mixed materials of your traditional piety into the crucible, and submit them to the fires of thought, and cleanse the dross from the pure gold. This process is inevitably severe, and to soft innocent natures brings many an unwelcome check. To challenge what is most dear and sacred to the heart, to hear how coldly it may be impugned and how poorly defended; to discover how, one after another, the props of authority give way, and the soul that has leaned on them has to stand up and to kneel down alone; to be led through the tangle of doctrine, and when pierced by its thorns and vexed by its contradictions, to find your own faith pointed out as its deadliest nightshade; to perceive how complete must be the re-construction of early Christian history, ere the story of the gospel is rightly conceived, and the love of Christ transferred from false grounds to true; all this is no doubt a stern discipline, trying to the weak, ennobling to the strong. We deliberately put you to the test. We cannot be satisfied with a blind enthusiasm. We aim to open out your implicit faith into explicit. We want no prophet *in a trance*, but clothed with light, like the angel standing in the Sun; and can never doubt the alliance of the highest Reason with the highest inspiration. While labouring towards that end, you could not but suffer a certain interregnum of suspense and provisional devotion; here and now, however, it ceases, not in death of any natural element of beauty or of good, but in its restitution under more glorious form; for "first cometh that which is natural, afterwards that which is spiritual." Fling yourselves freely then into the reopened arms of your first sacred love; only with deeper reverence; for it is the mortal that has put on immortality.

1884.

Prayer, at Valedictory Service.

O GOD, our everlasting Hope, who alone hast ever been, and wilt ever be! But for thy love that stoops to meet us, what are we that we should enter before thee, and speak to thee of things eternal? We are as children of yesterday, and can only lay at thy feet our wants and sins, and lift our eyes to thee for help. We have nothing, Lord, to say but what our fathers said, whose sighs and prayers went up as a memorial to thee. But thou seest how their strife, their thought, their sorrow, have come to us; and thy tender mercy will not weary of our everlasting cry. Every deeper moment of our life sends us back to thee, the light of every shadow, the repose of every fear, the chastener of every hope. No weakness wears us, when thou refreshest us with thy presence; no strength deceives us when it is rooted in thee. Send us, O Lord, whatsoever thou wilt; only living or dying, blind or seeing, at the beginning or the end of all our work, never let us be apart from thee, but simply go and simply be as thy spirit would have us.

O thou everliving God, who hast wakened in us the thirst for heavenly things and filled the wells of salvation from age to age! we bless thee that thou hast never left thyself without witness, but hast touched the souls of prophets and holy men to speak thy word and reflect thine image in the world; and hast shown us, by thy beloved Son, the path of uttermost trust and sacrifice that befits the children of the Highest. Still renew thy Spirit, Lord, in those who go forth to bear aloft his cross before the eyes of men, and witness for thee in his name; and especially kindle with thy purest altar-fire the heart and lips of thine untried servants whose vows and prayers are before thee this night. Plant thy Christ-like word within their souls; that they may be lifted above care and fear by a surrendering love. Join them to the glorious succession of the wise and faithful, whose memorials enrich their thought, and whose lives they desire to lead; and make them as living stones in thy latter temple, where the incense shall be all pure, and the love all true, and thy service a delight. Not in name only, but in their inmost mind, may they be followers of him who came to seek and to save the lost, to bear the children in his arms, and shame the guilty negligence of men. Amid the crush and crowd of this world give them the clear eye to catch the appealing look of sin and sorrow, and the deep heart to pity, and the strong hand to help. And often, O Lord, lest thy light grow dim, withdraw them to thy secret place; and, by the communings of thy Spirit, give them such knowledge of themselves and thee, as may exchange their strength for thine and open to them that kingdom of heaven which is within. So, O Lord, crown with thy blessing the labour and the hope of years, and accept it as our lowly offering to thee. And when we, for whom the shadows are declining, are summoned to our rest, may we leave more faithful watchmen to guard the city of our God; in every generation may the children serve thee better than the fathers; and may this, O Lord, be the fathers' joy and peace. Unite the labourers in thy field at length, where the toil and heat shall have passed, and he that soweth and he that reapeth may rejoice together. We ask it as disciples of Jesus Christ. AMEN.

Now the God of all grace, who hath called us to his peace by Christ Jesus, make you perfect, stablish, strengthen, settle you; and to him be glory and dominion for ever and ever. AMEN.

Address to a Congregation on Induction of a New Minister.

—◆—

My Christian Friends,

I well remember, though it be forty years ago, the solemn day which publicly dedicated to your service your late excellent minister, now withdrawn, amid the honour of us all, to his years of well-earned rest. There were spoken then, to you and to him, counsels of wise experience and words of modest hope; and to the Sanctifier of all, prayers grave and true for an almighty blessing. Pondering them deeply, under the broken lights of an unripe judgment and a heart on fire, I remember a certain youthful disappointment at their sober colouring;—a secret wonder whether the kingdom of God came so much by observation of what men might expect from themselves and from one another;—a longing to believe in some ministry of the spirit which should snatch us from self-distrust and self-reliance, and make us organs of diviner power. When I look round upon the altered scene to-day, and listen to the tone of its fervid voices, I find that early longing justified in everything except its criticism and complaint. Far more has been realized among you than was anticipated forty years ago; it has been realized, however, not by the enthusiasm which grasps at the whole, but by the quiet steadfastness which is faithful little by little. We have reached perhaps an age of freer affections, more open to the ministries, less suspicious of the sanctities, of life; but we have been brought to it by the scrupulous veracity, the shrinking from high profession, the unrequiring dutifulness, of predecessors who could serve their God and ask for nothing. It is the rigid fidelity of one generation which prepares the fresh fervours of another; nor at this moment are there any societies among us more abounding in healthful activities, more susceptible to the best impulses of the Christian life, than those which have been served, without pretension, simply by quiet sense and competent knowledge and noiseless conscientiousness.

Among you at least, my friends, the evidences of mutual fidelity between minister and people are so conspicuous, that I may dispense with the superfluous and uncongenial tone of good advice, and throw myself rather into the hopeful sympathies and earnest aspirations of this day. This fairer house, these fuller seats, those ampler schools, and all the various growth of the last forty years, are pledges for the future that you will not sleep, or suffer your spiritual industry to lag behind the material energies of this enterprising district. The chief danger perhaps to which in these parts the young minister is exposed is of being measured, in the discharge of a many-sided office, by the local habits of intense and productive activity running mainly in one direction. He is liable to be overwhelmed by a mass of expectations, no one of which, taken by itself, is ungenerous or out of place; but as each is formed by a different class, and quite out of view of all the rest, their combined demand would overtask half a dozen lives. Solicited by the various tastes of a mixed society, and tried by all their faculties in turn, he is by one expected, as pastor, to circulate freely over the vast area from which every Nonconformist Church is gathered; by another, as if he had a parochial charge, to look up the special district of his own chapel, and call the neighbours to his fold; by a third, to go forth as missionary into the villages around, and start fresh centres of kindred life; by a fourth, to work up the schools into the highest efficiency; by a fifth, to be active in the public institutions of the town; by a sixth, to be intellectually in the van of modern knowledge; and by all, to preach always with thought so fresh and heart so deep as to rouse the languid and not disappoint the wise. In the early church of Christ, as drawn for us in the living words of Paul, the gifts and graces were separately distributed, and divided to

every man his work, as the Spirit willed ; not all were
teachers ; nor all evangelists ; nor all interpreters ;
nor all administrators ; not all had the spirit of the
prophets ; nor all, the knowledge of the learned ; nor
all the tongue of fire. But in our time, there is
scarce an aptitude which someone is not found to
require in the minister ; not a defect, of nature, of
habit, or of culture which he is not made to feel.
Curate and bishop, catechist and missionary, expositor
and prophet, scholar and man of business, school
inspector and charity commissioner, all in one, he is
asked to go everywhere and do everything ; and is
placed side by side in speech, in thought, in action,
with men of practised and exclusive skill. As the
church too and the world grow old, and the riches
of history increase, our minds are insensibly occupied
by higher standards, and he is brought to a severer
test. The feeling with which we listen to his prayers
is formed by the choicest liturgies of the past, and is
the epitome of all that is deep and tender in the piety
of Christendom. His sermons are addressed to those
whose ideal of preaching has touches out of every age,
from Chrysostom to Robertson, whose hearts have been
kindled by the pages of Channing and of Parker, and
whose literary and poetic sense belongs to the ages of
Macaulay and Tennyson. He sits at the same board
of public affairs with men who represent the newest
economy of time and speech and the last refinements

of the mechanism of work. Does he expound the truths of natural religion? He speaks to a generation for whom a Lyell and a Darwin have changed the whole picture and reckoning of the world. Does he make the Bible his text-book in the class or the lecture room? He addresses those for whom Strauss and Newman have not written in vain; and he must find and mark the line between the eternal truth and the transitory form,—a line which cannot be cut like a trench upon the ground of time and place, but shoots through the air and light of our humanity, and warms it with the touch of God.

Living in the focus of so much light, searched by the scrutiny of so many demands, the minister is sure to find and to reveal his weaknesses, and fall short of others' hopes and of his own. What limit do then I ask you to put upon this excess of claim? Shall I beg you to forego a large portion of his functions, and select for him some narrow and defined beat of work which he may pace with finished round, and beyond which he shall never look? On the contrary, it is precisely the breadth and comprehensiveness of his sphere in which the very essence of him consists, and which fits him to represent the place of religion in the world; and I would pray you therefore, not so much to cancel this or that demand upon him, as in measuring each to remember all the rest; and whilst reducing the quantities all round within the bounds of reasonable strength, to look chiefly to the unity and faithfulness of Spirit that pervades the whole, the heart and hand quickened by the great Taskmaster's eye, the life of pure order and self-sacrifice that amid the selfish scramble of the world is a constant memento of Christ and God. If he is to interpret the Divine will which flows into every inlet of our life, and the Divine method which sways the universe, you cannot shut him into a corner, and bid him mind its business as his own. Righteousness, which it is his to uphold, is not a business, but a rule of all business. The spirit of Christ, which it is his to waken in the heart, is not a single art or virtue, but the very soul of noble action and the breath of highest love in all the world. The divine truth which it is his to bring into the light is no special Science, worked out upon this or that set of phenomena, but the mysterious realm of thought that holds all sciences, as Space holds the stars. If there is anything human, anything cosmical, which has no interest for him, he is less than the meaning of his name; and if he justifies his blind sympathy by false distinctions,—discharging *this* as secular, and *that* as political, and the other as scientific, and leaving only the residuary emptiness for religion,—he is self-convicted of incompetence and betrays his trust. When we complain of the meddlesomeness of the *Priest*, of his turning up everywhere to hang upon the springing steps of each new hope, we doubtless touch upon an evil of the first magnitude in social history ; but often, for want of clear perception, we look for its essence in the wrong place. The mischief lies, not in the *universality* but in the *quality*, of sacerdotal influence ; which, if it were true, would have divine right to go everywhere, but, being false, has only a Satan's plea for going anywhere ; which has no legitimate sphere in the nature of things at all ; and, if you drive it within narrower lines, is just as bad in the places where you leave it as it was in those which you shut against it. Wherein lies the falsehood of his pretension ? Not in asserting that every crisis should have its consecration ; that all life and love, all death and sorrow, may be turned from earthly to divine ; that to the incidents of the natural drama, the marriage, the birth, the funeral, not mutual joy and tears alone, but uplifted thanks and prayers are due ; that those of the spiritual history,—the child's unconsciousness, the youth's free will, the penitent's remorse, the saint's self-dedicating vow, should all draw us into communion with God ; and that nations, no more than individuals, can find their proper nobleness, if they cease to feel the eye of the all-righteous Judge. All this is true ; but the Priest's falsehood begins with the assumption that he, with his manipulations and his formulas, is the real consecrating thing, the vehicle of a patent salvation which no one can naturally reach, and none else can magically dispense. He is not wrong in saying that the divine authority of which he is the symbol is all-embracing as Omniscience, searching the depths of every human relation, and commanding what is supreme in human prerogative. He is wrong in identifying that authority with himself and his official habitudes of thought and act; and in daring to quote his enigmas and his rites against the grand primary pieties of the human heart. God has made over his claims upon us and his communion with us to no corporation, of believers or of magicians; he gives no charter except such as speaks for itself in the souls that he inspires; he delivers no insignia, except the sword of the spirit, the robe of purity, and the sceptre of devout Faith. The divine authority which encompasses our life is universal, not only as being *over* us all, but as being *in* us all —implicit in some, explicit in others,—the secret suspicion of the skulking conscience that shuts up and hides, the open discovery of the clear one that steals into the light, and even in its tears stands face to face with God. And the sense of this it is that makes the difference between the truth of the prophet and the falsehood of the priest. He does not pretend to do anything *for* man, from a level other than their own; but only to be *with* them, side by side, to own their weariness, to take on him as he can their heavy burdens, to grope with them, perhaps before them, through the dark and winding ways, and report the trembling

gleams which betray the fields of light. When he
speaks to them, he has but to interpret the inmost
experiences of our humanity, to find the pathetic
meanings which lie in the records of every soul, but
which, being writ in invisible ink, remain undeciphered
and dumb till the warm breath and the low music of
a congenial voice read them off into hymn and prayer.
This it is, this appeal to the men as " themselves also
taught of God," this key-note of a common sorrow
and a common sanctity,—that gave to the teaching of
Christ its unspeakable depth, and invested it with the
very authority which it seems to merge in sympathy.
And this it is which must ever be the true tone
and the chief function of the prophet. He has to
gather the hints, to follow the traces, of these infinite
relations, amid which Christ has set our life afloat, to
unveil the hiding places of God within us, and fix
upon the canvas the flitting foregleams of Immortality.
If our nature is fitted up upon that scale, if we are not
merely creatures but Sons of God, we surely carry, in
the constitution of our thought and love and conscience,
the marks of so great a lot; and whoever brings them
home to the hearts of men does the work of an evangelist. So, at last, may the wish of Christ be accomplished in the whole breadth of its spirit; and that
kingdom of God be established on earth which he
gave it to apostles to preach, and for which God
inspires all good men to pray.

Is this the function and attitude of the Christian preacher? Then we have only to turn the same thought the other way, to find the right mood for the Christian hearer. Does your minister, as a man among men, simply take the common platform with you? and will you not take it with him? Shall he spend himself in sympathy with experiences which are alike yours and his? and shall he want the help of a brotherly response? Shall he appeal to what is highest in you, in simple faith that the sleeping sanctities are there, and will you not go forth in heart to meet him, and lay yourself open to be found of him, and so save him from misgiving of his lonely visions? There is no dialogue between the pulpit and the pew to tell the feelings that pass to and fro; but, depend upon it, there is a silent free-masonry of souls at one, by which the secret flies, and as it breathes around, adds power to the most languid wing of aspiration, and sends Saul also among the prophets. Complaint is often made that the pulpit is turned into the Lecture desk; that criticism, evidences, metaphysics, history,—every husk that hangs about divine things, rather than the living kernel, is offered to a craving people; they ask for bread, and we give them a stone. A thousand times have I owned the truth to myself, and been humbled by it. But does the cause lie entirely with the preacher? Do you think that if his people are really thirsting, he will be perpetually dry? If their parched lips and eager eyes beseech him for the reviving drops, will he never dip his cup into the well of life? May it not sometimes be that his faith, his fervour, his tenderest pieties, are driven in, because, when they come out they seem to wander homeless and shiver in the cold air alone? May he not shrink from pouring forth the history of his inner strife and repose under the eye of the sceptic stranger, and from chanting his deepest psalm to the ear unmusical? The more doubtful he is of the sympathy around him, the more is he impelled, —instead of simply delivering the message of the spirit,—to insinuate it by logical bye-ways of approach, to support it by artifices of defence, to make apology for it before the critical faculties which cannot apprehend it. It is a fatal sign, when in the church itself their natural home, divine things, through the unsusceptible mood prevailing, are put upon their defence, and have even to go back to the beginning, and make good their own reality. Where heart is sure of heart, there will be no inventing of excuses for their common trust and love. Where in every hand the sacred torch is ready trimmed, and charged with the unwasting oil, it needs but the first to be on fire; one kindling touch, one rapid thrill from link to link, and the chain of flame is instantly complete, and the place is all aglow.

On you then, my friends, not less than on your minister, it depends to let this place be truly a house of prayer, and a nursery of all manly piety and sweet

affections. The more critical our age, the more
intense our secular activities, so much the more do we
need to guard some holy ground whence the voices of
disputation and the din of work may be banished,—
some refuge for the simplest affections and most
solemn trusts,—some retreat behind the shrine of
mystery and holy love, where we may be found of the
living God, and remember our kindred among the
saints of every age.   Reverence therefore the ends to
which this house is dedicated, and let the ideal of the
outer temple find its reality in this.   Once this is
secured, all else will follow; the highest term of
the soul includes all the rest.   Here is the citadel of
your strength ; and if this be maintained in high
allegiance to the Lord of our life and the cross of
Christ, there will be no betrayal upon the outposts of
duty.   United with your minister in his highest aims,
you will protect him in whatever is needful to sustain and
execute them.   You will respect his *time ;* and let him
rescue every day some fresh hours, to maintain the
fountains of thought clear and full, by resort to the
unwasting springs of Christian wisdom, and converse
with the great and good minds of every age.   You will
respect his *freedom ;* and being at one with him in the
essential spirit of life in Christ Jesus, on which all
the pieties and charities depend, will not expect him
always to spell it out in your favourite letters, or take
it amiss if for him the truth flows down into other

moulds. You will respect the limits of his power ; and by considerate forbearance will second his desire to do rather the *best* for you than the *most ;* knowing well how soon, if the standard once high is permitted to drop, the healthy vigour fails, and its order lapses into confusion. And you will volunteer to be partners in his active work ; going with him heart and hand, nay often before him, in every labour of mercy and of instruction ; and ever striving to make the moral space around this church wholesome, pure, and bright, not ashamed of the sunshine of God, or afraid of the scrutiny of men. So may the fruits of righteousness abound among you, and the work of people and pastor be owned, when the everlasting harvest is gathered in !

1864 (Bolton).

WOODFALL AND KINDER, PRINTERS, LONG ACRE, LONDON.

A Selection of Works

IN

THEOLOGICAL LITERATURE

PUBLISHED BY

MESSRS. LONGMANS, GREEN, & CO.

London: 39 PATERNOSTER ROW, E.C.

New York: 91 and 93 FIFTH AVENUE.

Bombay: 32 HORNBY ROAD.

Abbey and Overton.—THE ENGLISH CHURCH IN THE EIGHTEENTH CENTURY. By CHARLES J. ABBEY, M.A., Rector of Checkendon, Reading, and JOHN H. OVERTON, D.D., Canon of Lincoln. *Crown 8vo. 7s. 6d.*

Adams.—SACRED ALLEGORIES. The Shadow of the Cross —The Distant Hills—The Old Man's Home—The King's Messengers. By the Rev. WILLIAM ADAMS, M.A. With Illustrations. *16mo. 3s. net.*

The four Allegories may be had separately, *16mo. 1s. each.*

Aids to the Inner Life.

Edited by the Venble. W. H. HUTCHINGS, M.A., Archdeacon of Cleveland, Canon of York, Rector of Kirby Misperton, and Rural Dean of Malton. *Five Vols. 32mo, cloth limp, 6d. each; or cloth extra, 1s. each.*
OF THE IMITATION OF CHRIST. By THOMAS À KEMPIS.
THE CHRISTIAN YEAR.
THE DEVOUT LIFE. By ST. FRANCIS DE SALES.
THE HIDDEN LIFE OF THE SOUL. By JEAN NICOLAS GROU.
THE SPIRITUAL COMBAT. By LAURENCE SCUPOLI.

Arbuthnot.—SHAKESPEARE SERMONS. Preached in the Collegiate Church of Stratford-on-Avon on the Sundays following the Poet's Birthday, 1894-1900. Collected by the Rev. GEORGE ARBUTHNOT, M.A., Vicar of Stratford-on-Avon. *Crown 8vo. 2s. 6d. net.*

Baily-Browne.—Works by A. B. BAILY-BROWN.
A HELP TO THE SPIRITUAL INTERPRETATION OF THE PENITENTIAL PSALMS, consisting of Brief Notes from The Fathers, gathered from Neale and Littledale's Commentary. With Preface by the Rev. GEORGE BODY, D.D., Canon of Durham. *Crown 8vo. 1s. net.*
THE SONGS OF DEGREES; or, Gradual Psalms. Interleaved with Notes from Neale and Littledale's Commentary on the Psalms, *Crown 8vo. 1s. net.*

Bathe.—Works by the Rev. ANTHONY BATHE, M.A.

A LENT WITH JESUS. A Plain Guide for Churchmen. Containing Readings for Lent and Easter Week, and on the Holy Eucharist. 32mo, 1s.; *or in paper cover, 6d.*

AN ADVENT WITH JESUS. *32mo, 1s., or in paper cover, 6d.*

WHAT I SHOULD BELIEVE. A Simple Manual of Self-Instruction for Church People. *Small 8vo, limp, 1s. ; cloth gilt, 2s.*

Bathe and Buckham.—THE CHRISTIAN'S ROAD BOOK. 2 Parts. By the Rev. ANTHONY BATHE and Rev. F. H. BUCKHAM. Part I. DEVOTIONS. *Sewed, 6d. ; limp cloth, 1s. ; cloth extra, 1s. 6d.* Part II. READINGS. *Sewed, 1s. ; limp cloth, 2s. ; cloth extra, 3s. ; or complete in one volume, sewed, 1s. 6d. limp cloth, 2s. 6d. ; cloth extra, 3s. 6d.*

Benson.—Works by the Rev. R. M. BENSON, M.A., Student of Christ Church, Oxford.

THE FOLLOWERS OF THE LAMB : a Series of Meditations, especially intended for Persons living under Religious Vows, and for Seasons of Retreat, etc. *Crown 8vo. 4s. 6d.*

THE FINAL PASSOVER : A Series of Meditations upon the Passion of our Lord Jesus Christ. *Small 8vo.*

Vol. I.—THE REJECTION. 5s.
Vol. II.—THE UPPER CHAMBER.
Part I. 5s.
Part II. 5s.

Vol. III.—THE DIVINE EXODUS. Parts I. and II. 5s. each.
Vol. IV.—THE LIFE BEYOND THE GRAVE. 5s.

THE MAGNIFICAT ; a Series of Meditations upon the Song of the Blessed Virgin Mary. *Small 8vo. 2s.*

SPIRITUAL READINGS FOR EVERY DAY. 3 vols. *Small 8vo. 3s. 6d. each.*
I. ADVENT.   II. CHRISTMAS.   III. EPIPHANY.

BENEDICTUS DOMINUS : A Course of Meditations for Every Day of the Year. Vol. I.—ADVENT TO TRINITY. Vol. II.—TRINITY, SAINTS' DAYS, etc. *Small 8vo. 3s. 6d. each ; or in One Volume, 7s.*

BIBLE TEACHINGS: The Discourse at Capernaum.—St. John vi. *Small 8vo. 1s. ; or with Notes. 3s. 6d.*

THE WISDOM OF THE SON OF DAVID : An Exposition of the First Nine Chapters of the Book of Proverbs. *Small 8vo. 3s. 6d.*

THE MANUAL OF INTERCESSORY PRAYER. *Royal 32mo ; cloth boards, 1s. 3d. ; cloth limp, 9d.*

THE EVANGELIST LIBRARY CATECHISM. Part I. *Small 8vo. 3s.*

PAROCHIAL MISSIONS. *Small 8vo. 2s. 6d,*

Bickersteth.—YESTERDAY, TO-DAY, AND FOR EVER: a Poem in Twelve Books. By EDWARD HENRY BICKERSTETH, D.D.. late Lord Bishop of Exeter. 18mo. 1s. net. With red borders, 16mo, 2s. net.

The Crown 8vo Edition (5s.) may still be had.

Bigg.—UNITY IN DIVERSITY: Five Addresses delivered in the Cathedral Church of Christ, Oxford, during Lent 1899, with Introduction. By the Rev. CHARLES BIGG, D.D., Regius Professor of Ecclesiastical History in the University of Oxford. *Crown 8vo. 2s. 6d.*

Blunt.—Works by the Rev. JOHN HENRY BLUNT, D.D.

THE ANNOTATED BOOK OF COMMON PRAYER: Being an Historical, Ritual, and Theological Commentary on the Devotional System of the Church of England. *4to. 21s.*

THE COMPENDIOUS EDITION OF THE ANNOTATED BOOK OF COMMON PRAYER: Forming a concise Commentary on the Devotional System of the Church of England. *Crown 8vo. 10s. 6d.*

DICTIONARY OF DOCTRINAL AND HISTORICAL THEOLOGY. By various Writers. *Imperial 8vo. 21s.*

DICTIONARY OF SECTS, HERESIES, ECCLESIASTICAL PARTIES AND SCHOOLS OF RELIGIOUS THOUGHT. By various Writers. *Imperial 8vo. 21s.*

THE BOOK OF CHURCH LAW. Being an Exposition of the Legal Rights and Duties of the Parochial Clergy and the Laity of the Church of England. Revised by the Right Hon. Sir WALTER G. F. PHILLIMORE, Bart., D.C.L., and G. EDWARDES JONES, Barrister-at-Law. *Crown 8vo. 8s. net.*

A COMPANION TO THE BIBLE: Being a Plain Commentary on Scripture History, to the end of the Apostolic Age. *Two Vols. small 8vo. Sold separately.* OLD TESTAMEMT. 3s. 6d. NEW TESTAMENT. 3s. 6d.

HOUSEHOLD THEOLOGY: a Handbook of Religious Information respecting the Holy Bible, the Prayer Book, the Church, etc., etc. 16mo. *Paper cover, 1s. Also the Larger Edition, 3s. 6d.*

Body.—Works by the Rev. GEORGE BODY, D.D., Canon of Durham.

THE LIFE OF LOVE. A Course of Lent Lectures. 16mo. 2s. net.

THE SCHOOL OF CALVARY; or, Laws of Christian Life revealed from the Cross. 16mo. 2s. net.

THE LIFE OF JUSTIFICATION. 16mo. 2s. net.

THE LIFE OF TEMPTATION. 16mo. 2s. net.

THE PRESENT STATE OF THE FAITHFUL DEPARTED. *Small 8vo. sewed, 6d. 32mo. cloth, 1s.*

Book of Private Prayer, The. For use Twice Daily ; together with the Order for the Administration of the Lord's Supper or Holy Communion. *18mo. Limp cloth, 2s.; Cloth boards, 2s. 6d.*

Book of Prayer and Daily Texts for English Churchmen. *32mo. 1s. net.*

Boultbee.—A COMMENTARY ON THE THIRTY-NINE ARTICLES OF THE CHURCH OF ENGLAND. By the Rev. T. P. BOULTBEE. *Crown 8vo. 6s.*

Bright.—Works by WILLIAM BRIGHT, D.D., late Regius Professor of Ecclesiastical History in the University of Oxford.

THE AGE OF THE FATHERS. Being Chapters in the History of the Church during the Fourth and Fifth Centuries. *Two Vols. 8vo. 28s. net.*

MORALITY IN DOCTRINE. *Crown 8vo. 7s. 6d.*

SOME ASPECTS OF PRIMITIVE CHURCH LIFE. *Crown 8vo. 6s.*

THE ROMAN SEE IN THE EARLY CHURCH : And other Studies in Church History. *Crown 8vo. 7s. 6d.*

LESSONS FROM THE LIVES OF THREE GREAT FATHERS. St. Athanasius, St. Chrysostom, and St. Augustine. *Crown 8vo. 6s.*

THE INCARNATION AS A MOTIVE POWER. *Crown 8vo. 6s.*

Bright and Medd.—LIBER PRECUM PUBLICARUM EC-CLESIÆ ANGLICANÆ. A GULIELMO BRIGHT, S.T.P., et PETRO GOLDSMITH MEDD, A.M., Latine redditus. *Small 8vo. 5s. net.*

Browne.—AN EXPOSITION OF THE THIRTY-NINE ARTICLES, Historical and Doctrinal. By E. H. BROWNE, D.D., sometime Bishop of Winchester. *8vo. 16s.*

Campion and Beamont.—THE PRAYER BOOK INTER-LEAVED. With Historical Illustrations and Explanatory Notes arranged parallel to the Text. By W. M. CAMPION, D.D., and W. J. BEAMONT, M.A. *Small 8vo. 7s. 6d.*

Carpenter and Harford-Battersby. — THE HEXATEUCH ACCORDING TO THE REVISED VERSION ARRANGED IN ITS CONSTITUENT DOCUMENTS BY MEMBERS OF THE SOCIETY OF HISTORICAL THEOLOGY, OXFORD. Edited with Introduction, Notes, Marginal References, and Synoptical Tables. By J. ESTLIN CARPENTER, M.A. (Lond.) and G. HARFORD-BATTERSBY, M.A. (Oxon.). *Two vols. 4to. (Vol. I. Introduction and Appendices: Vol. II. Text and Notes).* 36s. *net.*

THE COMPOSITION OF THE HEXATEUCH : An Introduction with Select Lists of Words and Phrases. With an Appendix on Laws and Institutions. *(Selected from the above.)* 8vo. 18s. *net.*

Carter.—Works by, and edited by, the Rev. T. T. CARTER, M.A., late Hon. Canon of Christ Church, Oxford.

SPIRITUAL INSTRUCTIONS. *Crown 8vo.*

THE HOLY EUCHARIST. 3s. 6d.	OUR LORD'S EARLY LIFE. 3s. 6d.
THE DIVINE DISPENSATIONS. 3s. 6d.	OUR LORD'S ENTRANCE ON HIS
THE LIFE OF GRACE. 3s. 6d.	MINISTRY. 3s. 6d.

THE RELIGIOUS LIFE. 3s. 6d.

A BOOK OF PRIVATE PRAYER FOR MORNING, MID-DAY, AND OTHER TIMES. *18mo, limp cloth,* 1s. ; *cloth, red edges,* 1s. 3d.

THE DOCTRINE OF CONFESSION IN THE CHURCH OF ENGLAND. *Crown 8vo.* 5s.

THE SPIRIT OF WATCHFULNESS AND OTHER SERMONS. *Crown 8vo.* 5s.

THE TREASURY OF DEVOTION : a Manual of Prayer for General and Daily Use. Compiled by a Priest.
    18mo. 2s. 6d. ; *cloth limp,* 2s. Bound with the Book of Common Prayer, 3s. 6d. Red-Line Edition. *Cloth extra, gilt top.* 18mo. 2s. 6d. *net.* Large-Type Edition. *Crown 8vo.* 3s. 6d.

THE WAY OF LIFE : A Book of Prayers and Instruction for the Young at School, with a Preparation for Confirmation. *18mo.* 1s. 6d.

THE PATH OF HOLINESS : a First Book of Prayers, with the Service of the Holy Communion, for the Young. Compiled by a Priest. With Illustrations. *16mo.* 1s. 6d. ; *cloth limp,* 1s.

THE GUIDE TO HEAVEN : a Book of Prayers for every Want. (For the Working Classes.) Compiled by a Priest. *18mo.* 1s. 6d. ; *cloth limp,* 1s. *Large-Type Edition. Crown 8vo.* 1s. 6d. ; *cloth limp,* 1s.

THE STAR OF CHILDHOOD : a First Book of Prayers and Instruction for Children. Compiled by a Priest. With Illustrations. *16mo.* 2s. 6d.

SIMPLE LESSONS ; or, Words Easy to be Understood. A Manual of Teaching. I. On the Creed. II. The Ten Commandments. III. The Sacrament. *18mo.* 3s.

MANUAL OF DEVOTION FOR SISTERS OF MERCY. 8 parts in 2 vols. 32mo. 10s. Or separately :—Part I. 1s. 6d. Part II. 1s. Part III. 1s. Part IV. 2s. Part V. 1s. Part VI. 1s. Part VII. Part VIII. 1s. 6d.

UNDERCURRENTS OF CHURCH LIFE IN THE EIGHTEENTH CENTURY. *Crown 8vo.* 5s.

NICHOLAS FERRAR : his Household and his Friends. With Portrait. *Crown 8vo.* 6s.

Coles.—Works by the Rev. V. S. S. COLES, M.A., Principal of the Pusey House, Oxford.

LENTEN MEDITATIONS. *18mo. 2s. 6d.*

ADVENT MEDITATIONS ON ISAIAH I.-XII. : together with Outlines of Christmas Meditations on St. John i. 1-12. *18mo. 2s.*

Company, The, of Heaven : Daily Links with the Household of God. Being Selections in Prose and Verse from various Authors. With Autotype Frontispiece. *Crown 8vo. 3s. 6d. net.*

Conybeare and Howson.—THE LIFE AND EPISTLES OF ST. PAUL. By the Rev. W. J. CONYBEARE, M.A., and the Very Rev. J. S. HOWSON, D.D. With numerous Maps and Illustrations.

LIBRARY EDITION. *Two Vols. 8vo. 21s.* STUDENTS' EDITION. *One Vol. Crown 8vo. 6s.* POPULAR EDITION. *One Vol. Crown 8vo. 3s. 6d.*

Creighton.—Works by MANDELL CREIGHTON, D.D., late Lord Bishop of London.

A HISTORY OF THE PAPACY FROM THE GREAT SCHISM TO THE SACK OF ROME (1378-1527). *Six Volumes. Crown 8vo. 5s. each net.*

THE CHURCH AND THE NATION : Charges and Addresses. *Crown 8vo. 5s. net.*

THOUGHTS ON EDUCATION : Speeches and Sermons. *Crown 8vo. 5s. net.*

Day-Hours of the Church of England, The.   Newly Revised according to the Prayer Book and the Authorised Translation of the Bible. *Crown 8vo, sewed, 3s.* ; *cloth, 3s. 6d.*

SUPPLEMENT TO THE DAY-HOURS OF THE CHURCH OF ENGLAND, being the Service for certain Holy Days. *Crown 8vo, sewed, 3s.* ; *cloth, 3s. 6d.*

Edersheim.—Works by ALFRED EDERSHEIM, M.A., D.D., Ph.D.

THE LIFE AND TIMES OF JESUS THE MESSIAH. *Two Vols. 8vo. 12s. net.*

JESUS THE MESSIAH : being an Abridged Edition of 'The Life and Times of Jesus the Messiah.' *Crown 8vo. 6s. net.*

Ellicott.—Works by C. J. ELLICOTT, D.D., Bishop of Gloucester.

A CRITICAL AND GRAMMATICAL COMMENTARY ON ST. PAUL'S EPISTLES. Greek Text, with a Critical and Grammatical Commentary, and a Revised English Translation. *8vo.*

GALATIANS. *8s. 6d.*	PHILIPPIANS, COLOSSIANS, AND
EPHESIANS. *8s. 6d.*	PHILEMON. *10s. 6d.*
PASTORAL EPISTLES. *10s. 6d.*	THESSALONIANS. *7s. 6d.*

HISTORICAL LECTURES ON THE LIFE OF OUR LORD JESUS CHRIST. *8vo. 12s.*

English (The) Catholic's Vade Mecum: a Short Manual of General Devotion. Compiled by a PRIEST. *32mo. limp, 1s.; cloth, 2s.* PRIEST'S Edition. *32mo. 1s. 6d.*

Epochs of Church History.—Edited by MANDELL CREIGHTON, D.D., late Lord Bishop of London. *Small 8vo. 2s. 6d. each.*

THE ENGLISH CHURCH IN OTHER LANDS. By the Rev. H. W. TUCKER, M.A.

THE HISTORY OF THE REFORMATION IN ENGLAND. By the Rev. GEO. G. PERRY, M.A.

THE CHURCH OF THE EARLY FATHERS. By the Rev. ALFRED PLUMMER, D.D.

THE EVANGELICAL REVIVAL IN THE EIGHTEENTH CENTURY. By the Rev. J. H. OVERTON, D.D.

THE UNIVERSITY OF OXFORD. By the Hon. G. C. BRODRICK, D.C.L.

THE UNIVERSITY OF CAMBRIDGE. By J. BASS MULLINGER, M.A.

THE ENGLISH CHURCH IN THE MIDDLE AGES. By the Rev. W. HUNT, M.A.

THE CHURCH AND THE EASTERN EMPIRE. By the Rev. H. F. TOZER, M.A.

THE CHURCH AND THE ROMAN EMPIRE. By the Rev. A. CARR, M.A.

THE CHURCH AND THE PURITANS, 1570-1660. By HENRY OFFLEY WAKEMAN, M.A.

HILDEBRAND AND HIS TIMES. By the Very Rev. W. R. W. STEPHENS, B.D.

THE POPES AND THE HOHENSTAUFEN. By UGO BALZANI.

THE COUNTER REFORMATION. By ADOLPHUS WILLIAM WARD, Litt. D.

WYCLIFFE AND MOVEMENTS FOR REFORM. By REGINALD L. POOLE, M.A.

THE ARIAN CONTROVERSY. By the Rev. Professor H. M. GWATKIN, M.A.

Eucharistic Manual (The). Consisting of Instructions and Devotions for the Holy Sacrament of the Altar. From various sources. *32mo. cloth gilt, red edges. 1s. Cheap Edition, limp cloth. 9d.*

Farrar.—Works by FREDERIC W. FARRAR, D.D., Dean of Canterbury.

TEXTS EXPLAINED; or, Helps to Understand the New Testament. *Crown 8vo. 5s. net.*

THE BIBLE: Its Meaning and Supremacy. *8vo. 6s. net.*

ALLEGORIES. With 25 Illustrations by AMELIA BAUERLE. *Crown 8vo. gilt edges. 2s. 6d. net.*

Fosbery.—VOICES OF COMFORT. Edited by the Rev. THOMAS VINCENT FOSBERY, M.A., sometime Vicar of St. Giles's, Reading. *Cheap Edition. Small 8vo. 3s. net. The Larger Edition (7s. 6d.) may still be had.*

Gardner.—A CATECHISM OF CHURCH HISTORY, from the Day of Pentecost until the Present Day. By the Rev. C. E. GARDNER, of the Society of St. John the Evangelist, Cowley. *Crown 8vo, sewed, 1s.; cloth, 1s. 6d.*

Geikie.—Works by J. CUNNINGHAM GEIKIE, D.D., LL.D., late Vicar of St. Martin-at-Palace, Norwich.

THE VICAR AND HIS FRIENDS. *Crown 8vo. 5s. net.*

HOURS WITH THE BIBLE: the Scriptures in the Light of Modern Discovery and Knowledge. *Complete in Twelve Volumes. Crown 8vo.*

OLD TESTAMENT.

CREATION TO THE PATRIARCHS. *With a Map and Illustrations. 5s.*

MOSES TO JUDGES. *With a Map and Illustrations. 5s.*

SAMSON TO SOLOMON. *With a Map and Illustrations. 5s.*

REHOBOAM TO HEZEKIAH. *With Illustrations. 5s.*

MANASSEH TO ZEDEKIAH. *With the Contemporary Prophets. With a Map and Illustrations. 5s.*

EXILE TO MALACHI. *With the Contemporary Prophets. With Illustrations. 5s.*

NEW TESTAMENT.

THE GOSPELS. *With a Map and Illustrations. 5s.*

LIFE AND WORDS OF CHRIST. *With Map. 2 vols. 10s.*

LIFE AND EPISTLES OF ST. PAUL. *With Maps and Illustrations. 2 vols. 10s.*

ST. PETER TO REVELATION. *With 29 Illustrations. 5s.*

LIFE AND WORDS OF CHRIST.
Cabinet Edition. With Map. 2 vols. Post 8vo. 10s.
Cheap Edition, without the Notes. 1 vol. 8vo. 6s.
A SHORT LIFE OF CHRIST. *With 34 Illustrations. Crown 8vo. 3s. 6d. ; gilt edges, 4s. 6d.*

Gold Dust: a Collection of Golden Counsels for the Sanctification of Daily Life.

Translated and abridged from the French by E.L.E.E. Edited by CHARLOTTE M. YONGE. Parts I. II. III. Small Pocket Volumes. *Cloth, gilt, each 1s.*, or in white cloth, with red edges, the three parts in a box, 2s. 6d. *each net.* Parts I. and II. in One Volume. *1s. 6d.* Parts I., II., and III. in One Volume. *2s. net.*

*** The two first parts in One Volume, *large type, 18mo. cloth, gilt.* 2s. net.

Gore.—Works by the Right Rev. CHARLES GORE, D.D., Lord Bishop of Worcester.

THE CHURCH AND THE MINISTRY. *Crown 8vo. 6s. net.*
ROMAN CATHOLIC CLAIMS. *Crown 8vo. 3s. net.*

Goreh.—THE LIFE OF FATHER GOREH. By C. E. GARDNER, S.S.J.E. Edited, with Preface, by RICHARD MEUX BENSON, M.A., S.S.J.E., Student of Christ Church, Oxford. With Portrait. *Crown 8vo. 5s.*

Great Truths of the Christian Religion. Edited by the Rev. W. U. RICHARDS. *Small 8vo.* 2s.

Hall.—Works by the Right Rev. A. C. A. HALL, D.D., Bishop of Vermont.
CONFIRMATION. *Crown 8vo.* 5s. (*The Oxford Library of Practical Theology.*)
THE VIRGIN MOTHER: Retreat Addresses on the Life of the Blessed Virgin Mary as told in the Gospels. With an appended Essay on the Virgin Birth of our Lord. *Crown 8vo.* 4s. 6d.
CHRIST'S TEMPTATION AND OURS. *Crown 8vo.* 3s. 6d.

Hallowing of Sorrow. By E. R. With a Preface by H. S. HOLLAND, M.A., Canon and Precentor of St. Paul's. *Small 8vo.* 2s.

Hanbury - Tracy. — FAITH AND PROGRESS. Sermons Preached at the Dedication Festival of St. Barnabas' Church, Pimlico, June 10-17, 1900. Edited by the Rev. the Hon. A. HANBURY-TRACY, Vicar of St. Barnabas', Pimlico. With an Introduction by the Rev. T. T. CARTER, M.A. *Crown 8vo.* 4s. 6d. net.

Handbooks for the Clergy. Edited by the Rev. ARTHUR W. ROBINSON, B.D., Vicar of Allhallows Barking by the Tower. *Crown 8vo.* 2s. 6d. net each Volume.
THE PERSONAL LIFE OF THE CLERGY. By the Rev. ARTHUR W. ROBINSON, B.D., Vicar of Allhallows Barking by the Tower.
THE MINISTRY OF CONVERSION. By the Rev. A. J. MASON, D.D., Lady Margaret's Reader in Divinity in the University of Cambridge and Canon of Canterbury.
PATRISTIC STUDY. By the Rev. H. B. SWETE, D.D., Regius Professor of Divinity in the University of Cambridge.
FOREIGN MISSIONS. By the Right Rev. H. H. MONTGOMERY, D.D., formerly Bishop of Tasmania, Secretary of the Society for the Propagation of the Gospel in Foreign Parts.
THE STUDY OF THE GOSPELS. By the Very Rev. J. ARMITAGE ROBINSON, D.D., Dean of Westminster.
A CHRISTIAN APOLOGETIC. By the Very Rev. WILFORD L. ROBINSON, D.D., Dean of Albany, U.S.
PASTORAL VISITATION. By the Rev. H. E. SAVAGE, M.A., Vicar of South Shields. *Crown 8vo.* 2s. 6d. net.
* *Other Volumes are in preparation.*

Hatch.—THE ORGANIZATION OF THE EARLY CHRISTIAN CHURCHES. Being the Bampton Lectures for 1880. By EDWIN HATCH, M.A., D.D., late Reader in Ecclesiastical History in the University of Oxford. *8vo.* 5s.

A 2

Holland.—Works by the Rev. HENRY SCOTT HOLLAND, M.A., Canon and Precentor of St. Paul's.

GOD'S CITY AND THE COMING OF THE KINGDOM. *Crown 8vo. 3s. 6d.*

PLEAS AND CLAIMS FOR CHRIST. *Crown 8vo. 3s. 6d.*

CREED AND CHARACTER : Sermons. *Crown 8vo. 3s. 6d.*

ON BEHALF OF BELIEF. Sermons. *Crown 8vo. 3s. 6d.*

CHRIST OR ECCLESIASTES. Sermons. *Crown 8vo. 2s. 6d.*

LOGIC AND LIFE, with other Sermons. *Crown 8vo. 3s. 6d.*

GOOD FRIDAY. Being Addresses on the Seven Last Words. *Small 8vo. 2s.*

Hollings.—Works by the Rev. G. S. HOLLINGS, Mission Priest of the Society of St. John the Evangelist, Cowley, Oxford.

THE HEAVENLY STAIR ; or, A Ladder of the Love of God for Sinners. *Crown 8vo. 3s. 6d.*

PORTA REGALIS ; or, Considerations on Prayer. *Crown 8vo. limp cloth, 1s. 6d. net ; cloth boards, 2s. net.*

CONSIDERATIONS ON THE WISDOM OF GOD. *Crown 8vo. 4s.*

PARADOXES OF THE LOVE OF GOD, especially as they are seen in the way of the Evangelical Counsels. *Crown 8vo. 4s.*

ONE BORN OF THE SPIRIT ; or, the Unification of our Life in God. *Crown 8vo. 3s. 6d.*

Hutchings.—Works by the Ven. W. H. HUTCHINGS, M.A. Archdeacon of Cleveland, Canon of York, Rector of Kirby Misperton, and Rural Dean of Malton.

SERMON SKETCHES from some of the Sunday Lessons throughout the Church's Year. *Vols. I and II. Crown 8vo. 5s. each.*

THE LIFE OF PRAYER : a Course of Lectures delivered in All Saints' Church, Margaret Street, during Lent. *Crown 8vo. 4s. 6d.*

THE PERSON AND WORK OF THE HOLY GHOST : a Doctrinal and Devotional Treatise. *Crown 8vo. 4s. 6d.*

SOME ASPECTS OF THE CROSS. *Crown 8vo. 4s. 6d.*

THE MYSTERY OF THE TEMPTATION. Lent Lectures delivered at St. Mary Magdalene, Paddington. *Crown 8vo. 4s. 6d.*

Hutton.—THE SOUL HERE AND HEREAFTER. By the Rev. R. E. HUTTON, Chaplain of St. Margaret's, East Grinstead. *Crown 8vo. 6s.*

Inheritance of the Saints; or, Thoughts on the Communion of Saints and the Life of the World to come. Collected chiefly from English Writers by L. P. With a Preface by the Rev. HENRY SCOTT HOLLAND, M.A. *Crown 8vo. 7s. 6d.*

James.—THE VARIETIES OF RELIGIOUS EXPERIENCE: A Study in Human Nature. Being the Gifford Lectures on Natural Religion delivered at Edinburgh in 1901-1902. By WILLIAM JAMES, LL.D., etc., Professor of Philosophy at Harvard University. *8vo. 12s. net.*

Jameson.—Works by Mrs. JAMESON.

SACRED AND LEGENDARY ART, containing Legends of the Angels and Archangels, the Evangelists, the Apostles. With 19 Etchings and 187 Woodcuts. *2 vols. 8vo. 20s. net.*

LEGENDS OF THE MONASTIC ORDERS, as represented in the Fine Arts. With 11 Etchings and 88 Woodcuts. *8vo. 10s. net.*

LEGENDS OF THE MADONNA, OR BLESSED VIRGIN MARY. With 27 Etchings and 165 Woodcuts. *8vo. 10s. net.*

THE HISTORY OF OUR LORD, as exemplified in Works of Art. Commenced by the late Mrs. JAMESON ; continued and completed by LADY EASTLAKE. With 31 Etchings and 281 Woodcuts. *2 Vols. 8vo. 20s. net.*

Johnstone.—SONSHIP : Six Lenten Addresses. By the Rev. VERNEY LOVETT JOHNSTONE, M.A., late Assistant Curate of Ilfracombe. .With an Introduction by the Rev. V. S. S. COLES, M.A., Principal of the Pusey House, Oxford. *Crown 8vo. 2s.*

Jones.—ENGLAND AND THE HOLY SEE: An Essay towards Reunion. By SPENCER JONES, M.A., Rector of Moreton-in-Marsh. With a Preface by the Right Hon. VISCOUNT HALIFAX. *Crown 8vo. 3s. 6s. net.*

Joy and Strength for the Pilgrim's Day: Selections in Prose and Verse. By the Editor of 'Daily Strength for Daily Needs,' etc. *Small 8vo. 3s. 6d. net.*

Jukes.—Works by ANDREW JUKES.

LETTERS OF ANDREW JUKES. Edited, with a Short Biography, by the Rev. HERBERT H. JEAFFERSON, M.A. *Crown 8vo. 3s. 6d. net.*

THE NAMES OF GOD IN HOLY SCRIPTURE : a Revelation of His Nature and Relationships. *Crown 8vo. 4s. 6d.*

THE TYPES OF GENESIS. *Crown 8vo. 7s. 6d.*

THE SECOND DEATH AND THE RESTITUTION OF ALL THINGS. *Crown 8vo. 3s. 6d.*

Kelly.—Works by the **Rev. Herbert H. Kelly, M.A.,** Director of the Society of the Sacred Mission, Mildenhall, Suffolk.

A HISTORY OF THE CHURCH OF CHRIST. Vol. I. A.D. 29-342. *Crown 8vo.* 3s. 6d. *net.* Vol. II. A.D. 324-430. *Crown 8vo.* 3s. 6d. *net.*

ENGLAND AND THE CHURCH : Her Calling and its Fulfilment Considered in Relation to the Increase and Efficiency of Her Ministry. *Crown 8vo.* 4s. *net.*

Knox.—PASTORS AND TEACHERS : Six Lectures on Pastoral Theology. By the Right Rev. Edmund Arbuthnott Knox, D.D., Bishop of Coventry. With an Introduction by the Right Rev. Charles Gore, D.D., Bishop of Worcester. *Crown 8vo.* 5s. *net.*

Knox Little.—Works by W. J. Knox Little, M.A., Canon Residentiary of Worcester, and Vicar of Hoar Cross.

HOLY MATRIMONY. *Crown 8vo.* 5s. (*The Oxford Library of Practical Theology.*)

THE PERFECT LIFE : Sermons. *Crown 8vo.* 7s. 6d.

THE CHRISTIAN HOME. *Crown 8vo.* 3s. 6d.

CHARACTERISTICS AND MOTIVES OF THE CHRISTIAN LIFE. Ten Sermons preached in Manchester Cathedral, in Lent and Advent. *Crown 8vo.* 2s. 6d.

THE MYSTERY OF THE PASSION OF OUR MOST HOLY REDEEMER. *Crown 8vo.* 2s. 6d.

THE LIGHT OF LIFE. Sermons preached on Various Occasions. *Crown 8vo.* 3s. 6d.

SUNLIGHT AND SHADOW IN THE CHRISTIAN LIFE. Sermons preached for the most part in America. *Crown 8vo.* 3s. 6d.

Lear.—Works by, and Edited by, H. L. Sidney Lear.

FOR DAYS AND YEARS. A book containing a Text, Short Reading, and Hymn for Every Day in the Church's Year. 16mo. 2s. *net. Also a Cheap Edition,* 32mo, 1s.; *or cloth gilt,* 1s. 6d.; *or with red borders,* 2s. *net.*

FIVE MINUTES. Daily Readings of Poetry. 16mo. 3s. 6d. *Also a Cheap Edition,* 32mo. 1s.; *or cloth gilt,* 1s. 6d.

WEARINESS. A Book for the Languid and Lonely. *Large Type. Small 8vo.* 5s.

Lear. — Works by, and Edited by, H. L. SIDNEY LEAR.—*continued.*

DEVOTIONAL WORKS. Edited by H. L. SIDNEY LEAR. *New and Uniform Editions. Nine Vols.* 16mo. 2s. *net each.*

FÉNELON'S SPIRITUAL LETTERS TO MEN.

FÉNELON'S SPIRITUAL LETTERS TO WOMEN.

A SELECTION FROM THE SPIRITUAL LETTERS OF ST. FRANCIS DE SALES. Also *Cheap Edition,* 32mo, 6d. *cloth limp;* 1s. *cloth boards.*

THE SPIRIT OF ST. FRANCIS DE SALES.

THE HIDDEN LIFE OF THE SOUL.

THE LIGHT OF THE CONSCIENCE. Also *Cheap Edition,* 32mo, 6d. *cloth limp;* 1s. *cloth boards.*

SELF-RENUNCIATION. From the French.

ST. FRANCIS DE SALES' OF THE LOVE OF GOD.

SELECTIONS FROM PASCAL'S 'THOUGHTS.'

Leighton. — TYPICAL MODERN CONCEPTIONS OF GOD ; or, The Absolute of German Romantic Idealism and of English Evolutionary Agnosticism. With a Constructive Essay. By JOSEPH ALEXANDER LEIGHTON, Professor of Philosophy in Hobart College, U.S. *Crown 8vo.* 3s. 6d. *net.*

Liddon.—Works by HENRY PARRY LIDDON, D.D., D.C.L., LL.D.

SERMONS ON SOME WORDS OF ST. PAUL. *Crown 8vo.* 5s.

SERMONS PREACHED ON SPECIAL OCCASIONS, 1860-1889. *Crown 8vo.* 5s.

CLERICAL LIFE AND WORK : Sermons. *Crown 8vo.* 5s.

ESSAYS AND ADDRESSES : Lectures on Buddhism—Lectures on the Life of St. Paul—Papers on Dante. *Crown 8vo.* 5s.

EXPLANATORY ANALYSIS OF PAUL'S EPISTLE TO THE ROMANS. *8vo.* 14s.

EXPLANATORY ANALYSIS OF ST. PAUL'S FIRST EPISTLE TO TIMOTHY. *8vo.* 7s. 6d.

SERMONS ON OLD TESTAMENT SUBJECTS. *Crown 8vo.* 5s.

SERMONS ON SOME WORDS OF CHRIST. *Crown 8vo.* 5s.

THE DIVINITY OF OUR LORD AND SAVIOUR JESUS CHRIST. Being the Bampton Lectures for 1866. *Crown 8vo.* 5s.

ADVENT IN ST. PAUL'S. *Crown 8vo.* 5s.

CHRISTMASTIDE IN ST. PAUL'S. *Crown 8vo.* 5s.

PASSIONTIDE SERMONS. *Crown 8vo.* 5s.

[continued.

Liddon.—Works by HENRY PARRY LIDDON, D.D., D.C.L., LL.D.—*continued.*

EASTER IN ST. PAUL'S. Sermons bearing chiefly on the Resurrection of our Lord. *Two Vols. Crown 8vo. 3s. 6d. each. Cheap Edition in one Volume. Crown 8vo. 5s.*

SERMONS PREACHED BEFORE THE UNIVERSITY OF OXFORD. *Two Vols. Crown 8vo. 3s. 6d. each. Cheap Edition in one Volume. Crown 8vo. 5s.*

THE MAGNIFICAT. Sermons in St. Paul's. *Crown 8vo. 2s. net.*

SOME ELEMENTS OF RELIGION. Lent Lectures. *Small 8vo. 2s. net. [The Crown 8vo Edition (5s.) may still be had.]*

Luckock.—Works by HERBERT MORTIMER LUCKOCK, D.D., Dean of Lichfield.

THE SPECIAL CHARACTERISTICS OF THE FOUR GOSPELS. *Crown 8vo. 6s.*

AFTER DEATH. An Examination of the Testimony of Primitive Times respecting the State of the Faithful Dead, and their Relationship to the Living. *Crown 8vo. 3s. net.*

THE INTERMEDIATE STATE BETWEEN DEATH AND JUDGMENT. Being a Sequel to *After Death. Crown 8vo. 3s. net.*

FOOTPRINTS OF THE SON OF MAN, as traced by St. Mark. Being Eighty Portions for Private Study, Family Reading, and Instruction in Church. *Crown 8vo. 3s. net.*

FOOTPRINTS OF THE APOSTLES, as traced by St. Luke in the Acts. Being Sixty Portions for Private Study, and Instruction in Church. A Sequel to 'Footprints of the Son of Man, as traced by St. Mark.' *Two Vols. Crown 8vo. 12s.*

THE DIVINE LITURGY. Being the Order for Holy Communion, Historically, Doctrinally, and Devotionally set forth, in Fifty Portions. *Crown 8vo. 3s. net.*

STUDIES IN THE HISTORY OF THE BOOK OF COMMON PRAYER. The Anglican Reform—The Puritan Innovations—The Elizabethan Reaction—The Caroline Settlement. With Appendices. *Crown 8vo. 3s. net.*

Lyra Germanica: Hymns for the Sundays and Chief Festivals of the Christian Year. *Complete Edition. Small 8vo. 5s. First Series. 16mo, with red borders, 2s. net.*

MacColl.—Works by the Rev. MALCOLM MACCOLL, D.D., Canon Residentiary of Ripon.

THE REFORMATION SETTLEMENT: Examined in the Light of History and Law. Tenth Edition, Revised, with a new Preface. *Crown 8vo.* 3*s.* 6*d. net.*

CHRISTIANITY IN RELATION TO SCIENCE AND MORALS. *Crown 8vo.* 6*s.*

LIFE HERE AND HEREAFTER : Sermons. *Crown 8vo.* 7*s.* 6*d.*

Marriage Addresses and Marriage Hymns. By the BISHOP OF LONDON, the BISHOP OF ROCHESTER, the BISHOP OF TRURO, the DEAN OF ROCHESTER, the DEAN OF NORWICH, ARCHDEACON SINCLAIR, CANON DUCKWORTH, CANON NEWBOLT, CANON KNOX LITTLE, CANON RAWNSLEY, the Rev. J. LLEWELLYN DAVIES, D.D., the Rev. W. ALLEN WHITWORTH, etc. Edited by the Rev. O. P. WARDELL-YERBURGH, M.A., Vicar of the Abbey Church of St. Mary, Tewkesbury. *Crown 8vo.* 5*s.*

Mason.—Works by A. J. MASON, D.D., Lady Margaret's Reader in Divinity in the University of Cambridge and Canon of Canterbury.

THE MINISTRY OF CONVERSION. *Crown 8vo.* 2*s.* 6*d. net.* (*Handbooks for the Clergy.*)

PURGATORY; THE STATE OF THE FAITHFUL DEAD; INVOCATION OF SAINTS. Three Lectures. *Crown 8vo.* 3*s.* 6*d. net.*

THE FAITH OF THE GOSPEL. A Manual of Christian Doctrine. *Crown 8vo.* 7*s.* 6*d. Cheap Edition. Crown 8vo.* 3*s. net.*

THE RELATION OF CONFIRMATION TO BAPTISM. As taught in Holy Scripture and the Fathers. *Crown 8vo.* 7*s.* 6*d.*

Maturin.—Works by the Rev. B. W. MATURIN.

SOME PRINCIPLES AND PRACTICES OF THE SPIRITUAL LIFE. *Crown 8vo.* 4*s.* 6*d.*

PRACTICAL STUDIES ON THE PARABLES OF OUR LORD. *Crown 8vo.* 5*s.*

Medd.—THE PRIEST TO THE ALTAR; or, Aids to the Devout Celebration of Holy Communion, chiefly after the Ancient English Use of Sarum. By PETER GOLDSMITH MEDD, M.A., Canon of St. Albans. Fourth Edition, revised and enlarged. *Royal 8vo.* 15*s.*

Meyrick.—THE DOCTRINE OF THE CHURCH OF England on the Holy Communion Restated as a Guide at the Present Time. By the Rev. F. MEYRICK, M.A. *Crown 8vo.* 4*s.* 6*d.*

Monro.—SACRED ALLEGORIES. By Rev. EDWARD MONRO. *Complete Edition in one Volume, with Illustrations. Crown 8vo.* 3*s.* 6*d. net.*

Mortimer.—Works by the Rev. A. G. MORTIMER, D.D., Rector of St. Mark's, Philadelphia.

THE CREEDS: An Historical and Doctrinal Exposition of the Apostles', Nicene and Athanasian Creeds. *Crown 8vo.* 5s. *net.*

THE EUCHARISTIC SACRIFICE: An Historical and Theological Investigation of the Sacrificial Conception of the Holy Eucharist in the Christian Church. *Crown 8vo.* 10s. 6d.

CATHOLIC FAITH AND PRACTICE: A Manual of Theology. Two Parts. *Crown 8vo.* Sold Separately. Part I. 7s. 6d. Part II. 9s.

JESUS AND THE RESURRECTION: Thirty Addresses for Good Friday and Easter. *Crown 8vo.* 5s.

HELPS TO MEDITATION: Sketches for Every Day in the Year.
Vol. I. ADVENT TO TRINITY. *8vo.* 7s. 6d.
Vol. II. TRINITY TO ADVENT. *8vo.* 7s. 6d.

STORIES FROM GENESIS: Sermons for Children. *Crown 8vo.* 4s.

THE LAWS OF HAPPINESS; or, The Beatitudes as teaching our Duty to God, Self, and our Neighbour. *18mo.* 2s.

THE LAWS OF PENITENCE: Addresses on the Words of our Lord from the Cross. *16mo.* 1s. 6d.

SERMONS IN MINIATURE FOR EXTEMPORE PREACHERS: Sketches for Every Sunday and Holy Day of the Christian Year. *Crown 8vo.* 6s.

NOTES ON THE SEVEN PENITENTIAL PSALMS, chiefly from Patristic Sources. *Small 8vo.* 3s. 6d.

THE SEVEN LAST WORDS OF OUR MOST HOLY REDEEMER: with Meditations on some Scenes in His Passion. *Crown 8vo.* 5s.

LEARN OF JESUS CHRIST TO DIE: Addresses on the Words of our Lord from the Cross, taken as teaching the way of Preparation for Death. *16mo.* 2s.

Mozley.—Works by J. B. MOZLEY, D.D., late Canon of Christ Church, and Regius Professor of Divinity at Oxford.

ESSAYS, HISTORICAL AND THEOLOGICAL. *Two Vols.* *8vo.* 24s.

EIGHT LECTURES ON MIRACLES. Being the Bampton Lectures for 1865. *Crown 8vo.* 3s. *net.*

RULING IDEAS IN EARLY AGES AND THEIR RELATION TO OLD TESTAMENT FAITH. *8vo.* 6s.

SERMONS PREACHED BEFORE THE UNIVERSITY OF OXFORD, and on Various Occasions. *Crown 8vo.* 3s. *net.*

SERMONS, PAROCHIAL AND OCCASIONAL. *Crown 8vo.* 3s. *net.*

A REVIEW OF THE BAPTISMAL CONTROVERSY. *Crown 8vo.* 3s. *net.*

IN THEOLOGICAL LITERATURE.

Newbolt.—Works by the Rev. W. C. E. NEWBOLT, M.A., Canon and Chancellor of St. Paul's Cathedral.

APOSTLES OF THE LORD: being Six Lectures on Pastoral Theology. *Crown 8vo.* 3s. 6d. net.

RELIGION. *Crown 8vo.* 5s. (*The Oxford Library of Practical Theology.*)

WORDS OF EXHORTATION. Sermons Preached at St. Paul's and elsewhere. *Crown 8vo.* 5s. net.

PENITENCE AND PEACE: being Addresses on the 51st and 23rd Psalms. *Crown 8vo.* 2s. net.

PRIESTLY IDEALS; being a Course of Practical Lectures delivered in St. Paul's Cathedral to 'Our Society' and other Clergy, in Lent, 1898. *Crown 8vo.* 3s. 6d.

PRIESTLY BLEMISHES; or, Some Secret Hindrances to the Realisation of Priestly Ideals. A Sequel. Being a Second Course of Practical Lectures delivered in St. Paul's Cathedral to 'Our Society' and other Clergy in Lent, 1902. *Crown 8vo.* 3s. 6d.

THE GOSPEL OF EXPERIENCE; or, the Witness of Human Life to the truth of Revelation. Being the Boyle Lectures for 1895. *Crown 8vo.* 5s.

COUNSELS OF FAITH AND PRACTICE: being Sermons preached on various occasions. *Crown 8vo.* 5s.

SPECULUM SACERDOTUM; or, the Divine Model of the Priestly Life. *Crown 8vo.* 7s. 6d.

THE FRUIT OF THE SPIRIT. Being Ten Addresses bearing on the Spiritual Life. *Crown 8vo.* 2s. net.

THE MAN OF GOD. *Small 8vo.* 1s. 6d.

THE PRAYER BOOK: Its Voice and Teaching. *Crown 8vo.* 2s. net.

Newman.—Works by JOHN HENRY NEWMAN, B.D., sometime Vicar of St. Mary's, Oxford.

LETTERS AND CORRESPONDENCE OF JOHN HENRY NEWMAN DURING HIS LIFE IN THE ENGLISH CHURCH. With a brief Autobiography. Edited, at Cardinal Newman's request, by ANNE MOZLEY. 2 vols. *Crown 8vo.* 7s.

PAROCHIAL AND PLAIN SERMONS. *Eight Vols. Crown 8vo.* 3s. 6d. each.

SELECTION, ADAPTED TO THE SEASONS OF THE ECCLESIASTICAL YEAR, from the 'Parochial and Plain Sermons.' *Crown 8vo.* 3s. 6d.

FIFTEEN SERMONS PREACHED BEFORE THE UNIVERSITY OF OXFORD. *Crown 8vo.* 3s. 6d.

SERMONS BEARING UPON SUBJECTS OF THE DAY. *Crown 8vo.* 3s. 6d.

LECTURES ON THE DOCTRINE OF JUSTIFICATION. *Crown 8vo.* 3s. 6d.

₄ *A Complete List of Cardinal Newman's Works can be had on Application.*

Osborne.—Works by EDWARD OSBORNE, Mission Priest of the Society of St. John the Evangelist, Cowley, Oxford.

THE CHILDREN'S SAVIOUR. Instructions to Children on the Life of Our Lord and Saviour Jesus Christ. *Illustrated.* 16mo. 2s. net.

THE SAVIOUR KING. Instructions to Children on Old Testament Types and Illustrations of the Life of Christ. *Illustrated.* 16mo. 2s. net.

THE CHILDREN'S FAITH. Instructions to Children on the Apostles' Creed. *Illustrated.* 16mo. 2s. net.

Ottley.—ASPECTS OF THE OLD TESTAMENT: being the Bampton Lectures for 1897. By ROBERT LAWRENCE OTTLEY, M.A., Vicar of Winterbourne Bassett, Wilts; sometime Principal of the Pusey House. 8vo. 7s. 6d.

Oxford (The) Library of Practical Theology.—Edited by the Rev. W. C. E. NEWBOLT, M.A., Canon and Chancellor of St. Paul's, and the Rev. DARWELL STONE, M.A., Principal of the Missionary College, Dorchester. *Crown 8vo.* 5s. each.

RELIGION. By the Rev. W. C. E. NEWBOLT, M.A., Canon and Chancellor of St. Paul's.

HOLY BAPTISM. By the Rev. DARWELL STONE, M.A., Principal of the Missionary College, Dorchester.

CONFIRMATION. By the Right Rev. A. C. A. HALL, D.D., Bishop of Vermont.

THE HISTORY OF THE BOOK OF COMMON PRAYER. By the Rev. LEIGHTON PULLAN, M.A., Fellow of St. John Baptist's Oxford.

HOLY MATRIMONY. By the Rev. W. J. KNOX LITTLE, M.A., Canon of Worcester.

THE INCARNATION. By the Rev. H. V. S. ECK, M.A., St. Andrew's, Bethnal Green.

FOREIGN MISSIONS. By the Right Rev. E. T. CHURTON, D.D., formerly Bishop of Nassau.

PRAYER. By the Rev. ARTHUR JOHN WORLLEDGE, M.A., Canon and Chancellor of Truro.

SUNDAY. By the Rev. W. B. TREVELYAN, M.A., Vicar of St. Matthew's, Westminster.

THE CHRISTIAN TRADITION. By the Rev. LEIGHTON PULLAN, M.A., Fellow of St. John's College, Oxford.

BOOKS OF DEVOTION. By the Rev. CHARLES BODINGTON, Canon and Precentor of Lichfield.

HOLY ORDERS. By the Rev. A. R. WHITHAM, M.A., Principal of Culham College, Abingdon. *[In the press.*

THE HOLY COMMUNION. By the Rev. DARWELL STONE, M.A., Joint Editor of the Series. *[In preparation.*

[continued.

Oxford (The) Library of Practical Theology.—*continued.*

THE CHURCH CATECHISM THE CHRISTIAN'S MANUAL. By the Rev. W. C. E. NEWBOLT, M.A., Joint Editor of the Series.

[In preparation.

RELIGIOUS CEREMONIAL. By the Rev. WALTER HOWARD FRERE, M.A., Superior of the Community of the Resurrection, Examining Chaplain to the Bishop of Rochester. *[In preparation.*

VISITATION OF THE SICK. By the Rev. E. F. RUSSELL, M.A., St. Alban's, Holborn. *[In preparation.*

CHURCH WORK. By the Rev. BERNARD REYNOLDS, M.A., Prebendary of St. Paul's. *[In preparation.*

OLD TESTAMENT CRITICISM. By the Rev. HENRY WACE, D.D., Prebendary of St. Paul's Cathedral. *[In preparation.*

NEW TESTAMENT CRITICISM. By the Rev. R. J. KNOWLING, D.D., Professor of New Testament Exegesis at King's College, London. *[In preparation.*

Paget.—Works by FRANCIS PAGET, D.D., Bishop of Oxford.

CHRIST THE WAY: Four Addresses given at a Meeting of Schoolmasters and others at Haileybury. *Crown 8vo. 1s. 6d. net.*

STUDIES IN THE CHRISTIAN CHARACTER: Sermons. With an Introductory Essay. *Crown 8vo. 4s. net.*

THE SPIRIT OF DISCIPLINE: Sermons. *Crown 8vo. 4s. net.*

FACULTIES AND DIFFICULTIES FOR BELIEF AND DISBELIEF. *Crown 8vo. 4s. net.*

THE HALLOWING OF WORK. Addresses given at Eton, January 16-18, 1888. *Small 8vo. 2s.*

THE REDEMPTION OF WAR: Sermons. *Crown 8vo. 2s. net.*

Passmore.—Works by the Rev. T. H. PASSMORE, M.A.

THE THINGS BEYOND THE TOMB IN A CATHOLIC LIGHT. *Crown 8vo. 2s. 6d. net.*

LEISURABLE STUDIES. *Crown 8vo. 4s. net.*

CONTENTS.—The 'Religious Woman'—Preachments—Silly Ritual—The Tyranny of the Word—The Lectern—The Functions of Ceremonial—Homo Creator—Concerning the Pun—Proverbia.

Percival.—THE INVOCATION OF SAINTS. Treated Theologically and Historically. By HENRY R. PERCIVAL, M.A., D.D. *Crown 8vo. 5s.*

Powell.—CHORALIA : a Handy-Book for Parochial Precentors and Choirmasters. By the Rev. JAMES BADEN POWELL, M.A., Precentor of St. Paul's, Knightsbridge. *Crown 8vo. 4s. 6d. net.*

Practical Reflections. By a CLERGYMAN. With Preface by H. P. LIDDON, D.D., D.C.L., and the LORD BISHOP OF LINCOLN. *Crown 8vo.*

THE BOOK OF GENESIS. *4s. 6d.*	THE MINOR PROPHETS. *4s. 6d.*
THE PSALMS. *5s.*	THE HOLY GOSPELS. *4s. 6d.*
ISAIAH. *4s. 6d.*	ACTS TO REVELATION. *6s.*

Preparatio ; or, Notes of Preparation for Holy Communion, founded on the Collect, Epistle, and Gospel for Every Sunday in the Year. With Preface by the Rev. GEORGE CONGREVE, S.S.J.E. *Crown 8vo. 6s. net.*

Priest's Prayer Book (The). Containing Private Prayers and Intercessions ; Occasional, School, and Parochial Offices ; Offices for the Visitation of the Sick, with Notes, Readings, Collects, Hymns, Litanies, etc. With a brief Pontifical. By the late Rev. R. F. LITTLEDALE, LL.D., D.C.L., and Rev. J. EDWARD VAUX, M.A., F.S.A. *Post 8vo. 6s. 6d.*

Pullan.—Works by the Rev. LEIGHTON PULLAN, M.A., Fellow of St. John Baptist's College.

LECTURES ON RELIGION. *Crown 8vo. 6s.*

THE HISTORY OF THE BOOK OF COMMON PRAYER. *Crown 8vo. 5s. (The Oxford Library of Practical Theology.)*

Puller.—THE PRIMITIVE SAINTS AND THE SEE OF ROME. By F. W. PULLER, of the Society of St. John the Evangelist, Cowley. With an Introduction by EDWARD, LORD BISHOP OF LINCOLN. Third Edition, Revised and Enlarged. *8vo. 16s. net.*

Pusey.—Works by the Rev. E. B. PUSEY, D.D.

PRIVATE PRAYERS. With Preface by H. P. LIDDON, D.D., late Chancellor and Canon of St. Paul's. *Royal 32mo. 1s.*

SPIRITUAL LETTERS OF EDWARD BOUVERIE PUSEY, D.D. Edited and prepared for publication by the Rev. J. O. JOHNSTON, M.A., Principal of the Theological College, Cuddesdon ; and the Rev. W. C. E. NEWBOLT, M.A., Canon and Chancellor of St. Paul's. New and cheaper Edition. With Index. *Crown 8vo. 5s. net.*

Pusey.—THE STORY OF THE LIFE OF DR. PUSEY. By the Author of 'Charles Lowder.' With Frontispiece. *Crown 8vo. 7s. 6d. net.*

Randolph.—Works by B. W. RANDOLPH, D.D., Principal of the Theological College and Hon. Canon of Ely.

THE EXAMPLE OF THE PASSION : being Addresses given in St. Paul's Cathedral at the Mid-Day Service on Monday, Tuesday, Wednesday, and Thursday in Holy Week, and at the Three Hours' Service on Good Friday, 1897. *Small 8vo. 2s. net.*

MEDITATIONS ON THE OLD TESTAMENT for Every Day in the Year. *Crown 8vo. 6s.*

THE THRESHOLD OF THE SANCTUARY : being Short Chapters on the Inner Preparation for the Priesthood. *Crown 8vo. 3s. 6d.*

RIVINGTON'S DEVOTIONAL SERIES.
16mo, Red Borders and gilt edges. Each 2s. net.

BICKERSTETH'S YESTERDAY, TO-DAY, AND FOR EVER. *Gilt edges.*

CHILCOT'S TREATISE ON EVIL THOUGHTS. *Red edges.*

THE CHRISTIAN YEAR. *Gilt edges.*

HERBERT'S POEMS AND PROVERBS. *Gilt edges.*

THOMAS À KEMPIS' OF THE IMITATION OF CHRIST. *Gilt edges.*

LEAR'S (H. L. SIDNEY) FOR DAYS AND YEARS. *Gilt edges.*

LYRA APOSTOLICA. POEMS BY J. W. BOWDEN, R. H. FROUDE, J. KEBLE, J. H. NEWMAN, R. I. WILBERFORCE, AND I. WILLIAMS; and a Preface by CARDINAL NEWMAN. *Gilt edges.*

FRANCIS DE SALES' (ST.) THE DEVOUT LIFE. *Gilt edges.*

WILSON'S THE LORD'S SUPPER. *Red edges.*

*TAYLOR'S (JEREMY) HOLY LIVING. *Red edges.*

*———— ———— HOLY DYING. *Red edges.*

SCUDAMORE'S STEPS TO THE ALTAR.. *Gilt edges*

LYRA GERMANICA: HYMNS FOR THE SUNDAYS AND CHIEF FESTIVALS OF THE CHRISTIAN YEAR. *First Series. Gilt edges.*

LAW'S TREATISE ON CHRISTIAN PERFECTION. Edited by L. H. M. SOULSBY. *Gilt edges.*

CHRIST AND HIS CROSS: SELECTIONS FROM SAMUEL RUTHERFORD'S LETTERS. Edited by L. H. M. SOULSBY. *Gilt edges.*

* *These two in one Volume. 5s.*

18mo, without Red Borders. Each 1s. net.

BICKERSTETH'S YESTERDAY, TO-DAY, AND FOR EVER.

THE CHRISTIAN YEAR.

THOMAS À KEMPIS' OF THE IMITATION OF CHRIST.

HERBERT'S POEMS AND PROVERBS.

SCUDAMORE'S STEPS TO THE ALTAR.

WILSON'S THE LORD'S SUPPER.

FRANCIS DE SALES' (ST.) THE DEVOUT LIFE.

*TAYLOR'S (JEREMY) HOLY LIVING.

*———— HOLY DYING.

* *These two in one Volume. 2s. 6d.*

Robbins.—Works by WILFORD L. ROBBINS, D.D., Dean of the Cathedral of All Saints', Albany, U.S.

AN ESSAY TOWARD FAITH. *Small 8vo. 3s. net.*

A CHRISTIAN APOLOGETIC. *Crown 8vo. 2s. 6d. net. (Handbooks for the Clergy.)*

Robinson.—Works by the Rev. C. H. ROBINSON, M.A., Editorial Secretary to the S.P.G. and Canon of Ripon.

STUDIES IN THE CHARACTER OF CHRIST. *Crown 8vo. 3s. 6d.*

HUMAN NATURE A REVELATION OF THE DIVINE: a Sequel to 'Studies in the Character of Christ.' *Crown 8vo. 6s. net.*

Romanes.—THOUGHTS ON THE COLLECTS FOR THE TRINITY SEASON. By ETHEL ROMANES, Author of 'The Life and Letters of George John Romanes.' With a Preface by the Right Rev. the LORD BISHOP OF LONDON. *18mo. 2s. 6d. ; gilt edges. 3s. 6d.*

Sanday.—Works by W. SANDAY, D.D., LL.D., Lady Margaret Professor of Divinity and Canon of Christ Church, Oxford.

DIFFERENT CONCEPTIONS OF PRIESTHOOD AND SACRIFICE : a Report of a Conference held at Oxford, December 13 and 14, 1899. Edited by W. SANDAY, D.D. *8vo. 7s. 6d.*

INSPIRATION : Eight Lectures on the Early History and Origin of the Doctrine of Biblical Inspiration. Being the Bampton Lectures for 1893. *8vo. 7s. 6d.*

Sanders.—FÉNELON : HIS FRIENDS AND HIS ENEMIES, 1651-1715. By E. K. SANDERS. With Portrait. *8vo. 10s. 6d. net.*

Scudamore.—STEPS TO THE ALTAR: a Manual of Devotion for the Blessed Eucharist. By the Rev. W. E. SCUDAMORE, M.A. *Royal 32mo. 1s.*

On toned paper, and rubricated, 2s.: The same, with Collects, Epistles, and Gospels, 2s. 6d. ; 18mo, 1s. net; Demy 18mo, cloth, large type, 1s. 3d. ; 16mo, with red borders, 2s. net; Imperial 32mo, limp cloth, 6d.

Simpson.—Works by the Rev. W. J. SPARROW SIMPSON, M.A., Vicar of St. Mark's, Regent's Park.

THE CHURCH AND THE BIBLE. *Crown 8vo. 3s. 6d.*

THE CLAIMS OF JESUS CHRIST : Lent Lectures. *Crown 8vo. 3s.*

Skrine.—PASTOR AGNORUM : a Schoolmaster's Afterthoughts. By JOHN HUNTLEY SKRINE, Warden of Glenalmond, Author of 'A Memory of Edward Thring, etc. Crown 8vo. *5s. net.*

Soulsby.—SUGGESTIONS ON PRAYER. By LUCY H. M. SOULSBY. *18mo, sewed, 1s. net. ; cloth, 1s. 6d. net.*

Stone.—Works by the Rev. DARWELL STONE, M.A., Principal of Dorchester Missionary College.

OUTLINES OF MEDITATIONS FOR USE IN RETREAT. *Crown 8vo. 2s. 6d. net.*

CHRIST AND HUMAN LIFE: Lectures delivered in St. Paul's Cathedral in January 1901 ; together with a Sermon on 'The Fatherhood of God.' *Crown 8vo. 2s. 6d. net.*

OUTLINES OF CHRISTIAN DOGMA. *Crown 8vo. 7s. 6d.*

HOLY BAPTISM. *Crown 8vo. 5s.* (*The Oxford Library of Practical Theology.*)

Strange.—INSTRUCTIONS ON THE REVELATION OF ST. JOHN THE DIVINE: Being an attempt to make this book more intelligible to the ordinary reader and so to encourage the study of it. By Rev. CRESSWELL STRANGE, M.A., Vicar of Edgbaston, and Honorary Canon of Worcester. *Crown 8vo. 6s.*

Strong.—CHRISTIAN ETHICS : being the Bampton Lectures for 1895. By THOMAS B. STRONG, D.D., Dean of Christ Church, Oxford. *8vo. 7s. 6d.*

Stubbs.—ORDINATION ADDRESSES. By the Right Rev. W. STUBBS, D.D., late Lord Bishop of Oxford. Edited by the Rev. E. E. HOLMES, formerly Domestic Chaplain to the Bishop; Hon. Canon of Christ Church, Oxford. With Photogravure Portrait. *Crown 8vo. 6s. net.*

Waggett.—THE AGE OF DECISION. By P. N. WAGGETT, M.A., of the Society of St. John the Evangelist, Cowley St. John, Oxford. *Crown 8vo. 2s. 6d. net.*

Williams.—Works by the Rev. ISAAC WILLIAMS, B.D.

A DEVOTIONAL COMMENTARY ON THE GOSPEL NARRA- TIVE. *Eight Vols. Crown 8vo. 5s. each.*

THOUGHTS ON THE STUDY OF THE HOLY GOSPELS.
A HARMONY OF THE FOUR EVANGELISTS.
OUR LORD'S NATIVITY.
OUR LORD'S MINISTRY (Second Year).
OUR LORD'S MINISTRY (Third Year).
THE HOLY WEEK.
OUR LORD'S PASSION.
OUR LORD'S RESURRECTION.

FEMALE CHARACTERS OF HOLY SCRIPTURE. A Series of Sermons. *Crown 8vo, 5s.*

THE CHARACTERS OF THE OLD TESTAMENT. *Crown 8vo. 5s.*

THE APOCALYPSE. With Notes and Reflections. *Crown 8vo. 5s.*

SERMONS ON THE EPISTLES AND GOSPELS FOR THE SUN- DAYS AND HOLY DAYS. *Two Vols. Crown 8vo. 5s. each.*

PLAIN SERMONS ON CATECHISM. *Two Vols. Cr. 8vo. 5s. each.*

Wirgman.—THE DOCTRINE OF CONFIRMATION. By A. THEODORE WIRGMAN, D.D., D.C.L., Canon of Grahamstown, and Vice-Provost of St. Mary's Collegiate Church, Port Elizabeth, South Africa. *Crown 8vo. 3s. 6d.*

Wordsworth.—Works by CHRISTOPHER WORDSWORTH, D.D., sometime Bishop of Lincoln.

THE HOLY BIBLE (the Old Testament).   With Notes, Introductions, and Index.   *Imperial 8vo.*
> Vol. I. THE PENTATEUCH. 25s.   Vol. II. JOSHUA TO SAMUEL. 15s.
> Vol. III. KINGS to ESTHER. 15s.   Vol. IV. JOB TO SONG OF SOLOMON. 25s.   Vol. V. ISAIAH TO EZEKIEL. 25s.   Vol. VI. DANIEL, MINOR PROPHETS, and Index. 15s.
> *Also supplied in 13 Parts.   Sold separately.*

THE NEW TESTAMENT, in the Original Greek.   With Notes, Introductions, and Indices.   *Imperial 8vo.*
> Vol. I. GOSPELS AND ACTS OF THE APOSTLES. 23s.   Vol. II. EPISTLES, APOCALYPSE, and Indices. 37s.
> *Also supplied in 4 Parts.   Sold separately.*

CHURCH HISTORY TO A.D. 451.   *Four Vols.   Crown 8vo.*
> Vol. I. TO THE COUNCIL OF NICÆA, A.D. 325. 8s. 6d.   Vol. II. FROM THE COUNCIL OF NICÆA TO THAT OF CONSTANTINOPLE. 6s.   Vol. III. CONTINUATION. 6s.   Vol. IV. CONCLUSION, TO THE COUNCIL OF CHALCEDON, A.D. 451. 6s.

THEOPHILUS ANGLICANUS : a Manual of Instruction on the Church and the Anglican Branch of it.   12mo.   2s. 6d.

ELEMENTS OF INSTRUCTION ON THE CHURCH.   16mo.   1s. *cloth.*   6d. *sewed.*

THE HOLY YEAR : Original Hymns.   16mo.   2s. 6d. *and* 1s.   *Limp,* 6d.
> „   „   With Music.   Edited by W. H. MONK.   *Square 8vo.* 4s. 6d.

ON THE INTERMEDIATE STATE OF THE SOUL AFTER DEATH.   32mo.   1s.

Wordsworth.—Works by JOHN WORDSWORTH, D.D., Lord Bishop of Salisbury.

THE MINISTRY OF GRACE : Studies in Early Church History, with reference to Present Problems.   *Crown 8vo.* 6s. 6d. *net.*

THE HOLY COMMUNION : Four Visitation Addresses.   1891.   *Crown 8vo.* 3s. 6d.

THE ONE RELIGION : Truth, Holiness, and Peace desired by the Nations, and revealed by Jesus Christ.   Eight Lectures delivered before the University of Oxford in 1881.   *Crown 8vo.* 7s. 6d.

UNIVERSITY SERMONS ON GOSPEL SUBJECTS.   *Sm. 8vo.* 2s. 6d.

PRAYERS FOR USE IN COLLEGE.   16mo.   1s.

10,000/1/03.

Edinburgh : Printed by T. and A. CONSTABLE.

Lightning Source UK Ltd.
Milton Keynes UK
UKHW011336100219
336964UK00010B/805/P